EDUCATION
FOR ALL?

EDUCATION FOR ALL?

The Legacy of Free Post-Primary Education in Ireland

Edited by Judith Harford

Foreword by J.J. Lee

PETER LANG

Oxford • Bern • Berlin • Bruxelles • New York • Wien

Bibliographic information published by Die Deutsche Nationalbibliothek.
Die Deutsche Nationalbibliothek lists this publication in the Deutsche
National-bibliografie; detailed bibliographic data is available on the Internet at
http://dnb.d-nb.de.

A catalogue record for this book is available from the British Library.

Library of Congress Control Number: 2017961054

Cover image: pixabay.com.

Cover design: Peter Lang Ltd.

ISBN 978-1-78874-242-9 (print) • ISBN 978-1-78874-272-6 (ePDF)
ISBN 978-1-78874-273-3 (ePub) • ISBN 978-1-78874-274-0 (mobi)

Published by Peter Lang Ltd, International Academic Publishers,
52 St Giles, Oxford, OX1 3LU, United Kingdom
oxford@peterlang.com, www.peterlang.com

Printed in Germany

Contents

Acknowledgements

I would like to thank the scholars who contributed chapters to this book, all leading authorities in their fields. It has been my pleasure and privilege to work with them in bringing this volume to completion. I would also like to extend my thanks to Professor J. J. Lee for his support for this initiative from the outset and for penning a succinct and thought-provoking foreword. Similarly, I wish to thank Professor Tom O' Donoghue for his insight and expertise in this as in so many of my academic endeavours. I acknowledge funding provided by the College of Social Sciences and Law, University College Dublin, and the Department of Education and Skills for the Royal Irish Academy symposium from which this book emanated. Finally, thanks to Peter Lang and in particular Christabel Scaife for her expertise and professionalism.

J. J. LEE

Foreword

For all the vicissitudes of the past fifty years, it is clear that the 1967 free education scheme remains one of the most important developments in the history of independent Ireland. Although it is clear that much remains to be done, the initiative opened up unprecedented opportunities for further education beyond primary school to generations hitherto condemned to an educational system that equipped the vast majority of the population for an existence as only hewers of wood and drawers of water at home, and often not all that much better abroad for many first-generation emigrants. Even though numbers at second level were rising gradually, the pace of change remained grossly inadequate to provide opportunities for the large major- ity of children to either achieve their own individual potential or enhance their collective potential contribution to the economic, social and cultural welfare of the country. That the 1967 initiative occurred when it did, even if many of the measures might have emerged gradually, especially after our entry to the EU in 1973 – but nobody in 1967 could have been certain of that – was crucial in transforming attitudes towards the importance of education for Ireland's future. For all the intervening vicissitudes and frustrations, it is sobering to wonder where Ireland would be today had the pace of educational change remained so plodding. And so it might have, but for the idealism, energy and determination of a handful of politicians and civil servants determined to open up the wider opportunities for the next generation that had been largely denied to their own. Even after 1967, there would be numerous frustrations. Not all later policymakers, either in politics or the public service, would display a passion for fostering greater educational opportunity for all children, which in turn would have required far more extensive change in the wider socio-economic value system than the political culture would permit.

Among the multiple merits of this indispensable volume is the way it lifts the curtain on the manner in which a policy-making process driven by a relatively small number of people passionately committed to reforming an educational system based essentially on concepts of class privilege, however skillfully, even at times idealistically, enveloped in the capacious folds of both ecclesiastical and lay rhetoric, moved to one based primarily on the concept of human rights. For the brutal reality was that advance to second level in education, much less third level, was far more determined by pocket power than brain power. The residue of that mindset still remains. If far more young people now enter second level and indeed third level doors, the question has to be asked how many are still left on the outside, or at least stuck in the steerage levels of higher education, and why. That the divides between different levels of opportunity are happily no longer nearly as glaring as fifty years ago does not mean that much work does not remain to be done to ensure that no child is left behind through flaws in the education system itself.

This timely and significant publication draws together global thought leaders in the field of education. The editor has selected her contributors shrewdly, with chapter after chapter repaying not only reading, but rereading and deep reflection, while her pungently compact introduction provides so admirable a guide to the contents that it would be trying to gild the lily to seek to summarize it. What does emerge from the absorbing chapters by those at the coal face in lifting the curtain on the process from which Donogh O'Malley's 1967 free education scheme emerged, is the crucial difference that personality and hard-headed idealism can make, when expressed in the commitment of even a relatively small number of politicians, civil servants – and yes – academics, for all the differences of emphasis among them. What can only be inferred is the potential for resistance in conservative circles that obliged the Taoiseach, Sean Lemass – whose support was crucial but who sensed the potential for resistance – to play a canny game, worthy indeed of de Valera in tactical if not necessarily ideological terms – to facilitate the initiative while purporting to appear hesitant, at least up to a point. Indeed, one may wonder at how narrow may have been the window of opportunity to drive through such a scheme given O'Malley's untimely death and the premature resignation as Taoiseach on health grounds of Lemass himself. The role of Paddy Hillery, too, one of the most understated and underrated Irish politicians of his generation, and of Paddy Lynch, a seminal source of ideas to policymakers, can be seen to warrant yet further research. Equally, it is clear that Sean O'Connor and Bill Hyland both played significant roles. Given the speed of change in today's world, and the churning waters in which so frail a craft as Ireland has to navigate, it can be argued that over the medium term, much less the long term, as our educational system goes, so does Ireland go. This volume should be indispensable reading not only for professional educationalists, but for all those who care about the future of our country.

There always remains scope for improvement in every field of human endeavour, if only because progress by definition requires sustained raising of the bar. Among the many striking features of this collection is the astute editorial blending of accounts of the extraordinary achievements of the 1960s with expressions of impatience at challenges still to be overcome. The result is a volume that illuminates the remarkable achievements of the 1960s' revolution – and revolution is not too strong a term, however taken for granted it may now be – but the tendency of one generation to take for granted earlier achievements is itself the best tribute that can be paid to the inherited legacy. The challenge confronting the present generation may in some respects be even more formidable, for it requires significant shifts of perspective in the wider society that cannot be achieved by the earlier conjunction of the idealism, dedication and political commitment of a relatively small number of exceptional individuals in crucial political and administrative positions. The dynamic stimulated by this absorbing collection should in itself propel Ireland forward on the route towards the goal of an ever fairer, and ever more effective educational system in the widest possible national and individual interest.

JUDITH HARFORD

Introduction
Origins, Legacy and Impact: Reflections on the Free Education Scheme in Ireland

This book, commissioned to mark the fiftieth anniversary of the introduction of free post-primary education in Ireland, examines its origins, legacy and impact. Chapters are drawn from a range of scholars internationally recognized for their expertise in the fields of the history of education, the sociology of education, education policy and curriculum. It may be hard to imagine for school-goers today, but up until the introduction of free education, only a minority of young people went on to participate in post-primary schooling, with fewer still going on to third-level education. Participation at both second level and third level was directly contingent on social class and while some scholarships were available, they had a negligible impact on the promotion of equality. By the mid-1960s, one-third of all children were leaving full-time education upon completion of primary schooling and less than 60 per cent of all fifteen-year-olds were remaining in school, a scenario Donogh O'Malley (Minister for Education, 1966–8) described as 'a dark stain on the national conscience'.

While a number of scholars have elsewhere examined the significant social, political and economic developments of the 1960s (see, for example, Daly, 2016; Fleming and Harford, 2014; Walsh, 2009), there has been a paucity of research examining the significance of the 'free education scheme', and there has been even less research on the subject which blends both historical and contemporary commentary. Collectively, the chapters in this volume address this deficit, theorizing about the historical context of the introduction of free education, as well as the impact of the initiative on the promotion of equality of educational opportunity. The book takes a long view, bringing new knowledge to the field by examining previously unexamined primary sources, drawing on research on educational disadvantage, and assessing how policies have shifted over time. The early chapters, namely those of O'Donoghue, Hyland, Harford and Fleming, Coolahan and Mulcahy, explore the historical context for the introduction of the free education scheme and examine how such an initiative transformed the educational landscape. Identifying the 1960s as one of the most progressive periods in the history of education in Ireland, they identify the economic crisis of the 1950s as the trigger for a more ambitious and strategic policy approach. This was a time characterized by austerity, political instability, industrial and agricultural decline and mass emigration. For the majority during this period, education was not a priority; rather, it was a matter of survival. T. K. Whitaker, the noted economist and secretary of the Department of Finance, described the decade of the 1950s as one of stagnation, emigration and high unemployment, in which 'the mood of despondency was palpable' (Whitaker, 2006, p. 8). The later chapters by Smyth, Lynch and Crean, Boland, Gleeson and Sugrue adopt a more panoptic view, assessing the impact of the free education scheme over time. In doing so, they focus on implications for curricular reform, for the development of the institutes of technology and for teacher education. Central to these chapters is the enduring influence of social class across the educational experience.

The book commences with a foreword by Professor J. J. Lee, in which he reflects on the significance of the 1967 free education scheme in opening up unprecedented opportunities for further education beyond primary school to generations of pupils. Considering where Ireland would be today had 'the pace of educational change remained so plodding', Lee observes that the scheme remains one of the most important developments in the history of independent Ireland. He further contends that the execution of the scheme was down to the vision, resilience and political acumen of a handful of politicians and civil servants.

In Chapter 1, Tom O'Donoghue sets the scene for the expansion of education in the 1960s, charting patterns of attendance in the period from 1922 to 1965. In an analysis punctuated by interrogations of a number of 'invented traditions' (Hobsbawn and Ranger, 2017), he argues that, notwithstanding popular views to the contrary, the great majority of those who attended secondary school during the period were drawn from the socially advantaged sectors of Irish society. Furthermore, this particular sector constituted only a small percentage of the total potential secondary-school-going population at the time. In Chapter 2, Áine Hyland draws on her experience as a civil servant in the Department of Education from 1959 to 1964 and as a research assistant with the *Investment in Education* team from 1962 to 1964 to assess the significance of the *Investment in Education* (Government of Ireland, 1965) report and the role played by the Development Branch of the Department of Education in initiating and implementing the free education scheme. In line with subsequent chapters, Hyland identifies a conservative and insular approach to educational policymaking in the decades prior to the introduction of free education and an education system dominated by private interests. As later chapters illustrate, what this meant in practice was that the system favoured those in a financial position to participate in education, reinforced the dominant hegemony, in particular the values of a deeply conservative Catholic Church, and excluded those at the margins, who had neither the social nor the cultural capital to challenge the existing orthodoxy.

Building on Hyland's argument, in Chapter 3, Judith Harford and Brian Fleming examine the advocacy and agency of key individuals who collectively contributed to the reform agenda. Commencing their analysis in the 1950s, these authors illustrate how the dismal economic outlook was a key driver in instigating reform. The authors foreground the significance of 'cultural contrarians' (O'Sullivan, 2005, pp. 461–2) who began to advance a social justice agenda, highlighting for the first time the issue of equality of access for those from less well-off backgrounds. They also highlight the importance of international developments, in particular 'cultural strangers' (O'Sullivan, 1992) in the form of the OECD, and the multiple ways in which such developments led policymakers and politicians to argue that a strong link exists between a nation's level of education and the state of its economy. In particular, their chapter illustrates the extent to which a number of key politicians and civil servants, energized and emboldened by the potential for education to transform the existing educational landscape, responded to the social, political and economic cry to democratize post-primary education.

In his analysis of the impact and aftermath of the free education initiative in Chapter 4, John Coolahan charts the scale and breadth of the reform agenda, examining at the same time the practical challenges posed by the swift introduction of such a development. Situating the initiative in the context of a moribund educational system, overseen by a government department lacking in imagination and ambition, Coolahan considers the logistics of transporting increasing numbers of pupils around an expansive network of schools, as well as teacher education departments' struggling to cope with the rising numbers of entrants. Collectively, Chapters 2, 3 and 4 demonstrate how the economic agenda, coupled with an increasing emphasis on egalitarianism internationally, elevated education, and the education portfolio within government, to a new level, and raised public consciousness regarding the broader role of education within society. Similarly, they demonstrate how the 'policy choice' (Pierson, 2005) to invest in education brought new promise and potential to 1960s Ireland, which was evidenced in the development of new schools, a sophisticated transport system and the recruitment and preparation of a new generation of teachers.

Sensitive to the wider ambitions of the educational reform agenda, in Chapter 5, D. G. Mulcahy identifies a lack of a coherent framework of educational and pedagogical aims underpinning the introduction of free education and traces the implications of this for practical subjects, in particular. He advances the argument that a hierarchical curricular framework has resulted in practical subjects being considered as subjects of lower status. He casts a critical eye also on the inherent contradictions of emerging subjects, such as 'politics and society'. Absent from the contemporary curricular context, in his view, is a coherent framework of educational and pedagogical aims. What Mulcahy highlights in both contemporary and historical curricular contexts is a significant and worrying *disconnection* between ambition and implementation.

The subsequent chapters develop the discussion, questioning the impact of the free education scheme on pupils, on the higher education sector more broadly, on curricular reform and on teacher professionalism. Despite the introduction of free second-level education, Chapters 6 and 7 demonstrate that social differentiation is still a prominent factor in educational attainment and that, in the Irish context, educational level and grades have a significant impact throughout life, reinforcing social inequality in a range of outcomes. Taking *Investment in Education* (1966) as her starting point, in Chapter 6, Emer Smyth traces patterns of educational inequality in the post-1966 period, interrogating differences in educational outcomes according to individual social background and the extent to which unequal outcomes reflect differences in the social mix of students attending second-level schools.

In Chapter 7, Kathleen Lynch and Margaret Crean argue that assumptions and values associated with professionals' social and paradigmatic interests frame their educational and social imaginary. Acknowledging Ireland's educational achievements over the last fifty years, Lynch and Crean observe that educational expansion, while raising the national standards of education, has not led to any meaningful reduction in social-class inequalities. Using national and international evidence, they demonstrate that the generative site of social-class injustices is economic class relations. Because of this, equality of economic condition needs to be the guiding principle of equality in twenty-first-century Ireland; promoting equality of opportunity in education in an economically unequal society generally results in equal opportunities to become unequal. In Chapter 8, Tom Boland examines the inter-connectedness of the decision to introduce free second-level education and the implementation of what he regards as 'another pivotal decision', namely, the decision to establish a new kind of higher education institution, the institute of technology. Both policy developments, he contends, have had a profound effect on Irish society, culture and the economy. Boland examines how the development of the institutes of technology greatly expanded the opportunities for educational attainment, which then broadened access to higher education. This development was critical, he suggests, as it provided a local and technologically oriented alternative to the traditional universities and was also particularly important because it provided Ireland with the labour-market skills necessary for the development of the scientific, technological and pharmaceutical sectors. In Chapter 9, Jim Gleeson situates the ROSLA announcement in its wider educational and curriculum policy contexts and considers the post-primary curriculum prior to the 1983 establishment of the Interim Curriculum and Examinations Board (CEB) and its successor, the National Council for Curriculum and Assessment (NCCA). This chapter explores the work of the CEB and the NCCA, including the introduction of the Junior Certificate and subsequent developments under the statutory NCCA.

Finally, in Chapter 10, Ciaran Sugrue examines the professional challenges facing the teaching profession and policymakers in the context of the introduction of free education. He argues that while the expansion of the second-level system was a welcome development for the teaching profession, issues such as curriculum reform, assessment and pedagogy may have been neglected in the 'white heat' of an extended growth spurt and structural change. Following an overview of the major changes over time to the topography of the post-primary education system, Sugrue identifies the professional legacy issues that have emerged as significant shaping influences, as well as the challenges for the current and next generation of policymakers and practitioners.

Reflecting in the 1980s on the political victory of the roll-out of free second-level education less than two decades earlier, Lee (1982, p. 12) commented:

> At the level of high politics, potential Church/State conflict has been mediated with remarkable skill. The potentially explosive education issue was largely resolved in the 1960s, following an extraordinary surge of activity by the previously moribund Department of Education. If the strong feelings raised on both sides had not yet fully subsided, the observer must remain impressed with the relative smoothness of so striking a change in educational power structures.

Notwithstanding the political will and imagination necessary to democratize education, the promise and potential of the initiative did not provide the opportunities for social mobility that many expected. To quote Ferriter (2005, p. 598), 'what would remain contentious in this context ... was whether or not the changes introduced actually facilitated social mobility in practice, or just consolidated the advantages of the middle classes.' Ultimately, the chapters in this book demonstrate that the democratization of post-primary education – the notion that any child could continue their education, irrespective of their family's financial circumstances – while laudable as a principle and enshrined in the blueprint of the 'free education' scheme, was more complex than originally envisaged in its operationalization. Perhaps understandably, the impact of 'free education' was considerably less significant than its architects had envisaged. Notwithstanding the energy, vision and political goodwill engendered over the course of the 1960s, the largely economic rationale driving this momentum was never accompanied by rigorous policy formation based on considerations of social justice.

Bibliography

Daly, M. E. (2016). *Sixties Ireland: Reshaping the Economy, State and Society, 1957–73* (Cambridge: Cambridge University Press).

Ferriter, D. (2005). *The Transformation of Ireland, 1900–2000* (London: Profile Books).

Fleming, B., and Harford, J. (2014). 'Irish educational policy in the 1960s: a decade of transformation', *History of Education*, 43:5, pp. 635–56.

Hobsbawn, E., and Ranger, T. (2017). *The Invention of Tradition* (Cambridge: Cambridge University Press).

Lee, J. J. (1982). 'Society and Culture', in F. Litton (ed.), *Unequal Achievement: The Irish Experience 1957–82* (Dublin: Institute of Public Administration), pp. 1–18.

O'Sullivan, D. (1992). 'Cultural Strangers and Educational Change, The OECD's Report Investment in Education and Irish Educational Policy', *Education Policy*, 7:5, pp. 445–69.

O'Sullivan, D. (2005). *Culture, Politics and Irish Education since the 1950s* (Dublin: Institute of Public Administration).

Pierson, P. (2005). 'The Study of Policy Development', *Journal of Policy History*, 17:1, pp. 34–51.

Walsh, J. (2009). *The Politics of Expansion: The Transformation of Educational Policy in the Republic of Ireland, 1957–72* (Manchester: Manchester University Press).

Whitaker, T. K. (2006). *Protection or Free Trade: The Final Battle* (Dublin: Institute of Public Administration).

TOM O'DONOGHUE

1 Patterns of Attendance at Irish Secondary Schools from the Establishment of the Independent Irish State to the Introduction of the Free Education Scheme in 1967

Introduction

Fifty years ago, in 1967, the scheme of free education that eventuated in a great increase in attendance at second-level schools in Ireland got underway when the first cohort of eligible students was enrolled. In later years, associated issues, including issues related to changes in both the structure of the education system and the process of education, were identified and examined by various scholars. The spotlight at the time, however, was primarily on the greatly increased and improved access to second-level education that was expected to take place. This is not surprising since, up until 1967, only a minority of those who left primary school continued their schooling. For the majority of this minority, this meant attendance at a secondary school. A smaller proportion of the group attended continuation schools, which were run by local vocational education committees. Colloquially, these were known as 'vocational schools' or 'technical schools' – or, disparagingly, as 'techs'.

Secondary schools were fee-paying. Their material quality, while generally higher in the case of those attended by the better-off in society, left a lot to be desired overall. In 1965, 21 per cent of all secondary school classrooms in the state were 100 years old or more, and a further 18 per cent were eighty to ninety-nine years old (Government of Ireland, 1965).

Within the secondary schools, Catholic nuns, brothers and priests, largely teaching in schools of their own religious orders, constituted 55 per cent of the total population of secondary school teachers in the middle of the 1960s (Duffy, 1967). The focus in the schools was on religious instruction, a religious ethos, and a general academic education in the grammar school tradition. Students were prepared for the Intermediate Certificate examination, usually taken after three years of study, and the Leaving Certificate examination, usually taken after another two years. Those enrolled in the continuation schools were not permitted to sit these national examinations.

The full-time continuation courses offered by the continuation schools were only of two years' duration and were not designed to allow for transfer to secondary schools. Very few are likely to have followed the path of the Co. Limerick poet, the late Michael Hartnett. He left primary school at the age of fourteen in 1955 and went on to attend a continuation school. However, after two years, he was encouraged to sit an examination for a scholarship to attend a secondary school. He was successful and commenced his first year in secondary school at sixteen years of age. Accordingly, he was twenty years of age when he sat the Leaving Certificate examination (Murphy, 1987, p. 29).

The OECD-sponsored *Investment in Education* report (Government of Ireland, 1965), published in 1965, portrayed the economic, social and geographic inequalities of opportunity that existed in Ireland at the time: one-third of all children left full-time education upon completion of primary schooling and only 59 per cent of all fifteen-year-old children were actually in school. While this situation received widespread publicity nationally, it was less clear in the public mind at the time that levels of provision had been even bleaker at the time of the establishment of the state, and had not changed substantially over the succeeding four decades. It is arguable that such a lack of awareness still exists. Yet, there is sufficient evidence available to allow one to go some way towards rectifying this situation by outlining broad trends in attendance patterns in the early decades.

The emphasis in the rest of this chapter is on trends in the patterns of attendance in the secondary school sector during the first forty-five years of independent Ireland. A useful way of addressing this is by attempting to unmask a number of 'invented traditions', to use the memorable concept generated by Hobsbawn and Ranger (2017), and thus ensure they are not allowed to go uncontested. Accordingly, following a general portrayal of the economic and social conditions in Ireland from 1922 until the mid-1960s, and their relationship to secondary school attendance patterns, three of these invented traditions are considered, namely:

- that participation was steadily rising in the decade prior to the advent of the free education scheme and that, as a result, the period of expansion that commenced in 1967 was on the way anyway;
- that no child was ever turned away from a secondary school if he or she desired to attend one;
- that there were plenty of scholarships for 'bright' children of limited financial means.

These, I contend, are not 'straw men'; while one rarely reads of them in the academic literature, they are, I hold, part of regular discourse in 'general' Irish society and are circulated in a variety of ways.

The General Economic and Social Situation

Secondary schooling was not availed of by many of those in the poorer sectors of Irish society. This can be illustrated by considering the following points:

- As late as 1961, the children of professionals, managers and employers heavily outnumbered those from lower-status occupations in secondary schools, yet their parents constituted only 13 per cent of the workforce (Government of Ireland, 1965, p. 51).
- Children of unskilled or semi-skilled manual workers benefited least from secondary school education. They were also the most likely to drop out of secondary school at an early age (Government of Ireland, 1965, p. 51).

To a large extent, these trends can be attributed to family economic circumstances and associated attitudes and practices which became ingrained
during the 1920s, 1930s and 1940s. Agricultural prices had been high in the
years of the First World War, but this had given way to economic recession
by the 1920s (Brown, 1985, pp. 17–20). During the 1930s, the situation
remained bleak, with agricultural output falling by 6 per cent between
1931 and 1938 (Johnson, 1985, pp. 8–42). This had serious consequences
for the 53 per cent of the population involved in agriculture.

The unemployment situation in rural and urban Ireland also created a
high level of poverty. As a result of a slowing-down of emigration due to a
depressed economy internationally, unemployment in 1936 was, at 133,000,
twice the 1926 figure (Cullen, 1978, pp. 171–87) and there was little hope
of improving matters in the future.

The housing and health situations also left much to be desired. In 1926,
43 per cent of the population of Co. Mayo, 41 per cent of the population
of Co. Donegal, and 39 per cent of the population of Co. Galway lived in
crowded conditions of two persons per room (Culen, 1978, pp. 171–87).
While matters improved somewhat over the next decade, 14 per cent of
the population of Dublin still lived in conditions of four or more persons
to a room in 1936, and as late as 1937 tuberculosis still accounted for 7.5
per cent of all deaths in the state.

It is reasonable, then, to conclude that sending a son or daughter to
a secondary school, even when fees were waived, would have put a serious strain on the economic situation of many families. Although detailed
sociological evidence is not available, a certain amount of testimony allows
one to glean some insights. In 1931, the inspectors of the Department of
Education carried out an investigation to determine why children from
the intensely Irish-speaking areas of counties Galway, Mayo and Donegal
were not availing of secondary school education by taking up places in the
special secondary schools called preparatory colleges. In these colleges,
of which there were seven in all, selected children from Gaeltacht (Irish-
speaking) districts, and others with a high standard of spoken and written
Irish, were enrolled and received free secondary school education, before
progressing to the primary-school teacher-training colleges, where they
joined a number of those selected separately after graduating from 'regular'

secondary schools, again with a high standard of Irish (O'Donoghue and Harford, 2016).

One of the reasons put forward for the low acceptance of places was that the four years of study involved acted as a great deterrent to parents, who were anxious to supplement their meagre income with their children's earnings at the earliest possible date. The inspectors of the Department of Education also concluded that this outlook could not be easily changed. Later, in 1954, a similar investigation in a large area of under-provision around Carraroe in the County Galway Gaeltacht again led to the conclusion that parents in general felt they needed to send their children to work at a young age,[1] including to Britain, where there was plenty of unskilled work available because of the great post-war building programmes that were underway. Witnesses from around Ireland who presented themselves before the Commission on Emigration (Commission on Emigration, 1956) between 1948 and 1954 offered similar views, as did the Commission on Youth Unemployment (Commission on Youth Unemployment, 1952), which reported in 1952.

The requirement that, in order to attend a secondary school, fees must be paid (though they were sometimes waived by religious teaching orders for those deemed to be 'deserving cases'), then, was not the only influence at work. Author Frank Delaney depicted the situation in Co. Tipperary, where he grew up in the 1950s, as follows:

> The poverty of our parish was such that keeping the bodies and souls of many of the schoolchildren together was often as much as many parents could do. Where my four brothers and sisters were concerned, we received a secondary school education, perhaps the first entire family in our locality to do so. (1987, p. 366)

There are indications that a large cohort of people desired to send their children to a secondary school, but could not afford to do so, despite fees as low as £15 *per annum* for day pupils in over 66 per cent of secondary schools in 1961–2 (Government of Ireland, 1965). In the late 1950s, for example,

1   Mulcahy Papers. University College Dublin. Archives Department. File P/7/c/154, headed 'Minister's Note' and dated 21 June 1954.

parents from the farming working class, who were interviewed when a survey was carried out amongst the inhabitants of eight rural parishes in Co. Limerick (Newman, 1962), held that few of their children would have the opportunity to go to a secondary school even if it was free because of the cost of school attire and school books. Also, with only a subsistence wage of £5 per week, they could not afford to be without the labour or wages provided by a son or daughter who had reached school-leaving age.

At the same time, it would be remiss not to point to another cohort of parents, namely, those who, even if they could afford it, would not encourage a son or daughter to attend a secondary school as they saw no value in the experience. The Commission on Emigration in 1956 drew attention to this cohort, arguing that they saw secondary schooling as being too much geared towards 'white collar employment and professional careers'. Drawing again on the results of the Co. Limerick rural survey (Newman, 1962), members of the farming class said that they sent those sons deemed to be the brightest to secondary school and encouraged them to remain until they had achieved a Leaving Certificate so that they might be able to go on to study for the professions. On the other hand, a son who was going to inherit the farm, they held, should be sent to secondary school only for a year or two to gain some additional knowledge and make new friends before being physically strong enough to make a major contribution to work on the farm.

Attendance patterns also suggest that the dominant view amongst parents was that it was more important to provide a secondary school education for boys than it was for girls. More boys than girls attended secondary schools and sat the public examinations.

- In 1929–30, for example, only 1,580 girls sat the Intermediate Certificate examinations, while 2,363 boys were examined. In the same year, 856 boys sat the Leaving Certificate examinations, as opposed to only 443 girls (Department of Education, 1930).
- By 1939–40, this imbalance had not rectified itself, although the gap had narrowed somewhat, with 4,113 boys and 3,436 girls sitting the Intermediate Certificate examinations and 1,690 boys and 1,228 girls sitting the Leaving Certificate examinations (Department of Education, 1940).

While the evidence is not very clear, it is likely that the imbalance was due more to a lack of take-up by girls than to a lack of provision of secondary education for girls, since there was not a significant difference between the number of boys' and girls' secondary schools in the state. In fact, in 1930, the number of religious-managed Catholic boys' schools was equal to the number of religious-managed Catholic girls' schools. In the same year, female secondary school teachers, of which there were 1,406, outnumbered their male counterparts, of which there were 1,237 (Department of Education, 1930). Overall, these patterns suggest that the female religious orders were keen that a greater number of girls should attend secondary school.

Contesting Three Invented Traditions in Relation to Secondary School Attendance

Invented tradition no. 1: Participation was rising steadily in the decade prior to the advent of the free education scheme and, as a result, the period of expansion that commenced in 1967 was on the way anyway

In 1924, there were 493,382 students in primary schools in the state, while the private, state-subsidized secondary schools, which constituted the largest cohort within the second-level schooling sector, catered for only 22,897 students (Department of Education, 1926). Over the next four decades, the number of secondary school students increased only very gradually. By 1933–4, there were only 32,384 pupils in secondary schools, as opposed to 420,494 pupils attending primary schools (Department of Education, 1934). There was an improvement of only 1 per cent in this ratio by 1937–8, when 36,092 pupils were in attendance at secondary schools, as opposed to 398,544 pupils in attendance at primary schools (Department of Education, 1938). By 1955–6, the number of pupils in secondary schools had reached 59,306 (Department of Education, 1956).

The increase in attendance at secondary school between 1940 and 1962 was greatest between 1950 and 1962. This was due largely to an expansion in secondary school provision by the Catholic Church providers, which was made possible as a result of the building of extensions to and the development of existing schools, as opposed to the building of new schools. Also, between 1941 and 1956, the number of Catholic diocesan secondary schools and the number of Protestant secondary schools in the state remained at twenty-eight and forty-five respectively.

By 1962, there was still a great imbalance between the number of students attending primary schools and those attending second-level schools. Overall, what this meant at the time has been well summarized by Coolahan (1984, p. 184):

> When the pupils in secondary tops are added to those in secondary schools the grand total amounted to 87,041. The census of 1961 recorded a total of 233,832 in the age range 15 to 19. Taking 52,000 as a rough guide to the age cohort at the time, there would have been a total of 330,000 between the ages of 13 and 18 in 1961. Thus, while the numbers obtaining secondary education increased significantly in the 1950s, the great majority of the age range was still unaffected by it. About 30,000 pupils were in full-time attendance at vocational schools in 1961.

Thus, we can dismiss invented tradition no. 1, namely, that participation rising steadily in the decade prior to the advent of the free education scheme and that, as a result, the period of expansion that commenced in 1967 was on the way anyway. On the other hand, it is the case that by 1970, the introduction of free, second-level education resulted in an almost threefold increase in the number of secondary school students in the country.

Invented tradition no. 2: No child was ever turned away from a secondary school if he or she desired to attend

While it may be true that that no child was ever turned away from a secondary school if his or her parents approached the school authorities and expressed a desire for a free place to be allocated, to concentrate unduly on this can lead one to overlook the fact that for a particular cohort of potential students, making such a request would have made no sense because of the uneven distribution of secondary schools throughout the state. The north-west and south-west of the country, characterized by large stretches of poor land and very heavy emigration, are particularly noteworthy. For example, in the school year 1939–40, the following towns in the north-west and south-west of the country did not have a secondary school:

The North-West

1. Gweedore
2. Dunglow
3. Glenties
4. Killybegs
5. Donegal town
6. Bangor-Erris
7. Boyle
8. Castlerea
9. Claremorris
10. Clifden
11. Oughterard
12. Spiddal

The South-West

13. Sneem
14. Kenmare
15. Bantry

A small number of students from both of these areas were amongst those in the 30 per cent of the student population who were boarders. However, for reasons highlighted already, the majority of those of secondary school-going age, regardless of their geographical location, would not have been able to afford to pay boarding school fees.

Moreover, attendance patterns suggest that a great number of potential students are unlikely to have made a request to attend a secondary school, to have known that they could have made such a request, or to have been encouraged to make such a request. The following three attendance patterns, in particular, suggest that a greater number would have attended secondary school if it had been possible for them to do so:

- Some students attended secondary school for a year or two and then dropped out;
- A significant number of students continued to attend primary school after they had reached the compulsory age at which they could leave, namely, fourteen years of age;
- A large number numbers of girls attended 'secondary tops'.

The statistical evidence for each of these points is now outlined briefly.

Regarding the evidence that some students attended secondary school for a year or two and then dropped out

The evidence suggests the possibility that a greater proportion of boys and girls might have stayed on at secondary school if the economic situation of their parents had been better. The pattern was more prominent in the case of boys than it was in the case of girls. Regarding boys, from the mid-1920s to the mid-1960s, a pattern was established whereby a certain proportion of boys attended secondary schools for a year or two and then dropped out:

- In 1932–3, 4,527 boys commenced their first year of secondary schooling (Department of Education, 1933). By the second year, 10 per cent of them had dropped out of school and by the third year, 21 per cent of the original group had left;
- Of the 4,817 boys who entered secondary school in 1936–7, only 3,766, or 78 per cent of the original group, were still in school in 1938–9 (Department of Education, 1937).

As the rate of attendance at secondary school increased over the next decades, so too did the drop-out rate:

- Of the 5,244 boys who entered the first year of secondary school in 1943–4, 25 per cent had dropped out by 1945–6 (Department of Education, 1946);
- Of the 6,971 boys who entered first year in 1953–4, 27 per cent had dropped out by 1955–6 (Department of Education, 1956).

Regarding girls, while approximately two girls entered the first year of secondary school for every three boys throughout the period under consideration, most of them were still in secondary school four years later.

The various costs involved in educating pupils for four or five years would seem to suggest that the vast majority of girls who attended secondary school were from the better-off sections of society.

Regarding the evidence that significant number of students continued to attend primary school after they had reached the compulsory age at which they could leave, namely, fourteen years of age

This evidence suggests that a greater number of girls might have attended a 'regular' secondary school if it had been possible to do so. In the school year 1927–8, 7.5 per cent of the primary school population in the state consisted of pupils between fourteen and sixteen years of age (Department of Education, 1928). This percentage was down to 6.13 per cent by the school year 1936–7 (Department of Education, 1937). Nevertheless, the latter percentage represented 29,536 pupils, a number which was not very far behind the number of pupils in secondary schools and secondary tops combined (the former being 35,890 and the latter being 3,155). Of the 29,536 pupils, 6,538 were fifteen years of age or over, and 2,845 were sixteen years of age or over. The figures also indicate that the tendency was more or less the same throughout the individual counties, at around 6 per cent, with the Kerry figure high at 9 per cent and the Dublin City (as opposed to the Dublin County) figure low at 3.7 per cent.

It is difficult to explain with any degree of certainty the tendency to stay on at primary school. Some, no doubt, commenced their education at six or seven years of age and were completing the normal primary-school education cycle. Others may have been what came to be called 'slow learners' and were encouraged to remain on to reach what was considered to be an acceptable standard of education. Others, one imagines, were pupils who were waiting to enter the work force. The likelihood is that at least some in these different groups would have attended a secondary school if it had been possible to do so. This proposition is supported by statistics demonstrating a continuing decline over the decades in the number of pupils in the cohort in question as more places became available in secondary schools and some new schools were built.

- The figure for 1936–7, it will be recalled, was 6.13 per cent;
- By 1949–50, it was down to 4.05 per cent;
- By 1956–7, it was down to 3.22 per cent.

Yet, we must not forget that, overall, as was indicated at the outset, the majority of children of second-level attendance age, were not in attendance.

Regarding the evidence that a large number of girls attended 'secondary tops'

The evidence that a large number of girls attended 'secondary tops' also suggests that a greater number of girls would have attended a 'regular' secondary school if it had been possible to do so. The secondary tops were primary schools which provided secondary school courses recognized by the Department of Education and which, from June 1925, were allowed to admit pupils to the Intermediate and Leaving Certificate examinations.

By the school year 1930–1, there were thirty-seven secondary tops in the state. These were staffed by primary school teachers who had received no specific preparation (Department of Education, 1931). The secondary tops increased throughout the 1940s and 1950s. There were:

- Sixty-one of them in the school year 1939–40;
- Seventy-three in the school year 1946–7;
- Seventy-two in the school year 1950–1;
- Eight-seven in the school year 1956–7.

The number in 1939–40 represented one secondary top for every ten secondary schools in the state. By 1956–7, the ratio had only dropped a little, to one secondary top for every eight secondary schools (Department of Education, 1957).

It is likely that the Department of Education allowed the development of secondary tops to take place as they provided a relatively cheap way of extending the provision of secondary school education without the state becoming involved directly in the building of new secondary schools and having to meet associated capital expenses. In 1954, General Mulcahy, as Minister for Education, urged the officials in the Department of Education to 'crystallize' their attitude in order to 'encourage in every way the development of the secondary-tops'.[2] The ASTI took an opposing view, drawing attention to the fact that the secondary tops catered mainly for girls and arguing that they 'were only cramming centres' (ASTI, 1959, p. 23) which offered no more than the minimum of six subjects and provided no cultural background for the students. However, it was not until the introduction of major changes in Irish education in the 1960s that the secondary tops began to be phased out.

Invented tradition no. 3: There were plenty of scholarships for 'bright' children of limited financial means

This is another 'invented tradition' that does not hold up to scrutiny. The level of provision of local authority scholarships was totally inadequate as an aid and as an incentive for those in the lower social groups to pursue a secondary school education. In 1950, for example, the number of scholarships awarded expressed as a percentage of the number of students in the sixth class of primary school was only 1.54 per cent. Also, scholarships were not distributed equitably on a regional basis. For example, in the school year 1950–1 (Department of Education, 1951):

---

2   Mulcahy Papers. University College Dublin. Archives Department. File P/7c/154, headed 'Minister's Note' and dated 21 June 1954.

- Dublin County Council Borough (as distinct from Dublin County Council) offered one scholarship for every ten students in sixth class of primary school;
- Offaly County Council offered one scholarship for every twenty-eight students;
- Laois County Council offered one scholarship for every thirty students.

At the other end of the spectrum were counties Dublin, Galway and Cork, whose county councils offered only one scholarship for every 202, 227 and 281 students respectively in sixth class in primary school. Furthermore, the value of scholarships was only barely sufficient to pay the annual school fees. All other expenses had to be paid by parents, or were made available through the benevolence of those who managed the schools. Apart from County Monaghan, those counties in the north-west of the country that had the lowest provision of second-level schools in the state also had a very low level of scholarship provision. In 1950–1, for example, counties Donegal, Cavan and Leitrim provided only one scholarship for every 145, 121 and 112 pupils respectively in sixth class in primary school (Department of Education, 1951). County Monaghan was an exception in that it provided one scholarship for every forty-three pupils in primary school. Finally, it was not until 1961 that the central government began to make a financial contribution to the scholarship scheme. This took place as a result of the passing of the Local Authorities (Education Scholarships) (Amendment) Act.[3] The government of the day preferred the resulting extension of scholarships to raising the school-leaving age.

3   Local Authorities (Education Scholarships) Amendment Act, 1961.

Conclusion

The trends in patterns of attendance outlined in this chapter can assist in providing a deeper understanding than has been available to date of the nature and extent of what was eventually achieved as a result of the implementation of the free education scheme. Education expanded dramatically following its introduction. Also, in the 1970s and early 1980s, students spent much longer in school than students in earlier eras. In saying this, I am acutely aware of the work of various academics, who have demonstrated that while overall class differences in educational attainment declined, class barriers were not removed. As Raftery and Hout (1993) have observed, the differences simply became less consequential because the education system expanded to the point where it could afford to be less selective. Overall, the results of their research led them to generate the hypothesis of maximally maintained inequality and conclude that the 1967 'reforms' appeared to have had no effect on equality of education opportunity. Lynch (2014) and Smyth (1999) have done much to deconstruct the dynamics of inequality in Irish education and Lynch's (1987) early work unmasked an assumption in much education discourse in Ireland whereby individuals are characterized by the possession of a quantifiable entity called 'intelligence' or 'ability', which is generally interpreted as a given entity and as something which remains fixed through time.

My view is that there is a need to generate an equally powerful *corpus* of research taking a longer historical view of the situation. There is plenty of room for such research in the field so that nuanced accounts, supported by a more substantial body of evidence, can be provided. One direction associated projects could take would be to extend our current understanding of the general patterns of secondary school attendance portrayed in this chapter for the period 1922–65, so that we can come to a better understanding of how powerful sectors in society hid their practice of using schools to reproduce social privilege and continue to keep this hidden through the perpetuation of 'invented traditions', which are still voiced today. Essentially, the sectors to which I am referring are the Catholic Church and the state, which worked together to control secondary school education in Ireland

in order to meet their dual interests of producing priests, brothers and
nuns, and a loyal middle class (O'Donoghue, 1999). To highlight this in
relation to the secondary school attendance patterns considered in this
chapter is to take on board the argument of Southgate (2005, p. 62) that
'myth-breaking' must continue to be an important task for the historian.
By engaging in 'myth-breaking', we can, as Aldrich (2003, p. 135) has put
it, fulfil our 'duty to our own generation'.

Bibliography

Aldrich, R. (2003). 'The three duties of the historian of education', *History of Education*, 32:2, pp. 133–43.

ASTI (1959). *The School and College Yearbook for 1959* (Dublin: ASTI).

Brown, T. (1985). *Ireland: A Social and Cultural History 1922–85* (London: Fontana Press).

Commission on Emigration (1956). *Reports of the Commission on Emigration and Other Population problems, 1948–54* (Dublin: Stationery Office, 1956).

Commission on Youth Unemployment (1952). *Commission on Youth Unemployment 1951–Report* (Dublin: Stationery Office).

Coolahan, J. (1984). *The ASTI and Post-Primary Education in Ireland, 1909–84* (Dublin: ASTI).

Cullen, L. (1978). *An Economic History of Ireland Since 1660* (London: B. T. Batsford).

Delaney, F. (1987). 'The Library Boxes', in A. N. Jeffares and A. Kamm (eds), *Irish Childhoods: An Anthology* (London: Collins).

Department of Education (1926). *Report of the Department of Education for the School Year 1924–7 and the Financial and Administrative Year 1924–5–6* (Dublin: Stationery Office).

Department of Education (1928). *Report of the Department of Education for the School Year 1924–7 and the Financial and Administrative Year 1927–8* (Dublin: Stationery Office).

Department of Education (1930). *Report of the Department of Education for the School Year 1929–30* (Dublin: Stationery Office).

Department of Education (1931). *Report of the Department of Education for the School Year 1930–1* (Dublin: Stationery Office).

Department of Education (1932). *Report of the Department of Education for the School Year 1930–1* (Dublin: Stationery Office).

Department of Education (1934). *Report of the Department of Education for the School Year 1932–3* (Dublin: Stationery Office).

Department of Education (1937). *Report of the Department of Education for the School Year 1936–7* (Dublin: Stationery Office).

Department of Education (1938). *Report of the Department of Education for the School Year 1937–8* (Dublin: Stationery Office).

Department of Education (1940). *Report of the Department of Education for the School Year 1939–40* (Dublin: Stationery Office).

Department of Education (1944). *Report of the Department of Education for the School Year 1943–4* (Dublin: Stationery Office).

Department of Education (1946). *Report of the Department of Education for the School Year 1945–6* (Dublin: Stationery Office).

Department of Education (1947). *Report of the Department of Education for the School Year 1946–7* (Dublin: Stationery Office).

Department of Education (1951). *Report of the Department of Education for the School Year 1950–1* (Dublin: Stationery Office).

Department of Education (1954). *Report of the Department of Education for the School Year 1953–4* (Dublin: Stationery Office).

Department of Education (1956). *Report of the Department of Education for the School Year 1955–6* (Dublin: Stationery Office).

Department of Education (1957). *Report of the Department of Education for the School Year 1956–7* (Dublin: Stationery Office).

Duffy, P. J. (1967). *The Lay Teacher* (Dublin: Fallons).

Government of Ireland (1965). *Investment in Education: Report of the Survey Team Appointed by the Minister of Education in October 1962* (Dublin: Stationery Office).

Hobsbawn, E., and Ranger, T. (2017). *The Invention of Tradition* (Cambridge: Cambridge University Press).

Johnson, D. (1985). *The Interwar Economy in Ireland* (Dublin: The Economic and Social History Society of Ireland).

Lynch, K. (1987). 'Dominant Ideologies in Irish Educational Thought: Consensualism, Essentialism and Meritocratic Individualism', *Economic and Social Review*, 18:2, pp. 101–22.

Lynch, K. (2014). 'Economic Inequality Creates Educational Inequalities and Class-Based Cuts to Education, an Engine for Equality, Subvert other Rights and Goods for the most Vulnerable', *Village: Ireland's Political and Cultural Machine* <http://villagemagazine.ie/index.php/2014/02/>.

Murphy, D. (1987). *Education and the Arts: A Research Report* (Dublin: Trinity College, Dublin, School of Education, 1987).

Newman, J. (1962). *The Limerick Rural Survey. Third Interim Report: Social Structure* (Tipperary: Muintir na Tíre).

O'Donoghue, T. (1999). *The Catholic Church and the Secondary School Curriculum in Ireland, 1922–65* (New York: Peter Lang).

O'Donoghue, T., and Harford, J. (2016). *Secondary School Education in Ireland: Memories and Life Histories, 1922–67* (London and New York: Palgrave Macmillan).

Raftery, A. E., and Hout, M. (1985). 'Does Irish Education approach the Meritocratic Ideal?', *Sociology of Education*, 16:2, pp. 115–40.

Raftery, A. E., and Hout, M. (1993). 'Maximally Maintained Inequality: Expansion, Reform, and Opportunity in Irish Education, 1921–75', *Sociology of Education*, 66:1, pp. 41–62.

Smyth, E. (1999). *Do Schools Differ?* (Dublin: Oak Tree Press and the Economic and Social Research Institute).

Southgate, B. (2005). *What is History For?* (London: Routledge).

ÁINE HYLAND

2 The Birth of the Free Education Scheme

Background

This chapter provides a backdrop to the birth of free second-level education in Ireland in September 1967. It is written from the perspective of this author, who was a civil servant in the Department of Education from 1959 to 1964 and worked as a research assistant with the *Investment in Education* team from September 1962 to September 1964. The chapter does not pretend to be a comprehensive analysis or critique of events of the period nor does it claim to be dispassionate or neutral. It is an insider's view of educational developments during the period from 1962 to September 1967, and, as well as drawing on published and unpublished material, some of which has not previously been in the public domain, it is based on the author's own recollection of events. The chapter analyses and discusses the influence of the *Investment in Education* report (Government of Ireland, 1965) and the role played by the Development Branch of the Department of Education in initiating and implementing the free education scheme. The setting-up of a development unit was recommended by the *Investment in Education* report, and its formation was formally announced by Minister George Colley in his estimates speech in July 1965 (Dáil Debates, 16 June 1965).

The *Investment in Education* team began its survey of Irish education in summer 1964 and its report was published in December 1965. The team was chaired by Professor Patrick Lynch, Professor of Economics in University College Dublin, and it had three other members: William (Bill) J. Hyland, statistician in the United Nations office in New York; Martin O'Donoghue, lecturer in Economics in Trinity College Dublin, and Pádraig Ó Nualláin, Inspector of Mathematics in the Department of Education.

The secretary of the team was Charles Smith and this author was seconded from the Department of Education, where she was an Executive Officer, to provide research assistance for the team. An earlier paper by this author, which was published in *Irish Educational Studies* in 2014, discussed the workings of the *Investment in Education* team and the conditions under which it operated (Hyland, 2014). In spring 1966, having returned to his post in the UN eighteen months previously, Bill Hyland was contacted by the Department of Education in Dublin and offered the post of senior statistician in the newly formed Development Branch of the department. Bill had been a statistician at the Central Statistics Office in Dublin in the late 1940s and early 1950s. He was appointed statistician at the United Nations office in New York in 1952. Ten years later, he was seconded back to Ireland for a two-year period as a member of the *Investment in Education* team. He was the main drafter of the 500-page *Investment in Education* report and was single-handedly responsible for the report's 750 pages of annexes and appendices.[1] At the end of his secondment period in summer 1964, he returned to the United Nations (to the Economic Commission for Europe office in Geneva) and remained in contact with the other members of the *Investment in Education* team, drafting and re-drafting sections of the report and the annexes and appendices until the final copy went to the printers in mid-1965. Having accepted the post of statistician in the Development Branch in summer 1966, he was a key member of its staff until it was prematurely closed down by Richard Burke, Minister for Education, in 1973.[2]

Bill was passionately committed to equality of educational opportunity, and throughout his period on the survey team, he was deeply engaged in trying to come up with solutions to the inequalities uncovered by the

[1]   The full text of the report (over 500 pages) and the annexes and appendices (750 pages) can be accessed online at <http://www.education.ie/en/Publications/Policy-Reports/?pageNumber=5>. I am grateful to the Secretary General of the Department of Education and Skills, Seán Ó Foghlú, for arranging to digitize and make the report available online to mark the fiftieth anniversary of its publication.

[2]   For more information on Bill Hyland's contribution to the *Investment in Education* report, and his views on education, see Áine Hyland, 'The investment in education report 1965 – recollections and reminiscences' in *Irish Educational Studies*, 33:2 (June 2014).

Investment in Education research. In early 1964, he began to collate and analyse data which culminated in the chapter in the annexes and appendices entitled 'School Location Analysis'. This author spent many hours with Bill in the early months of 1964, trying to develop a statistical model which could be applied to educational planning in Ireland, with a special focus on developing a model which would ensure that every young person in the country could access post-primary education. Various successful and unsuccessful attempts at developing a statistical model were filed away and kept by this author as were drafts of sections of the report which were dismissed by other members of the team, as well as some initial drafts of papers which Bill prepared during his early months in the Development Branch in summer 1966. These papers were consulted in the writing of this chapter. Because of the marriage ban, the author had to retire from her post in the Department of Education on her marriage to Bill in 1964, but she remained interested and involved in educational debate about opening up access to education. How the challenges surrounding full participation in second-level schooling would be resolved dominated conversations between the author and her husband throughout 1965 and 1966, leading to the birth of free second-level education – as well as the birth of two of our children, the first in May 1965 and the second in September 1966 – just two weeks after Minister for Education Donogh O'Malley announced his plans to introduce free second-level education in Ireland.

The Provision of Second-Level Education in Ireland before 1967

Before 1967, post-primary education was provided in (voluntary) secondary schools; vocational schools; secondary tops; preparatory colleges and juniorates of religious orders and congregations. Although government funding for voluntary secondary schools was limited, and all schools had to charge fees, the numbers of pupils attending secondary education grew from the mid-1920s to the mid-1960s, as Table 2.1 shows.

Table 2.1: Numbers of Secondary Schools and Pupils in Selected Years between 1926–7 and 1962–3 (Reports of the Department of Education for the School Years 1927–63)

Year	No. of secondary schools	No. of pupils in secondary schools
1926–7	283	24,766
1936–7	329	35,890
1946–7	393	42,927
1956–7	480	62,429
1960–1	526	76,843
1961–2	542	80,400
1962–3	557	84,916

Enrolments in secondary schools had almost quadrupled in the thirty-five years following Independence. Until the early 1960s, those involved in educational policy saw no need for ministerial intervention to improve participation rates in post-primary education. In 1949, the then Minister for Education, General Richard Mulcahy, had likened the role of the minister to that of a plumber, stating:

> I regard the position as Minister in the Dept. of Education as that of a kind of dungaree man, the plumber who will make satisfactory communications and streamline the forces and potentialities of the educational workers and educational management in this country. (DÉ, 19 July 1956, c. 1494)

Twenty more years were to pass before a Minister for Education would take the initiative to introduce free post-primary education.

The Report of the Council of Education on the Curriculum of the Secondary School, 1962

A Council of Education was set up by Minister Richard Mulcahy in 1950 to advise the government on the development of primary education in Ireland. It was an unrepresentative council of almost forty members, twenty-six of whom were professional educators and eleven of whom were clerics of various denominations, chaired by a Catholic cleric. Trade unions were not represented, nor was there a representative of the Inspectorate or of parents (McManus, 2014, p. 82). In November 1954, the council was asked to report on the secondary-school curriculum. Its deliberations were long drawn out, and its *Report of the Council of Education – The Curriculum of the Secondary School* (Department of Education, 1962b) was not completed and submitted to the Minister for Education until 1960. The report, which was not published until 1962, was a conservative report, and while it contained some interesting analyses of the secondary school curriculum of the time, it saw no need for any significant expansion of secondary schooling, stating:

> Even a superficial examination of the demand (for free secondary education for all) will show that in this unqualified form it is untenable ... An unqualified scheme of 'secondary education for all' would be both financially impractical and educationally unsound. Only a minority would be capable of benefiting from such education and standards would fall. The voluntary system has worked well and preserves a sense of the value of education. Better State grants and more scholarships are needed to further stimulate it. (Department of Education, 1962b)

It was subsequently suggested that the reason for the delay in publishing the Council of Education report was because it no longer reflected the predominant views of politicians or policymakers. T. K. Whitaker's first report on economic expansion had been published in 1958, and in October 1959, within six months of his appointment as Minister for Education, Patrick Hillery had announced that government policy was to 'bring about a situation in which all children will continue their schooling until they are at least 15 years of age ... Our immediate policy is to increase the facilities for post-primary education' (Dáil Debates, vol. 177, cols 470–1, 28 October 1959, quoted in McManus, 2014, p. 103).

Interim Report of a Department of Education Committee on Post-Primary Education, December 1962

In June 1962, a committee was set up within the Department of Education to consider the future development of post-primary education, 'particularly in its social aspects'. The committee was chaired by Dr Duggan, Chief Inspector of Secondary Education, and its secretary and author of the report was Dr Finbarr O'Callaghan, an inspector in the Technical Instruction Branch. It would be interesting to know why the committee was set up, given that the same month, the Minister for Education, Patrick Hillery had announced the setting-up of the *Investment in Education* survey team. One explanation is that it was expected that the *Investment in Education* survey team would confine its deliberations to the economic aspects of education and the internal departmental group would focus on the social aspects (Hyland and Milne, 1992, p. 555). The committee was not expected to report until 1963, but in November 1962, it was asked to produce an interim report before 8 December 1962. The interim report unhesitatingly recommended 'a compulsory and free period of post-primary education for all Irish children':

> a comprehensive system ... a common form of post-primary course, extending over a three year period, should be available both in existing vocational and secondary schools ... The units we envisage following this common course would be termed 'Junior Secondary Schools'. They should aim at operating with a minimum of 120 pupils i.e. an annual intake of a minimum of 40 pupils ... (Department of Education, 1962a)

However, the committee was equally clear that senior-cycle courses should not be free, stating 'we are not prepared to recommend that senior second-ary school courses should be available free to all pupils who wish to partake of them'. From that point onwards, until September 1966 when Minister O'Malley announced his free education scheme, the position held by senior policymakers in the department was that a common junior cycle should be provided for all pupils, that an annual intake of forty pupils would be suf-ficient to maintain a viable second-level school, but that free senior-cycle secondary school courses should not be free.

Investment in Education Report, 1965

In one short chapter, it would be impossible to summarize the findings of the *Investment in Education* report, which was completed in mid-1965 and published in December of that year. The report was a fact-finding, empirical

analysis of the Irish educational system. It highlighted significant disparities
in participation rates in full-time education according to social group. It
pointed out that 35 per cent of pupils left full-time education either during
or at the end of primary school; fewer than 50 per cent completed junior-
cycle education and only 20 per cent completed the Leaving Certificate.
Fewer than 4 per cent of the cohort (about 2,000) went on to university,
and up to 20 per cent of these either failed to get a degree or dropped out
before completion. Young people from professional backgrounds were at
least five times more likely to complete the senior cycle than children of
the unskilled workers or the unemployed, and were more than twenty-five
times more likely to enter university. There were also significant disparities
in participation between those from rural backgrounds and those from
urban backgrounds, with distance from the nearest post-primary school
identified as a barrier to participation. Table 2.2 summarizes the participation rates by age of young people in full-time schooling.

Table 2.2: Participation by Young People in Full-Time Schooling in Ireland by Type
of School and Selected Age Group, February 1963 (<http://www.education.ie/en/
Publications/Policy-Reports>)

	6–12 years	*13 years*	*14 years*	*15 years*	*16 years*
National Schools	389,739	31,039	5,843	938	254
Sec. Schools and Sec. Tops	6,832	17,715	21,139	19,472	15,438
Vocational Schools	135	4,714	10,268	8,334	4,185
Population (est.)	401,400	56,600	56,400	56,600	56,200
Participation (%)	*98.8*	*94.6*	*66.4*	*51.6*	*36.8*

Various commentaries on the *Investment in Education* report correctly
emphasize that it made only one recommendation, that is, that a development unit should be set up within the Department of Education. However,
many of those commentaries understate the conclusions of the various
chapters of the report, including 'conclusions based on an analysis of

participation rates in full-time education', which were effectively recommendations under a different name. In relation to participation, these
conclusions stated that 'the main areas in which improvements might be
sought are as follows':

1. The number who leave school without having reached primary cer-
    tificate level;
2. The low rate of participation in post-primary by children from social
    groups F and G (unskilled, semi-skilled, unemployed, etc.);
3. The high rate of early school leaving from junior cycle;
4. The small proportion of continuation pupils who reach third level;
5. The low rate of participation in university – and the relatively low
    certificate attainment of many entrants.

The report contained numerous statistical and analytical tables which were
to provide an invaluable basis for subsequent educational planning. There
would no longer be any excuse for basing educational policy on surmise
and anecdote. *Investment in Education* provided an immense evidence base
for subsequent education policymaking. Much has been written about the
influence of the report on subsequent educational policy. The National
Industrial and Economic Council, writing in May 1966, stated:

> The sober and detailed factual analysis in *Investment in Education*, by challenging
> complacency and conventional wisdom and leaving no excuse for ignorance of rel-
> evant facts, has given an impetus towards that critical examination of our educational
> system in all aspects that alone can lay the basis for permanent improvements ... if we
> are to move towards the ideal of equal opportunity for all, these causes of the present
> inequalities must as far as possible be removed. (NIEC, 1966, p. 31)

In 1986, Seán O'Connor, who was head of the Development Branch and
subsequently secretary of the department wrote:

> The importance of the [*Investment in Education*] report to the Department of
> Education cannot be over-emphasised. The public were now aware of the deficien-
> cies and inequalities of the system and remedial action could no longer be postponed.
> (O'Connor, 1986, p. 10)

Writing in 1989, Seamus Ó Buachalla stated:

> *Investment in Education* offered the quantitative basis for a coherent rational policy which might well tax the political energies and economic resources of an enthusiastic government for a few decades. It illustrated convincingly the nature and the extent of inequality; it drew attention to the low rate of participation in post compulsory education by children of the lower social groups ... (Ó Buachalla, 1988, p. 72)

And in a scholarly analysis of the period, John Walsh commented:

> The [*Investment in Education*] report's conclusions not only illuminated the failures of educational policy in the past, but also charted a way forward for constructive development in the future. Investment was a devastating analysis of the Irish educational system, and made a compelling case for radical reform. (Walsh, 2009, p. 120)

Annexes and Appendices of the *Investment in Education* Report

Six months after the *Investment in Education* report was published, a 750-page volume of annexes and appendices was published. The timing of the publication of the *Annexes and Appendices* coincided with the publication of the National Industrial and Economic Council's report on *Investment in Education*, by which time the government had effectively accepted the findings of the report and had decided that action would have to be taken to address the inequalities which had been highlighted. As a result, the annexes and appendices, which contained wide-ranging and previously unavailable statistical detail, received little or no publicity, although they included material and data which had very significant implications for subsequent policy development.

This was particularly true of the 'School Location Analysis' (Chapter XII.B of the *Annexes and Appendices*) which suggested a number of different options for a nationwide system of post-primary education. The language and terminology used in the chapter was detached, dense and technical, and, in retrospect, understated the richness of the data provided and its potential implications for policy. However, this chapter was to have a profound effect on the development of post-primary education in subsequent decades. The 'Location Analysis' was made possible as a result of a nationwide census of schools, carried out by the survey team in February and June 1963 and again in February 1964 (Government of Ireland, 1965, pp. 393–453). As indicated by this author in another paper, one of the major challenges initially faced by the team was the paucity of statistical data – not only in relation to schools, pupils and teachers, but in relation to the population generally (Hyland, 2014). Following a preliminary analysis of the 1963 February census, it was decided to collect additional information, through the Inspectorate, about primary schools, including the age and physical condition of the schools and their distance from the nearest post-primary school. This data enabled the team to analyse the implications of making post-primary education accessible to all young people and to evaluate the consequences of using different catchment areas as a basis for developing post-primary facilities.

Bill Hyland conceptualized and led the 'Location Analysis' and it was one of the main areas of work that this author, as research assistant, was asked to undertake during the early months of 1964. It was a mammoth task, requiring detailed and painstaking work. This author still has the papers which set out the theoretical framework underpinning the analysis. Given the considerable number of mathematical options that were theoretically possible, Bill decided that he would have to try to get access to a computer, which would enable him to try out various statistical models. In the appendix to the *Investment* report, he explained why:

> One of the most important technical aspects of educational planning is the development of techniques for accurate and detailed evaluation of the consequences of alternative strategies. This has always proved very difficult in the past. The advent of the computer has meant a significant transformation of the conditions under which such evaluations are made. It is now possible to programme a computer to analyse in great detail the consequences of a large number of different strategies.

In 1963, an international technology firm, International Computers and Tabulators, had opened a new facility at the junction of Dublin's Adelaide

Road and Harcourt Street, where they had installed one of their then new mainframe ICT series 1300 computers, time on which could be rented on a commercial basis. It was physically a huge machine, requiring 700 sq. ft of floor space and weighing 5 tons. It had 20 bytes of memory – miniscule by today's standards! Bill persuaded the Department of Education to rent some time on this machine and he taught himself computer programming in order to analyse various simulations and strategies.[3] Over a period of a few months in early 1964, I would deliver the programmed punch cards to the ICT facility on my way home from work, they would be run through the computer during the night, and I would collect the results on my way into the office the following morning.

Bill initially suggested that a possible option for analysing educational date might be 'units already in use in connection with the provision of services e.g. those units used in the administrative organisation of the Public Health Services'. In support of this approach, he pointed out that the organization of the Public Health Services was based on the Registrars' Districts and the Dispensary Districts, and that population data for Registrars' Districts were available from the Central Statistics Office by gender and five-year age group. He suggested that these data could provide a basis for local planning and asked 'whether the catchment areas defined by these districts might also have some function in the administration of education and other social services?'

However, the eventual analysis was not based on civic or census areas. Since the national school system was a denominational system and national schools had historically been provided on a parish and diocesan basis, there had been no tradition of planning educational facilities on a civic boundary basis. Consequently, a more pragmatic approach to catchment-area planning was adopted and so-called 'major' and 'general' centres were identified. The 'major centres', were selected primarily on the basis of population. As they all had full post-primary facilities (in 1964), they were regarded as a minimal group of centres. The 'general centres' were defined by reference to population, geographical location and existing facilities. All of the

3   Bill subsequently graduated (in 1969) with a Master's degree in Computer Science from Trinity College Dublin.

general centres either already had some post-primary facilities (e.g. at least junior-cycle provision) or there were plans to provide such facilities in those centres. Data was also provided for Superintendent Registrars' Districts (total 126) and the Registrars' Districts (total 655), but ultimately these areas were not used for educational planning. The analysis was undertaken on a county basis – therefore, when it was decided to undertake consultation about post-primary provision on a county-by-county basis, the statistical data to undertake this exercise was already available. The potential of the statistical analysis that had been undertaken was recognized in the appendix:

> While the location survey has been used initially to measure the size of catchment areas in terms of the numbers of children in national schools and potentially in post-primary schools, it will be clear that the data may be useful also in the planning of a variety of social services apart from education.

A key table in the 'School Location Analysis' was the table showing the distance of national school pupils from their nearest post-primary school.

Table 2.3: Distance of National School Pupils from the Nearest Post-Primary School, June 1964 (<http://www.education.ie/en/Publications/Policy-Reports>)

Type of School	Under 1 mile	1–4 miles	5–9 miles	10 miles and over
Boys' secondary	50.2%	11.2%	24.1%	14.5%
Boys' vocational	53.1%	14.5%	25.4%	6.9%
Nearest boys' post-primary school	55.1%	16.1%	23.9%	4.9%
Girls' secondary	54.9%	12.2%	22.7%	10.2%
Girls' vocational	54.3%	13.5%	25.2%	7.0%
Nearest girls' post-primary school	58.1%	15.4%	22.4%	4.1%

Another important table in the *Annexes and Appendices* was Table 18 of Appendix V, which showed the proportion of pupils attending secondary schools charging various levels of (tuition) fees. This table showed that 62 per cent of all day pupils attended schools which charged less than £15 per annum; 74 per cent of pupils attended schools which charged less than £20 per annum. and 81 per cent of pupils attended schools which charged less than £25 per annum. With this information, it would be possible to estimate the cost of abolishing tuition fees and introducing a grant in lieu of fees, when free second-level education was introduced.

The statistical information provided in the annexes and appendices to the *Investment in Education* report was invaluable. For instance, the realization that almost 40 per cent of young people were attending a national school which was located at least 5 miles from the nearest post-primary school meant that the number of children for whom transport arrangements would have to be made could be estimated with a high degree of accuracy. The 'School Location Analysis' also provided information on the age of school buildings, the facilities available in them and the potential costs of replacing or upgrading school buildings where necessary. Because of the information provided in the report and appendices, future policy decisions could be evidence-based. So, for example, when Donogh O'Malley made his historic announcement about the introduction of free post-primary education in September 1966, he made that announcement with knowledge of the resource implications of such a policy, as will be seen in a later section of this chapter.

George Colley, Minister for Education, May 1965 to July 1966

George Colley was appointed Minister for Education in May 1965. Within two months of his appointment, he introduced to the Dáil his first Estimates as Minister for Education. Colley did not believe that a Minister for Education should play a passive role. In his view, 'the role of the Minister is to think, decide, initiate, affect, and finally guide educational reform' (*Irish Independent*, 7 February 1966). This was a decidedly different interpretation of the role of Minister for Education to that articulated by Richard Mulcahy fifteen years earlier.

During Colley's term of office, he continued the annual increase in the education estimates which had begun with his predecessor, Patrick Hillery. Colley initiated the restructuring of post-primary provision, appealing (as

his predecessor Patrick Hillery had done) for collaboration between secondary and vocational schools, with a view to providing a comprehensive
curriculum for pupils. His intention was to raise the school-leaving age
to fifteen in 1970, and to develop a system of secondary education which
would provide junior-cycle schooling for all, to be followed by two years
in senior cycle. This would coincide with extending the then two-year
course in vocational schools to three years. Post-primary education would
be organized on comprehensive lines 'wherever conditions are favourable'
(Dáil Debates, 5 February 1964).

In his speech in July 1965, Colley also formally announced the
setting-up of a Development Branch in the Department of Education.
The *Investment in Education* report had recommended that a development unit be set up and that a new post of assistant secretary, who would
be directly responsible for long-term planning work, should be created.
The report had stated that 'the professional head of the development unit
should be a first-class statistician who, ideally should have considerable
administrative experience as well'. The unit should also have the services
of 'at least one full-time economist and an inspector of schools'. A fourth
professional member should 'possess skills in the application of quantitative methods to decision-making processes' and 'to complete the professional personnel of the unit, a sociologist would be needed' (*Investment
in Education*, 1965, p. 466). However, when the unit was set up in 1966,
it was but a pale imitation of what had been envisaged in the report. Seán
O'Connor was appointed head of the Development Branch, at assistant
secretary level. Bill Hyland, who was appointed as statistician, was never
given the title of professional head of the unit and the only other professionals appointed within the first year were inspectors seconded on a
short-term basis from within the Department of Education. There was no
economist, no sociologist and no other professionals.[4] Bill was regarded
by his colleagues in the department as an outsider and was not deemed
eligible for promotion under either of the two professional promotion pillars – the administrative pillar or the Inspectorate pillar. In the early years

4   A few years later, Torlach O'Connor was appointed as the department's first
     psychologist.

of the Development Branch, he had some influence and his views were listened to by policymakers, but as time went by, he became increasingly marginalized and many of his proposals were regarded as too radical or challenging, particularly by Minister Richard Burke, who closed down the Development Branch in 1973.

Two 'Planning' Papers: *Notes on the Organization of Secondary Education in a Sample Rural Area*, and *Financial Assistance for Post-Primary Students*

While Bill Hyland had kept in touch with the thinking in the department in relation to expanding post-primary provision during 1965 and early 1966, when he returned to Dublin in June 1966 to take up the post of statistician in the Development Branch, he got down to work immediately, and drafted a number of papers suggesting how post-primary schooling for all could be delivered in Ireland. Among his papers, this author has found two documents which were written in summer 1966, months before Donogh O'Malley's announced the free education scheme on 20 September 1966. The first paper was entitled *Notes on the Organization of Secondary Education in a Sample Rural Area*, and the second was entitled *Financial Assistance for Post-Primary Students*.

Notes on the Organization of Secondary Education in a Sample Rural Area

This twenty-page paper started off by asking 'whether the limitations and the uneconomic use of resources of the present system accurately pinpointed in the Report *Investment in Education* will be sufficiently countered by the proposals for the development and reorganization of secondary education which seem likely to prevail in the rural areas in the future?' The paper expressed scepticism about the department's plans at that time for expanding post-primary provision: 'Are they bold enough? Do they go far enough? The contention of these notes is that they may not.' The paper then set down the 'Present Situation and Intentions'. These included the development of a system of secondary education, which, starting in 1970, would provide three years of compulsory post-primary education in the junior or first cycle for all, to be followed by two further years in a senior cycle and to move, 'wherever conditions were favourable', towards the organization of post-primary education on comprehensive lines. It criticized proposals for the extension and reorganization of secondary education, which were based on minimum units for the junior cycle of six classes and 150 pupils (an intake of fifty pupils per annum) and four classes and 100 pupils for the senior cycle. It went on to set out a number of general planning considerations, emphasizing the issues of school size and geographical location, and stated:

> In the majority of West European countries with which Ireland will have increasing economic and other ties, far reaching transformations in the education system have already or are in the process of taking place. The time of change is not by any means at an end. Ireland has the inestimable advantage of deciding relatively late on the reshaping of its own system and is able to profit from the mistakes and experiments of others. It would be a great pity if this advantage was whittled away and she entered on the task of educational renewal with one hand tied behind her back *because of an insufficiently bold forward view*. (Author's emphasis)

Concern was expressed in the paper that:

> the present plan based largely on minimum sizes of secondary school of 150 and 100 will fix on the rural areas of the country a system of secondary education by the lowest common denominator, restrictive of educational opportunity, ill adapted to change and limited in its ability to utilise high cost resources economically and efficiently ... The first major move forward in Irish secondary education is likely in the rural areas to be based too often on the smallest equivalent unit. *The national eye should surely be lifted for this vital service towards a somewhat loftier horizon.* (Author's emphasis)

The paper went on to discuss factors to be taken into account in determining the size of the school unit in relation to effective resource use. It discussed the deployment of teachers, especially in subjects where there was

a scarcity of teachers, for example, 'Science, Maths, Modern Languages'.
It explored the probability of far-reaching changes in teaching methods
in the next generation, 'which are likely to alter both the size and nature
of teaching groups', and the implications of these changes for the design
of school buildings. Taking Co. Mayo as an example, the paper set out
detailed projections, based on statistics collected for the 'School Location
Analysis', of the likely enrolment at the seventeen centres in the county
which at that time had some form of post-primary provision. The paper
then categorized these centres into groups, geographically and by size, on
the basis that none of the schools would have fewer than a four-form entry
every year, that is, that each school would have an enrolment of at least
300 in the junior cycle and 200 in the senior cycle. Where a centre could
not achieve this size, the paper envisaged that the centre would be deemed
unviable and would be amalgamated into the next geographically viable
centre. The second paper, prepared at around the same time was entitled
Financial Assistance for Post-Primary Students.

Financial Assistance for Post-Primary Students (prepared in the development branch)

This provided a detailed analysis and cost estimates of providing free post-
primary education for all pupils up to the age of fifteen. It suggested that
one possibility would be to offer a grant in lieu of fees of £10 per pupil in
junior cycle to schools with a stated fee of £15 and a grant of £15 to schools
with a stated fee of £20. (The justification for not offering a grant that was
the same as the fee charged, in lieu of fees, was that 'all secondary give free
places and accept reduced fees in hardship cases and in addition they have
collection difficulties'.) However, on balance, it was recommended that it
would be better to offer a flat grant in lieu of fees of £15 per pupil to all
secondary schools willing to forego school fees.[5]

---

5   In the context of the current practice of many secondary schools of seeking a 'volun-
     tary contribution' from parents, it is worth noting that the paper added: 'It would be

The paper also stated that financial assistance would be required for 'poor children' in the junior cycle to meet the cost of books, stationery, transport, etc. 'So far as the very poor child is concerned free tuition is not enough – he will not have the money to pay for the books and stationery he will need ... It is necessary therefore to ensure that the poor child will be provided with the books and accessories needed for his course.' The paper estimated that approximately 10 per cent of pupils would require such extra financial assistance. The paper also emphasized that free education, including 'a larger subsidy for books and accessories', should be available for 'poor children' to take their education up to the Leaving Certificate. It argued that there was no need to provide a grant in lieu of fees to all senior-cycle pupils, stating that 'school fees in this country, with some exceptions are very moderate and well within the compass of middle-income groups'. The paper stated that a scheme of financial assistance should be available, 'based on ability and graduated according to income to the low-income group to enable them to proceed to university or technological college'. It proposed 'to confine additional State support to the group with income below say £12 a week ... and for those we propose an additional grant of £15 per pupil to the school'.

As indicated earlier in this chapter, the thinking within the department from late 1962 until this time was that free education would be introduced for all pupils up to fifteen years of age, when the school-leaving age would be raised to fifteen, which was expected to occur in 1970. (In the event, the school-leaving age was not raised to fifteen until 1972.) The head of the Development Branch, Seán O'Connor, and his colleagues, including the secretary of the department, T. Ó. Raifeartaigh and influential leaders within the department, such as Finbarr O'Callaghan, were not in favour of introducing it sooner, nor did they anticipate introducing free education for pupils in senior cycle (Fleming, 2016, p. 238). Bill Hyland clearly differed from his colleagues in this regard. He not only envisaged free junior-cycle education for all, sooner rather than later, but he held strong views about removing barriers to participation for

---

an express condition of the State grant that the school would provide free education for all day pupils taking the Intermediate Certificate course'.

children of 'poorer' families, by providing additional financial support (including grants to compensate for loss of earnings) up to and including third-level education.[6]

Appointment of Donogh O'Malley as Minister for Education, 13 July 1966

On 7 July 1966, shortly before the Dáil went into summer recess, the Taoiseach, Seán Lemass, made an important speech on education in which he stated that the recent National Industrial and Economic Council commentary on the *Investment in Education* report emphasized the need for a very considerable expansion of financial outlay on educational development. He added:

> To an ever-increasing extent the policy of the Government will be directed to this, and we will have to endure the political criticisms which it may evoke from the unthinking, as other desirable developments are necessarily slowed down to enable this essential educational programme to be fulfilled. (Cited in Walsh, 2009, p. 159)

In his speech, Lemass pledged that the government would give education 'the priority it deserves' in the future allocation of government funds. On 13 July 1966, Lemass appointed Donogh O'Malley as Minister for Education. A fortnight later, in a letter to the Taoiseach dated 29 July, O'Malley made it clear that he had more radical and immediate plans than his predecessors, including the rapid completion of three comprehensive schools (which had been delayed due to lack of funding); the establishment of new comprehensive schools in other areas; a national transport

6   Bill regularly raised the issue of 'opportunity costs', arguing that fees, transport and other costs associated with school attendance were not the only barriers which prevented those from lower socio-economic backgrounds from participating in education. He was of the view that the loss of potential earnings had to be factored into any scheme that targeted full participation in post-primary education.

scheme for post-primary pupils; a school meals service for primary schools and a scheme of grants for audio-visual aids for schools. He stated: 'This is an imposing list of new and extended services but in my short period as Minister for Education, it has become abundantly clear that we shall have to introduce them quickly if we want to make any progress in education' (Letter from O'Malley to Lemass, 29 July 1966, National Archives, D/T 97/6/437, S.17913).

Memorandum from Donogh O'Malley to the Taoiseach, 7 September 1966

Shortly after his appointment as Minister for Education, O'Malley raised the question of free post-primary education with Seán O'Connor, who advised the minister to wait until 1970, when the school leaving age would be raised (O'Connor, 1986, p. 141). This had been the policy of department officials since 1962. However, as indicated earlier, Bill Hyland had reservations about this policy and had already drawn up a plan, including costings, for introducing free post-primary education. Consequently, when O'Malley asked that a scheme of free post-primary education be prepared by the Development Branch, much of the material for such a scheme was already available. Seán O'Connor admitted as much some years later. When O'Malley asked him how long it would take to draft a plan for free education, O'Connor said, 'Six weeks'. O'Malley wanted it 'for the following Monday' and O'Connor acknowledged that a short deadline could be met because 'in fact a fair amount of the work had already been done in the Department and we weren't really starting from scratch' (Christina Murphy, 10 September 1986, quoted in O'Dubhlaing, 1997). Within a week or two, Seán O'Connor, Bill Hyland and Seán O'Mahony had drafted the outline of the proposals which formed the basis of O'Malley's memorandum to the Taoiseach on 7 September (O'Connor, 1986). This outline contained much of the material that Bill Hyland had included in his earlier musings and papers.

The memorandum of 7 September 1966 set out two possible schemes for free post-primary education. Scheme A provided for free education up to Intermediate Certificate level for all pupils in vocational and comprehensive schools, as well as all day pupils in secondary schools which charged an annual fee of no more than £20. Senior-cycle education would be means-tested and would be free for pupils whose family income was less than £12 a week. Scheme B would provide free post-primary education for all pupils up to Leaving Certificate level in vocational and comprehensive schools and in secondary schools which charged fees of £20 or less. The memorandum also included details of a transport scheme and additional subsidies for pupils from disadvantaged backgrounds. In a covering letter with this memorandum, O'Malley told the Taoiseach that he proposed to make a speech shortly in which he would refer to some of the matters referred to in the memorandum (Horgan, 1997, pp. 298–9).

Announcement by Minister for Education, Donogh O'Malley, 10 September 1966

Three days later, before the Taoiseach or the Cabinet had an opportunity to consider the schemes outlined in the memorandum, O'Malley made his now famous speech at the annual conference of the National Union of Journalists in Dun Laoghaire, announcing that as of September 1967, every child in the country would be able to avail of free post-primary education. In his speech, he condemned the inequalities in the Irish education system, pointing out that 'every year some 17,000 of our children finishing their primary school course do not receive any further education'. He continued:

> This means that almost one in three of our future citizens are cut off at this stage from the opportunities of learning a skill, and denied the benefits of cultural development that go with further education. This is a dark stain on the national conscience. For it means that some one-third of our people have been condemned – the great majority through no fault of their own – to be part-educated unskilled labour, always the weaker, who go to the wall of unemployment or emigration.

He proposed to introduce a scheme 'from the coming school year' whereby no child would be prevented by lack of funds from completing the Intermediate and the Leaving Certificate courses. As well as providing free education in vocational and comprehensive schools, and abolishing fees 'in the general run of secondary schools', he announced that funding would be made available to provide books and equipment to pupils whose families could not afford to buy them. He also intimated that a lack of finances would no longer be a barrier to participation in higher education, although he did not elaborate on this. The publicity he achieved for his announcement was more than either he or any of his advisers had antici-pated. While some officials in the Development Branch, including Bill Hyland, were aware that O'Malley was planning to give this speech (they had been involved in preparing a draft speech during the previous week), they had not anticipated the huge coverage it achieved in the national newspapers. The *Sunday Press* and the *Sunday Independent* the following day (11 September) gave details of the speech on their front pages. The three daily newspapers covered the announcement on Monday, the 12th, with an editorial in the *Irish Press* stating that O'Malley's proposal would 'help to lift poorer children out of the serfdom of ignorance'. An editorial in the *Irish Times* stated:

> Caution, not untinged with scepticism, may well be the first reaction of many because of the pace and timing of this burst of speed, but it should be welcomed. The scheme will cost us dear, but a sense of proportion will remind us that if we can pay £15 a head subsidy for a heifer or a calf, we can afford to think in generous terms for the education of a child.

But reaction back in the Department of Finance was much less enthusias-tic. Both the secretary of the Department of Finance, T. K. Whitaker, and the Minister for Finance, Jack Lynch, were annoyed that the announce-ment had been made without the prior approval of the department or the Minister for Finance. Jack Lynch was out of the country at the time and had no prior knowledge of O'Malley's proposal. Whitaker was critical of O'Malley's failure to follow usual procedures and to obtain approval from the Department of Finance in advance. Whitaker complained to Lemass by memorandum on 12 September that the free schooling policy had not been approved at government level, and that the budget had not been agreed (NAI, DT, 96/6/356, S12891F, Whitaker to Lemass, 12 September, 1966).

However, it is likely that Lemass knew when he met O'Malley on 7 September, that O'Malley was planning to make the announcement. In a subsequent letter, Whitaker said that when he met the Taoiseach to discuss his (Whitaker's) memorandum of 12 September, 'while he (Lemass) did not expressly say so, I deduced from what he said (and the smile on his face) that he had personally authorized Donogh O'Malley to make this announcement' (O'Dubhlaing, 1999). Thirty years later, in 1996, when this author was a member of the Constitution Review Group chaired by T. K. Whitaker, she raised the issue of O'Malley's announcement with him. Whitaker was still angry about O'Malley's precipitate action. In the context of a suggestion to Whitaker at that time that the Constitution Review Group might recommend that Article 42.4 of the Constitution be amended to remove the word 'for' and that the state's provision of free education be extended to include post-primary education, Whitaker visibly bristled and refused to include such a recommendation.[7] While in many ways Whitaker was an extraordinary civil servant, totally committed to the public good, he refused to accept, even then, that the way in which O'Malley had introduced free post-primary education was appropriate, and he expressed doubt as to whether every child in the country should have a right to free post-primary education.

There was widespread support for O'Malley's announcement, which pre-empted the publication of the Fine Gael policy document, *Towards a Just Society*, in November 1966. Tom O'Donnell, then a Fine Gael TD in O'Malley's constituency, later stated:

7   The 1922 Constitution stated that 'All citizens of the Irish Free State have the right to free elementary education'. This was amended in the 1937 Constitution to read: 'The State shall provide for free primary education and shall endeavour to supplement and give reasonable aid to private and corporate educational initiative, and when the public good requires it, provide other educational facilities or institutions, with due regard however, for the rights of parents, especially in the matter of religious and moral formation'. The report of the Constitution Review Group (pp. 343–4) includes a long explanation (drafted by Whitaker) regarding why the provisions of the 1922 Constitution in relation to free education were amended in the 1937 Constitution.

It was a bold and brilliant move. Donogh was very pragmatic; he always saw the bigger picture. The idea of free education didn't originate with him but that's beside the point. He saw an opportunity to enact a massive change and he delivered on it. He knew exactly what he was doing ... (cited in Browne, 2006, pp. 86–7)

Seamus Ó Buachalla wrote:

O'Malley's free education and transport schemes were formed from some very deep convictions on the social role of education, the innate injustice of inequality and the long-term national benefit to be derived from expanding educational opportunity. ... He was keenly aware of the fate of those, 17,000 in number, who never transferred from primary to post-primary, whose formal education ended at 14 ... (Ó Buachalla, 1988, p. 284)

Subsequent commentators have highlighted the significance of O'Malley's decision. In 2005, Dermot Keogh wrote:

The most dramatic development in the educational sector in the 1960s was when Donogh O'Malley announced the introduction of free post-primary education. The announcement, made on 11th September 1966, may have taken cabinet colleagues by surprise, but it is almost certain that the O'Malley speech was a ploy used often by Lemass to anticipate opposition and get a radical shift in policy approved by acclamation. This pre-empted interminable cabinet discussion and blocking tactics by the Department of Finance. Educational planning in the 1960s had been moving inexorably in that direction. (Keogh 2005, p, 284)

Memorandum to the Government, 11 November 1966

Developments between the time O'Malley made his announcement in September 1966 and the introduction of free post-primary education a year later have been well researched and documented and will not be elaborated on in this chapter (see Walsh, 2009; Fleming and Harford, 2014). A subsequent and detailed submission from the Department of Education to the Department of Finance on 11 November 1966 provided costings of the proposed scheme under four headings: Free Tuition, Free Books and

Maintenance, University Education, and Transport. However, the proposals that were eventually approved by the Department of Finance did not include the additional subsidy for maintenance for 'poorer children' that had been proposed in Bill Hyland's paper, so that the dream of 'equality of educational opportunity' was never fully realized. The path to implementation was not without its obstacles. Between O'Malley's announcement in September 1966 and the implementation of his plan a year later, O'Malley encountered some bitter opposition, but he was determined to proceed with his plan. His speech in the Senate in February 1967 encapsulated his frustration but also his determination:

> I know I am up against opposition and serious organised opposition but they are not going to defeat me on this. I shall tell you further that I shall expose them and I shall expose their tactics on every available occasion whoever they are. I see my responsibilities very clearly to the Irish people and to the Irish children. No vested interest group whoever they may be, at whatever level, will sabotage what every reasonable-minded man considers to be a just scheme … Christian charity how are you. (Senate reports, vol. 62, 9 February 1967)

Conclusion

O'Malley's decision in September 1966 to introduce free post-primary education together with a country-wide transport scheme was a game changer, and while it did not remove all the inequalities in education, it made a significant difference to participation at all levels of Irish education. While O'Malley's predecessors, Hillery and Colley, had each played an important role in expanding the educational horizons of Ireland's young people, O'Malley's appointment as Minister for Education came at a crucial time, when political and public opinion was ready for a 'big bang' approach. The statistics and the analysis carried out by the *Investment in Education* team had provided crucial evidence of the need for the expansion of post-primary provision. The 'Location Analysis' in the *Annexes and Appendices* of the *Investment in Education* report provided a template and a development plan for a nationwide system of post-primary education, accessible to all. By summer 1966, the work which underpinned the county reports had already been done and the timing of O'Malley's appointment as Minister for Education in July 1966 could not have been better. O'Malley proved himself willing and able to ride roughshod over the innate caution of some of the senior civil servants and to overrule their advice that free second-level education should await the raising of the school-leaving age to fifteen – then planned for 1970. Twenty years later, Seán O'Connor, who had initially been of the view that free second-level education should not be introduced until 1970, and that it should be limited to junior-cycle pupils, wrote:

> I now believe that events proved Donogh O'Malley to be right. Had free educa-
> tion been delayed until 1970, I believe that the scheme would have been employed
> only to students under fifteen, or at most to students following the Intermediate
> Certificate course, and that there would have been no provision for students following
> the Leaving Certificate course. By 1970, Seán Lemass had left the government and
> without his help, no Minister for Education would have been able to overcome the
> resistance of the Minister for Finance and his Department. (O'Connor, 1986, p. 153)

Bibliography

Bonel-Elliott, I. (1994). 'Lessons from the Sixties: Reviewing Dr. Hillery's Educational Reform', *Irish Educational Studies*, 13, pp. 32–45.

Bonel-Elliott, I. (1996). 'The Role of the Duggan Report (1962) in the Reform of the Irish Education System', *Administration*, 44, pp. 42–60.

Breen, R., Hannan, D., Rottman, D., and Whelan, C. (1990). *Understanding Contemporary Ireland: State, Class and Development in the Republic of Ireland* (Dublin: Gill and Macmillan).

Browne, P. J. (2006). *Unfilled Promise: Memories of Donogh O'Malley* (Dublin: Currach Press).

Coolahan, J. (1984). *Irish Education: its History and Structure* (Dublin: Institute of Public Administration).

Daly, M. E. (2016). *Sixties Ireland: Reshaping the Economy, State and Society, 1957–73* (Cambridge: Cambridge University Press).

Department of Education (1962a). *Interim Report of Committee on Post-Primary Education* (unpublished).

Department of Education (1962b). *Report of the Council of Education – The Curriculum of the Secondary School* (Dublin: Stationery Office).

Fleming, B. (2016). *Irish Education, 1922–2007: Cherishing All the Children?* (Dublin: Mynchen's Field Press).

Fleming, B., and Harford, J. (2014). 'Irish Educational Policy in the 1960s: A Decade of Transformation', *History of Education*, 43:5, pp. 635–56.

Garvin, T. (2010). *News from a New Republic: Ireland in the 1950s* (Dublin: Gill and Macmillan).

Government of Ireland (1965). *Investment in Education: Report of the Survey Team Appointed by the Minister of Education in October 1962* (Dublin: Stationery Office).

Government of Ireland (1965). *Investment in Education: Annexes and Appendices* (Dublin: Stationery Office).

Healy, J. (1988). 'The Wild One', *Magill*, March.

Horgan, J. (1997). *Seán Lemass: The Enigmatic Patriot* (Dublin: Gill and Macmillan).

Hyland, Á. (2014). 'The Investment in Education Report 1965: Recollections and Reminiscences', *Irish Educational Studies*, 33:2, pp. 123–40.

Hyland, Á., and Milne, K. (1992). *Irish Educational Documents Vol. 2* (Dublin: Church of Ireland College of Education).

Keogh, D. (2005). *Twentieth Century Ireland: Revolution and State Building* (Dublin: Gill and Macmillan).

Lee, J. J. (1989). *Ireland 1912–85: Politics and Society* (Cambridge: Cambridge University Press).

McManus, A. (2006). *Irish Education: The Ministerial Legacy, 1919–99* (Dublin: The History Press Ireland).

Mulcahy, D. G., and O'Sullivan, D. (1989). *Irish Educational Policy: Process and Substance* (Dublin: Institute of Public Administration).

Murphy, C. (1986). 'How O'Malley launched Free Schooling', *The Irish Times*, 10 September.

Ó Buachalla, S. (1988). *Education Policy in Twentieth Century Ireland* (Dublin: Wolfhound Press).

O'Connor, S. (1986). *A Troubled Sky: Reflections on the Irish Educational Scene 1957–68* (Dublin: Educational Research Centre).

O'Dubhlaing, S. (1997). *Donogh O'Malley and the Free Post-Primary Education Scheme* (unpublished MEd dissertation, Maynooth University).

O'Flaherty, L. (1992). *Management and Control in Irish Education: The Post-Primary Experience* (Dublin: Drumcondra Teachers' Centre).

O'Sullivan, D. (2005). *Cultural Politics and Irish Education since the 1950s: Policy Paradigms and Power* (Dublin: Institute of Public Administration).

Randles, E. (1975). *Post-Primary Education in Ireland 1957–70* (Dublin: Veritas Publications).

Walsh, J. (2008). *Patrick Hillery: The Official Biography* (Dublin: New Island).

Walsh, J. (2009). *The Politics of Expansion: The transformation of educational policy in the Republic of Ireland, 1957–72* (Manchester: Manchester University Press).

3 Agency and Advocacy: The Key Actors behind the Free Education Initiative

Context for Reform

On 10 September 1966, the Minister for Education, Donogh O'Malley, famously surprised the nation when he announced plans for free second-level education. In the public memory, the introduction of 'free education' is so closely associated with O'Malley's name that the terms are virtually synonymous. The dramatic nature of his statement, the fact that he bypassed normal government procedures in announcing a significant change in policy, an air of mystery surrounding the exact role of the Taoiseach Seán Lemass in this manoeuvre, and O'Malley's death, at a relatively young age, a couple of years later, have collectively contributed to O'Malley being viewed as 'the folk-hero of Irish education' (O'Connor, 1986, p. 192). O'Malley was perceived to have been both the architect and the mastermind of free education. The reality, of course, was infinitely more complex.

The government in 1922 inherited a system of education which was controlled by the Churches and funded, albeit inadequately, by the state. This arrangement had been copper-fastened in the 1937 Constitution, which clearly defined the system of education as state-aided rather than provided. Walsh (2009, p. 1) suggests that education policy at this time was characterized by a 'conservative consensus, which was shared by politicians, senior officials and educational authorities'. This consensus was based on the assumption that the state should exercise a limited role in providing education and in shaping policy, ceding control to private interest groups, in particular the Catholic Church, which enjoyed at this time 'a grip on education of unique strength' (Whyte, 1980, p. 16). This stance is probably best illustrated by the following statement from the Minister for Education, Richard Mulcahy, expressing his view of the Irish educational system to the Dáil in July 1956:

> You have your teachers, your managers and your churches and I regard the position as Minister in the Department of Education as that of a kind of dungaree man, the plumber who will make satisfactory communications and streamline the forces and potentialities of the educational workers and educational management in this country. He will take the knock out of the pipes and will link up everything. I would be blind to my responsibility if I insisted on pontificating or lapsed into an easy acceptance of an imagined duty to philosophise here on educational matters. (DÉ 19 July 1956, c.1494)

These remarks have been frequently derided by commentators. The reality is that they represent an honest assessment of the role of the Minister for Education as Mulcahy perceived it. It is also a fair appraisal of the approach of each his predecessors.

Cultural Contrarians

O'Sullivan identifies the important contribution to bringing about change that can be made by those whom he describes as '"cultural contrarians" … those who, while indigenous to the culture, nonetheless think otherwise in some significant regard' (O'Sullivan, 2005, pp. 461–2). Fortunately, in relation to this period of Irish education, there were some very capable and committed contrarians, although they were few in number. A prominent critic of educational policy at the time was John O'Meara, Professor of Latin at University College Dublin and Irish correspondent of the *Times Education Supplement*. He synthesized his views on the deficiencies in the education system in a lecture delivered in March 1958. This synthesis was easily the most comprehensive critique of the Irish education system to date, and was subsequently published as a booklet (O'Meara, 1958). In his opening remarks, O'Meara recognized the 'heroic role' the Church had played in the provision of education over several decades; however, he was scathing in his assessment of the state's performance:

> Hardly more than a ripple or two has come to disturb that stagnant pond which is the Department of Education since the State was founded – and it would seem that hardly a ripple ever will – for that Department seems to share some of the qualities of the natural law; it seems to be immutable. It would rest undisturbed until there is severe pressure put upon the government – and that, I hope, is not too far away ... The Department assumes the minimum possible responsibility for the secondary schools. The Church guarantees her own interests, in the first place, and provides almost a free education, of a special kind to a very large number. But in between the interest of the country as a whole is not served. This is the State's responsibility and it cannot be shirked. (1958, p. 6)

This analysis was compounded by claims that many teachers at post-primary level were unqualified and that advertisements for teaching posts often required teachers to teach eight or nine subjects (*The Irish Times*, 20 August 1953). Post-primary at the time consisted of secondary, vocational and a small number of comprehensive schools.

There were, at this time, around fifty secondary schools in Ireland which were managed and owned by lay people, compared to approximately 550 schools under the control of the Catholic Church. There were also vocational schools and a small number of comprehensive schools, both of which were run by lay committees with significant clerical membership. A federation representing lay secondary schools had been formed in 1947. At about the same time, Patrick Cannon and his wife Eileen founded Sandymount High School, a co-educational, non-denominational secondary school. Cannon joined the Federation of Irish Lay Secondary Schools in 1952 and quickly became prominent within the organization. 'A bugbear of clerical educationalists because of his liberal views' (Garvin, 2004, p. 142), Cannon periodically used his annual prize-giving address as a forum for critiquing educational policy. In a 1954 address, he contrasted the low progression rate of Irish children from primary to post-primary schooling with European norms (*The Irish Times*, 24 May 1954). Two years later, he linked the pressing need for investment in education to the economic future of the nation. Meanwhile, the federation was gaining traction as it was tapping into an issue of growing public importance. A memorandum produced in 1956 called for action to be taken to deal with the poor progression rates from primary to post-primary education, which were, it claimed, the lowest in Europe (*Irish Independent*, 13 March 1956).

In his presidential address at the federation's annual conference in 1959, Cannon returned to the theme of investment in education, suggesting that free post-primary education for all was necessary in order to secure economic growth (*The Irish Times*, 9 June 1959). By taking this position, Cannon was aligning himself with the growing number of economists internationally who were developing the theory of human capital. Some years later, the federation compiled a significant report entitled *Investment in Education in the Republic of Ireland with Some Comparative Statistics* (The Federation, 1962), which contained a detailed statistical analysis of educational provision in Ireland and neighbouring jurisdictions. The report noted that financial provision for primary education calculated on a *per capita* basis was about 75 per cent of that in England and Wales and, at post-primary level, approximately one-third. In an editorial, the *Irish Independent* described the report as 'refreshingly direct and incisive', endorsing its call for increased resources for education and the establishment of a permanent planning unit in the Department of Education (*Irish Independent*, 12 May 1962).

Around the same time, Tuairim, an intellectual movement which challenged the existing orthodoxy, emerged as an influential think tank. With branches throughout Ireland, including Belfast, and also in London, the association produced a number of key publications on public policy issues. In 1962, both the Dublin and London branches issued policy documents on Irish education. While broadly similar, the London document was more strident because, according to *The Irish Times*, 'distance has lent disenchantment' (*The Irish Times*, 2 October 1962):

> Education has remained static for so long in Ireland because it suits powerful sections of society, the middle classes, the Churches and the politicians ... the State cannot be expected to subsidize private institutions out of the public purse unless it has complete control over the way in which these subsidies are spent. (Tuairim, 1962, pp. 4–5)

The London document was particularly critical of politicians, suggesting that they were reluctant to advocate reforms in education for fear that they 'might offend the various pressure groups'. Ministers for Education were described as having 'played safe' and 'this political paralysis appears to have permeated the whole department' (*Irish Independent*, 18 April 1963).

Key Implementation Triggers

A number of key individuals who collectively transformed the policy agenda emerged at this point. Seán Lemass (1899–1971) took over as Taoiseach (Prime Minister) from Éamon de Valera (1882–1975) in 1959, quite late in his career. Succeeding the towering figure of de Valera inevitably meant that expectations of how he would fill the role were limited. He was granted 'no more than a guarded welcome' by the press and there was no sign of public enthusiasm for his accession (Lee, 1998, p. 365). He had served as Tánaiste (Deputy Prime Minister) since 1945, every time his party had been in power, and was fifty-nine when he became Taoiseach. Some may have assumed that this prolonged period as second-in-command, and a relatively late appointment to the top position, might have resulted in a low-key, transitional term of office. The reverse was the case, as the challenge facing the country in the 1950s prompted a very active premiership. 'Even during this depressing period Seán Lemass represented a restless frustrated potential which ... in the agonies of the country's gravest hour, symbolised Ireland's determination to survive recover and grow' (*Nusight*, 1969, p. 81).

Determined to reform the economy following the deep recession of the previous decade, he saw education as central to this ambition, a view shared by his close associate T. K. Whitaker, secretary of the Department of Finance. Whitaker describes the period post-Independence as one of stagnation, emigration and high unemployment, during which 'the mood of despondency was palpable' (Whitaker, 2006, p. 8). Like many of his contemporaries, he cautioned that 'something had to be done or the

achievement of national Independence would prove to have been a futility'
(Whitaker, 1983, p. 9). Noël Browne (1915–97), physician and Minister
for Health (1948–51), and Declan Costello (1926–2011), Fine Gael TD
(Teachta Dála, member of Dáil Éireann, the lower house of the Oireachtas
or Irish Parliament), also linked the need for action on education with the
efforts and ideals of the state's founders.

Browne noted:

> I would suggest then to the Minister that what he should aim at would be an educa-
> tional system that, first of all, gives a child, no matter whose child, the same chance
> as he would expect from a child of wealthy parents ... the aim of the men in the 1919
> Dáil was to provide a democratic programme, cherishing equally all the children of
> the nation. The Minister now has a magnificent opportunity of deeming that great
> pledge made on behalf of men who sacrificed so much thirty or forty years ago in
> order to establish a militant democratic republic, of putting an end to a system estab-
> lished by the British regime and which we have retained practically unchanged in
> the fundamentals. (DÉ, 2 May 1957, cc. 690–1)

Costello subsequently commented:

> Forty years ago in this State, a political revolution occurred when part of this coun-
> try, at least, obtained its freedom. It is time now that a social revolution occurred
> in this State. Our society is stratified into very rigid classes, mainly as a result of our
> educational system, and it is time we had in this country what can only be called a
> revolution in our educational system ... We have in this country at the present time
> a system whereby it is largely true that the child of poor parents finds it extremely
> difficult to get adequate education. That system must change ... we must be prepared
> to make whatever financial sacrifices are necessary to provide the educational services
> to bring this system about. (DÉ, 7 June 1961, c.1612)

Developing a Reform Agenda

Over the seven years of his premiership, Lemass appointed as Minister
for Education, in turn, three ambitious, young politicians, Patrick Hillery
(1923–2008), George Colley (1925–83) and Donogh O'Malley (1921–68).

During the summer of 1962, education was the subject of much consideration at government level. The Council of Education, which had begun its review of the secondary school curriculum in 1954, had submitted its report to the government in 1960. It was a conservative, unimaginative report, variously described as 'a big disappointment' (Coolahan, 1981, p. 80) and 'a disaster' (O'Connor, 1986, p. 69). Its position on free second-level education was as follows:

> Secondary education for all is utopian if only for financial reasons. The financial burden would have to be assumed by the State ... There are also objections on educational grounds. One of these is that only a minority of pupils would be capable of profiting by secondary (grammar school) education, as is attested by the experience of many countries. Furthermore, if secondary education were universally available free for all ... standards would inevitably fall. (Department of Education, 1962, p. 252)

An opportunity for reflection and reform soon emerged *via* the Organisation for Economic Cooperation and Development (OECD), which was then embarking on an analysis of a series of education systems, and was seeking participants. The Irish government was one of the few to respond positively to the opportunity, a bold decision given the potential impact of a full-scale review of the existing system. The survey team, under the leadership of a prominent economist, Paddy Lynch, began work in 1962. The other members of the group were Martin O'Donoghue, a Trinity economist, Bill Hyland, a statistician on secondment from the United Nations Statistics Office in New York, and Pádraig Ó Nualláin, a member of the Inspectorate in the Department of Education. Two department officials, Charles Smith and Áine Hyland (then Áine Donlon), acted as secretary and researcher for the group. A national steering committee under the chairmanship of Seán MacGearailt, assistant secretary of the department, was appointed to oversee the process. Unlike previous review groups, this committee was a broadly based group not dominated by clerical figures.

Lemass included the topic of education in a number of his speeches during the summer of 1962: 'It is in the growth and improvement of our education system that the foundations of our future prosperity must be firmly based' (*Irish Independent*, 9 July 1962). Some weeks later, he announced that Hillery was 'working on a scheme which envisaged a new type of post-primary school with a curriculum which, although broadly based, would have a definite practical bias' (*Irish Independent*, 15 July 1962). Away from the public eye, there was new thinking within the department as senior officials prepared some material for the *Second Programme for Economic Expansion*, which was to be published in 1963 (Department of Finance, 1963). Their *Forecast of Developments* document was wide-ranging, although its thinking on secondary education was limited. Having said that, it included a proposal for the provision of comprehensive education in parts of the country where no secondary schools were available.

Of perhaps more significance was the establishment of an internal department committee of inspectors in June 1962, under the chairmanship of Dr Maurice Duggan, to 'consider the present position of post-primary education, particularly in its social aspects, and to make recommendations' (Hyland and Milne, 1992, p. 555). Dr Finbarr O'Callaghan, who had been a member of the Technical Instruction Branch (TIB) of the Inspectorate since 1955, was appointed secretary to the Duggan committee. Ultimately, he became not only the secretary of the Duggan committee, but the author of the report it produced. He recalls that the minister had begun to bring pressure to bear for the report to be completed early (in conversation with Brian Fleming, 2013), an indication of Hillery's commitment to the reform agenda. The committee reported at the end of 1962 and recommended free compulsory post-primary education for all children between the ages of twelve and fifteen, with a suggestion that, in due course, this should be extended to sixteen years. The committee also recommended that free places be made available at senior-cycle level for pupils showing the ability to benefit from such provision. The need for the extension of provision to those areas currently without any provision was highlighted as a priority.

In August 1962, the Taoiseach made a speech in which he referred to proposals for a new type of post-primary school on which Hillery was working. It had been preceded by some robust internal debate on the topic, caused by the *Report of the Interdepartmental Committee on the Problems of Small Western Farms*, which was circulated to government departments for comment. As his department had not been represented on the committee, Hillery responded with a detailed memorandum in July 1962 (NAI, DT, S 12891, D/2/62). He highlighted the fact that there were many areas in the country that were not served by post-primary facilities, particularly in the western counties, and proposed a new type of junior post-primary school, offering a comprehensive curriculum. In his view, the state should bear in full the capital and running cost of these regional post-primary schools. The Department of Finance voiced strong opposition in response, largely on financial grounds, but also observing that educational interests, including those of the Churches, would have to be consulted before any such initiative could be introduced. Hillery reacted in a forthright manner, again emphasizing areas in which there was no provision. Lemass, in speeches on education at that time, was somewhat understated, but clearly supported Hillery's stance; the evidence suggests that these addresses were drafted within the Department of Education (NAI, DT, S 12891, D/1/62). The minister continued to develop his proposals and, in January 1963, he submitted a plan to Lemass for comprehensive schools to be established as a pilot scheme in areas without suitable facilities locally, notwithstanding the considerable expense involved and the likely opposition:

> I would like you to regard the suggestions as the archetype of a system of post-primary education which should apply to the whole country ... It will be expensive but it is necessary and probably inevitable ... Certain 'vested interests' in education would be annoyed at the introduction of such a school on a national basis but in these particular areas the interests have not provided for the children and cannot therefore object to State action. Once a beginning is made the general application of this system to the whole country would follow slowly over time. (NAI, DT, 17405, C/63)

Lemass's support for the proposals, as his colleague steered them to fruition, was hugely important. Interestingly, he encouraged Hillery to announce his proposals publicly as otherwise, he cautioned, 'you will never get it through the government' (Walsh, 2009, p. 87). Farrell (1971, p. 68) contends that Lemass was 'an adroit exploiter of the inspired leak, willing to organise press speculation on matters of concern'. At a press conference on 20 May 1963, Hillery released a detailed statement, in

---

which he highlighted 'two main weaknesses' in existing provision. The first related to areas of the country where there were no post-primary schools within geographic reach. The second related to the state's duty to provide for the education of those:

> ... whose parents pay their share of taxes and rates which help to provide post-primary education for others ... whose voice amid the babel of competing claims from the more privileged has hitherto been scarcely heard. As I see it, the equality of educational opportunity towards which it is the duty of the State to strive must nowadays entail the opportunity of *some* post-primary education for *all*. (Original italics, cited in Randles, 1975, p. 331)

Although ambitious, Hillery did not go as far as the Duggan committee, which had recommended universal, free junior-cycle post-primary provision; however, there is some evidence that this may have been part of his long-term vision. Based on her conversations with him in the early 1990s, Bonel-Elliott suggests that he was concerned that such an initiative would be difficult to implement because of 'the accepted assumption of a very limited role for the State in education, the Department of Finance's fear of cost and its penny-pinching attitude, and the Church's propriety attitude to the running of education' (Bonel-Elliott, 1996, p. 58).

A Priority Issue

By the mid-1960s, reform of the education system had reached the active policy agenda, with all parties contributing to the debate. The Labour Party issued *Challenge and Change in Education*, a comprehensive policy document, based on a fundamental belief that post-primary education should be free to all in 1963:

> Education in Ireland today, despite the fact that increasing numbers of children are receiving post-primary education of one sort or another, remains essentially a part of a structure of social and financial class privileges which serve to prevent the full

utilisation of the human resources of the community and which are in complete opposition to Labour's concept of a good society. (1963, p. 1)

In particular, the party called for significant change at post-primary level. 'If we are to "cherish all the children equally" we must radically alter the system of secondary education by which in the past the financial contribution of the State tended to endorse the rich and buttress privilege' (Labour, 1963, pp. 10–11). In 1965, Fine Gael released its policy document, *Towards a Just Society*. Although comprehensive, the section on education was limited and devoted mainly to the revival of the Irish language. In relation to access to education, it stated that 'Fine Gael will introduce a system to enable every child capable of benefitting from further education to proceed from national school right through to university irrespective of the financial circumstances of the child's parents' (Fine Gael, 1965, p. 23).

The Significance of *Investment in Education*

Following an election in April of 1965, the Fianna Fáil government of Seán Lemass was returned to power and George Colley was appointed Minister for Education. He served a short time in that role, although he was in office when the *Investment in Education* report was submitted late in 1965. Under its terms of reference, it was clear that the report was designed to be analytical, forecasting the future manpower needs of the economy. As such, the team was required to assess the likely demand for educational facilities, forecast future enrolments and their implications for teacher training and employment, and outline the financial consequences for the state. This was, as the report itself described it, a 'limited task ... the prosaic one of examining those resources which are indispensable to any system of education' (OECD, 1965, p. xxxiii). In accordance with that brief, the group made no educational policy proposals. However, Áine Hyland, who was assigned by the Department of Education as a researcher for the group, recalls that they were influenced in their analysis by the criticisms of existing provision emanating from Pat Cannon and the Federation of Irish Secondary Schools, John O'Meara, and Tuairim (Hyland, 2014). Their single formal recommendation was organizational, namely that a planning unit should be established within the Department of Education. The group's influence was such that this proposal was implemented almost six months before the report was published. Colley described the unit's role as overseeing 'the implementation of improvements and reforms' (DÉ, 16 June 1965, cc. 977–8). Seán O'Connor was assigned head of the unit. Bill Hyland of the OECD survey team was also appointed as a member.

The team's survey of the currently available provision was highlighted in considerable detail. At a time when the collection of national statistics was not as advanced as it is today, to provide such a complete picture of the Irish education system was a remarkable achievement. Credit is due to Bill Hyland, the statistician on the team. Indeed, one of his fellow unit members, Pádraig Ó Nualláin, has described the report as 90 per cent the work of Bill Hyland (Ó Nualláin, 2012). The appointment of a team of two economists, a statistician and one educationalist to carry out a manpower study under the aegis of the OECD might have resulted in a report dominated by economic imperatives. However, while economic issues were addressed, the report's core messages related to the inherent social inequalities in the existing educational system. The key variables flagged in relation to inequality were social class and geographical location. The team also underscored the high drop-out rate, noting that more than one-third of the cohort examined left education after primary level. Of those who went on further, less than 30 per cent completed the Leaving Certificate. Among fifteen- to nineteen-year-olds, in excess of 46 per cent of those whose families were in the professional, business-executive or salaried categories were in full-time education. The corresponding figure for those in the semi-skilled or unskilled categories was less than 12 per cent. At third level, the contrast was even starker, the respective figures being 8 per cent and 0.25 per cent. The report noted the challenges involved in providing a more equitable system of education:

> The influence of such factors – social group, location etc. – on participation in education has of course been observed in many countries. Experience in other countries has shown that a significant improvement in participation by certain social groups can be a very slow and expensive process. (Report of the Survey Team, 1966, p. 176)

Careful to avoid making recommendations, the team skilfully circumvented restrictions in the terms of reference by noting that there was 'clearly a need for public policy to concern itself with these anomalies' (Report of the Survey Team, p. 389). The stark analysis contained in the report represented a comprehensive indictment of the Irish education system. Prompted by Lemass, who was concerned that the technical nature of the report might limit its impact (NAI, DT, 97/6/437, S. 17913), Colley prepared and released a summary of the document with the result that the findings of the survey team received widespread coverage, including favourable editorial comment (*The Irish Times* and *Irish Independent*, 23 December 1965). The team emerged in the public eye as honest brokers with no vested interest. Its analysis of existing provision was so stark that it provided a useful basis for George Colley to continue the reforming work of his predecessor.

The 'Folk-Hero of Irish Education'?

Seán Lemass announced a cabinet reshuffle in July 1966, which resulted in a number of changes. The appointment of Donogh O'Malley as Minister for Education was described as 'the greatest surprise', causing 'the greatest speculation' (*Irish Independent*, 7 July 1966), and 'most controversial' (*The Irish Times*, 7 July 1966). In previous government positions, O'Malley had established a reputation for getting things done quickly and efficiently. Commenting on his appointment, *The Irish Times* noted, 'Mr O'Malley will have less respect for tradition in the sense of red tape than many of his predecessors and if he rips through the Department of Education, he will have most of the parents of the country behind him' (7 July 1966). In

·

making this appointment, Lemass, who by that time was contemplating retirement, chose someone whom he expected to complete the education reform agenda without delay. The new minister was perceived as a forceful, if somewhat impetuous, politician. Seán O'Connor, whose book *A Troubled Sky: Reflections on the Irish Education Scene* provides the only first-hand account of these events, observed:

> He had a reputation as a 'hell-raiser', as being impetuous, and as having little respect for convention, which blinded many to his ability and his deep concern and sympathy for the underdog ... From O'Malley, we expected fast and furious action. (1986, p. 139)

O'Connor recalls that O'Malley raised the question of free education with him only days after taking up his portfolio. The minister asked O'Connor to brief him on the work of both the Secondary Branch and the Development Branch. Up until that point, all planning in the department had been based on the proposed increase in the school leaving age to fifteen, which was due to be implemented in 1970. The thinking was that free education up to that age would be introduced at the same time. In addition, some form of initiative at senior-cycle level to improve progression rates was considered necessary. O'Connor left that initial briefing believing O'Malley to be satisfied with that approach and commenced his annual leave. While on leave, O'Malley asked to meet him in a Dublin hotel and made it clear that he wanted more immediate action. Following O'Connor's return from leave, O'Malley raised the question of free education immediately. At a meeting one Thursday, he was asked by the minister how long it would take to draw up a plan for free education. O'Connor's suggestion was that a period of six weeks would be required, to which O'Malley responded, 'Right you have till Monday'. Thus, O'Connor and his two colleagues in the Development Branch, Bill Hyland and Seán Ó Mathúna, worked through the weekend. He recalls 'in fact, a fair amount of work had already been done in the Department and we weren't really starting from scratch' (*The Irish Times*, 10 September, 1986). They presented two options to the minister the following Monday morning. Scheme A consisted of free tuition and transport up to Intermediate Certificate level (a state examination usually taken at fifteen years of age, now known as the Junior Certificate). This arose from the work of the Duggan committee and the subsequent *Investment in Education* report. This scheme also included the option that provision could be extended to Leaving Certificate level, but that this element would be contingent on a means test. Scheme B removed the proposed means test and amounted to free schooling and transport at second level. O'Connor recalled that he and his colleagues favoured the more limited option:

> Mr O'Malley was not enthusiastic ... he said that the Taoiseach did not like means tests and he would have to consult with him. After lunch he came back and said a means test was not acceptable. I did not believe he had consulted the Taoiseach at all and I said as much to him when we were alone. All I got in reply was a laugh. (1986, p. 142)

Irrespective of the merits of either scheme, O'Connor and his two colleagues saw no rationale for the immediate introduction of such an initiative as the vocational system would require time to adapt to a new programme, enabling schools in that sector to provide courses leading to the Intermediate Certificate examination. (The vocational system catered for smaller numbers at post-primary level and provided practical rather than academic subjects in the main.) Despite hesitation on the part of his officials, O'Malley proceeded with his plan and submitted a memorandum to the Taoiseach on 7 September 1966 which was labelled 'preliminary' (NAI, DT, 96/6/356, S.12891F). He used the *Investment in Education* findings to great effect in highlighting deficiencies in existing provision, and cautioned that Fine Gael was about to launch their own plan.

The members of the Development Branch were well aware of the need for a wide range of reforms to meet the needs of poorer families. This first draft by Hyland set out the case. The handwritten comments are almost certainly O'Connor's and his call to 'be specific and not shirk the issue' was reflected in all subsequent memoranda.

Part B - Special assistance for the Needy Pupils.

10. For the under-privileged group, free tuition will not be sufficient to enable them to participate in post-primary education up to the end of the Leaving Certificate cycle. Financial assistance to enable them to purchase books and other school accessories is essential. They will be lacking in reading opportunity and cultural interest and these initial disadvantages will be aggravated by their inability to purchase the text books they need. These environmental disadvantages are now accepted as a primary cause of the inferior achievement of children of these groups. Furthermore, for poor children who live long distances from a post-primary school a special grant for transport is necessary, as there would be little point in having a scheme for free books and accessories, if these pupils could not attend school because of inability to pay their share of the cost of transport under the State subsidised transport scheme referred to later in this memorandum.

11. Special provision will also need to be made for (really) poor parents who have to send their children out to work when they reach the school leaving age in order to supplement the family earnings. These parents cannot afford not to have their children earning. The idea is that some amount by way of a maintenance allowance would be payable and would be confined

-/.....

[handwritten margin notes:] Who is going to define. Let's be specific in our proposals and not shirk the issue.

[handwritten margin note:] What is a "poor" child.

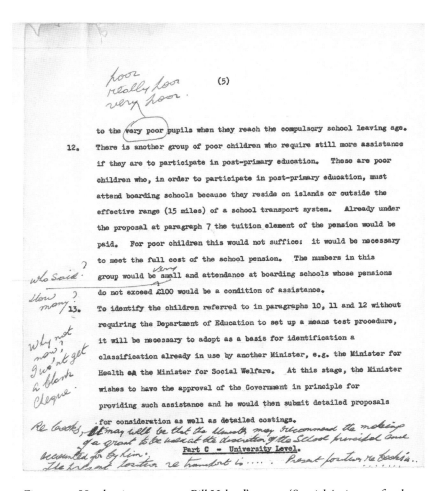

Figure 3.1: Hand-written notes on Bill Hyland's memo, 'Special Assistance for the Needy Pupils'. (Courtesy of Áine Hyland)

A Surprise Announcement

In his first major speech as Minister for Education on 10 September 1966, O'Malley condemned the inequalities of the current provision and described the fact that one-third of young people received no education beyond primary level as 'a dark stain on the national conscience'. He noted:

> I have always been concerned with the dilemma of parents ... who in the matter of post-primary education wish to do their very best for their children but find that the school fees – even when they are quite modest – are quite beyond their means. I propose, therefore, from the coming school year, beginning in September of next year, to introduce a scheme whereby, up to the completion of the Intermediate Certificate course, the opportunity for free post-primary education will be available to all families ... Going on from there I intend to make provision, whereby no pupil will, for lack of means, be prevented from continuing his or her education to the end of the Leaving Certificate course. (*The Irish Times*, 12 September 1966)

This was a cleverly worded passage. Essentially it amounted to an endorsement of scheme B, but was vague enough in relation to arrangements at senior cycle to allow for a scaling-back to scheme A if necessary. As O'Malley most probably anticipated, the vagueness went unnoticed and the proposal gained its own momentum. It represented a major step forward from the reforming proposals of his predecessors, which had tended to be gradualist in nature. As the speech was made to a gathering of journalists, it received extensive coverage. The editorial in *The Irish Times* noted:

> Startling is the word for the speech made by the Minister for Education on Saturday. It startles firstly because, in the world of cutbacks, it indicates a considerable investment; priority for education had been promised by the Taoiseach, but no one can have expected either so sudden or so mighty a leap forward. (12 September 1966)

Although, in principle, there was widespread support for the democratization of post-primary education, the operationalization of such a proposal was the focus of considerable comment and debate (*The Irish Times*, 13 September 1966).

Away from the public eye, a major row was ensuing. O'Malley's proposals had not been authorized by the government and, in particular, the Department of Finance had no knowledge of them. The department's secretary, T. K. Whitaker, 'exploded' (Horgan, 1997, p. 298):

> This 'free schooling' policy has not been the subject of any submission to the Department of Finance, has not been approved by the government, has certainly not been examined from the financial (whatever about the educational) aspect, and therefore should have received no advance publicity, particularly of the specific and definite type involved in Mr O'Malley's statement. (NAI, DT, 96/6/356, S12891F, Whitaker to Lemass, 12 September 1966)

The Minister for Finance, Jack Lynch, was abroad at this time, but it seems highly probable that Whitaker had discussed the contents of this letter with the minister before issuing it. In the same letter, Whitaker noted that the Department of Health had been left 'gravely insolvent' following O'Malley's departure. In Whitaker's view, it was 'astonishing that a major change in educational policy should be made by the Minister for Education in such a public fashion'.

It has been the focus of much speculation over the years whether or not the Taoiseach was completely *au fait* with O'Malley proposals in advance. We know that, on 7 September 1966, O'Malley, having submitted a memorandum to the Taoiseach's office, followed up by meeting with Lemass to discuss its contents. This was a private meeting between the two and no record of what transpired exists. Walsh considers it to be 'highly implausible' (2009, p. 190) that Lemass approved O'Malley's speech in detail before it was delivered. Horgan takes a somewhat more nuanced view, suggesting that perhaps O'Malley had 'general approval' (1997, p. 299), without Lemass necessarily having full knowledge of the specifics. Either way, there seemed to be a general awareness that consultation between the two men had taken place. Farrell recounts that five cabinet members had told him that they believed Lemass had seen the speech and arranged for parts to be amended before it was delivered (Farrell, 1971, pp. 69–70). This view tallies with that of Seán O'Connor. Interviewed twenty years later, he was 'quite certain that Lemass knew all about what was going on' and described O'Malley as the Taoiseach's 'stalking horse' (*The Irish Times*,

10 September 1986). Even more persuasive is the evidence of Whitaker. After he lodged his protest at O'Malley's announcement, he was called to a meeting with the Taoiseach. He recalls that 'while he (Lemass) did not expressly say so, I deduced from what he said (and the smile on his face) that he had personally authorized Donogh O'Malley to make this announce-ment' (O'Dubhlaing, 1997, p. 31). In retirement, Lemass agreed to one detailed interview about his time in politics with Michael Mills of the *Irish Press*, during which he observed: 'One of the methods by which the head of a Party, or the head of a Government, leads his party along a particular line of action is to speak in public in favour of a line of action before the government or the Party had decided on it' (*Irish Press*, 3 February 1969). The free education announcement was a case in point; although on this occasion, Lemass facilitated his minister's use of the tactic.

On the Monday following the speech, Lemass wrote to O'Malley, advising him that the announcement did not imply a commitment on the part of the government (NAI, DT, 96/6/356). Walsh describes this as 'a rebuke' (2009, p. 191). However, if it were a rebuke, it was certainly a mild one, and arguably reads more as though Lemass was protecting himself against a possible backlash. O'Malley's spirited response reminded the Taoiseach that both of them knew that Fine Gael was about to unveil a comprehensive education policy. In his view, it would have been 'dis-astrous politically' to be left trailing after the main opposition party on this matter (NAI, DT, 96/6/356). Apologizing for 'a misapprehension in believing that I had your support for my announcement', he asked Lemass for 'full support in getting my plans approved by government'. In a com-ment that reveals much about his character, he continued: 'I believe that it is essential for a government from time to time to propound bold new policies which would catch the imagination of the people and respond to some widespread, if not clearly formulated demand on their part' (NAI, DT, 96/6/356). A serious struggle ensued as O'Malley sought to have his policies endorsed by the government, and the Department of Finance made strenuous objections for financial reasons. Having discussed the matter further with the Minister for Finance, Lemass issued a rather more robust letter to O'Malley, stressing the necessity to follow proper procedure (NAI, DT, 96/6/356). Thereafter, the Taoiseach kept a watchful eye on events. When two deputies (Brendan Corish, leader of the Labour Party and Gerry L'Estrange of Fine Gael) submitted parliamentary questions seeking further details of the scheme and how it was to be financed, it was Lemass who determined the wording of the response, which was vague and non-committal (NAI, DT, 96/6/357).

O'Malley submitted his first detailed memorandum to the Taoiseach's department on 14 October 1966. On this occasion, the usual supplementary information, including projected costs of the scheme, were included. Yet again, he tried to circumvent normal procedure by attaching an 'urgency certificate' to the documents, which stated that a government decision was required before a television debate seven days later (NAI, DT, 97/6/638, S. 12891F). On this occasion, Lemass blocked the move. More significantly, Lemass suggested that the scheme be amended in favour of 'what it may be possible to achieve in the next few years ... at a lower cost' (Lemass to Malley, 17 October 1966, NAI, DT, 97/6/638, S. 12891F).

The second memorandum was circulated on 11 November, which was, as it happens, a day after Lemass had retired (he was replaced by Jack Lynch). It presented a strong argument for reform. The evidence gathered by the *Investment in Education* team, which indicated the 'extent to which ability to pay governs the rates of participation in post-primary education', was cited. There was also an emphasis on skills shortages in particular sectors of the economy and the need to address these in order for the economy to develop (NAI, DT, F.111668). Permission was sought for four initiatives: the abolition of tuition fees in post-primary schools opting into the new scheme, the introduction of assistance in the case of poorer children consisting of a 'free book scheme' and in particularly necessitous cases a maintenance grant, and the provision of a school transport scheme. In a speech on 10 September, O'Malley had also referred to the fact that a Commission on Higher Education was sitting at that time and commented that he wished to see some form of financial support so that poorer children could attend university. In fact, he included a proposal to introduce a university grants scheme in the memorandum to government. The Department of Finance response was issued on 17 November 1966 (NAI, DT, 97/6/683). It was made clear that no agreement had been reached in discussions between the two departments and the Department of Finance asked the government to 'view very critically proposals which will add substantially to public expenditure' as new taxation would be required to implement the plan. The department suggested that the 'proper course would be to defer these proposals, however desirable they may be in themselves, until funds sufficient to pay for them become available at present taxation levels'. However, recognizing the political reality, the memorandum suggested various modifications in the event that 'the government considers that something in the form of these proposals should be announced now' (NAI, DT, 97/6/638).

Cabinet Approval

The education issue was listed on the agenda for cabinet meetings on 18 and 25 November but not discussed. This may have been mere chance but it seems more likely that the delay reflected ongoing debate in government circles. It was considered by the cabinet later that month. The fact that O'Malley had made his proposals public, together with Fine Gael's launch of a policy document on education somewhat similar to his own, forced the government's hand. In O'Connor's view, 'the issue of the Fine Gael policy document silenced any opposition to the proposals within the government' (1986, p. 146). Although he had had to amend his initial proposal somewhat, for example, reducing the *per capita* payment to secondary schools joining the 'free' scheme, O'Malley more or less maintained the substance and aims of the original memorandum with respect to post-primary education, but his proposal for a university grants scheme was rejected. As well as the inclusion of various forms of financial assistance for less well-off families, such as grants for books, the proposal suggested that a special grant of £40 *per annum* be paid to the families of 'very poor pupils' who continued in full-time education beyond the minimum school-leaving age (NAI, DT, 97/6/638, S12891F, F11668). It was estimated that 3,000 families would require such assistance. The Department of Finance voiced strong opposition: 'The Minister for Finance feels that publication of this proposal might attract pressure for a higher scale of maintenance grant and a wider spread of beneficiaries with consequent increased cost' (NAI, DT, 97/6/638, S12891F, F11668). This particular issue was deferred for further consideration and it was agreed that 'the terms of the announcement in this regard [would] be settled between the Ministers for Finance and Education' (NAI, 95/5/1, G.C.12/2, Cabinet minutes).

O'Malley outlined the details of a scheme, including the grants to replace fees for those schools opting into the new arrangement, in the Dáil the next day. He also gave details of the school transport scheme, which was to be provided at the expense of the state. In the majority of cases, the fees traditionally paid by parents were quite modest, and indeed anecdotal evidence at the time suggests that they were often waived in necessitous circumstances. Taking this into consideration, although the abolition of fees is foremost in the public memory of the time, the reality is that the introduction of a school transport system probably contributed more to opening up access to post-primary education. O'Malley also mentioned the case of extremely necessitous families: 'When ... I have had an opportunity to assess the extent of the problem, I shall have to see what special provision for such cases should be made' (DÉ, 30 November 1966, c. 1890). As we now know, that proposal never saw the light of day, notwithstanding the cabinet decision referred to earlier.

Concluding Thoughts

In theorizing regarding policy shifts, Kingdon (2011) notes how 'windows of opportunity' emerge at key junctures when a range of variables or 'streams' converge. Hall (1993) suggests that policy failure over a prolonged period of time often acts as a catalyst for radical reform. It was the dismal economic performance leading to widespread emigration that brought about a paradigm change in the Irish approach to policymaking. There was a stable period in Irish education for four decades before a window of opportunity was opened, prompted by economic considerations and the promulgation of the human capital theory by the OECD. The confluence of a set of ideas promoted by a range of policy actors, along with the socio-economic climate in which such an agenda was being articulated, resulted in the introduction of significant reform. Such was the nature of this reform that had one variable been absent, the likelihood is that reform would have been stymied and maybe even prevented.

On taking up office as Taoiseach, Seán Lemass began implementing significant economic policy change. Altered economic policies inevitably led to social changes and a growing awareness of the importance of education in the public consciousness. Commenting on the inevitable knock-on effect of the economic policy changes on society more broadly, David Thornley (1935–78), Labour politician and academic, noted 'we have set in train certain great and far reaching processes within the material culture which inevitably will have great and far reaching effects in other dimensions' (quoted in Brown, 1981, p. 243). A growing awareness of the link between education and the economy meant that the education portfolio was viewed from the late 1950s as a prestigious cabinet post (Ó Buachalla, 1988). The economic policy reorientation which had commenced in the 1950s was gradually translated into education policy under a series of younger ministers born or raised after Irish Independence (Fleming and Harford, 2014; Walsh, 2009).

For Lemass, and indeed Whitaker, the motivation was economic regeneration. With the OECD highlighting human capital theory, the focus on educational provision was a natural consequence. Each of the education ministers during that period played an important role. O'Malley is often celebrated, but the important preparatory work undertaken by Hillery is under-appreciated. Without Hillery's groundwork, O'Malley's announcement of free education in September 1966 would not have been possible. Colley, although minister for a relatively short period, continued that work and established, in the public mind, the primary importance and responsibility of a minister and his department in the making of policy. Among the politicians, however, the major credit must go to Lemass. It was he who brought education onto the active agenda of government and he whose support and advice at critical junctures enabled his various ministers to introduce reform. He was the 'true radical in the government'

(O'Connor, 1986, p. 162) and, in Hillery's view, were it not for him, educational 'expansion would not have happened' (Walsh, 2009, p. 324). It is interesting that the window of opportunity for further reform in Irish education closed upon his retirement. As Lee (1989, p. 371) observes of Lemass, 'it was neither his manner of gaining power, nor his manner of holding it, that distinguished him uniquely among Irish prime ministers. It was his manner of using it'.

Often omitted in the historical memory of the period are the public servants who essentially work anonymously, arguably for more altruistic reasons. There is no doubt that *Investment in Education*, which crystallized the link between education and economy in its very title, provided the catalyst which brought the ambition for reform to the public consciousness. *Investment in Education* was 'the key contribution' (Lee, 1989, p. 361) and, in O'Connor's view, its importance could not be 'over-emphasised' (O'Connor, 1986, p. 120). The report provided an irrefutable case for reform. As well as their obvious expertise, each member of the survey team brought with them a strong sense of social justice. This was particularly true of the team's dominant personalities. While Hyland's contribution is obvious, Lynch's hand is clear in the understated but effective language used in the report. He also used his diplomatic skills, together with those of Mac Gearailt, to reassure the members of the steering committee charged with overseeing the process. It is important not to overlook the impact, also, of the Duggan Report. The choice of O'Callaghan, who had already established a reputation within the department as an innovative thinker (Coolahan with O'Donovan, 2009, p. 176), as secretary of the group, was critical. Presumably credit for this must go to Tarlach Ó Raifeartaigh, secretary of the department. For a government seeking to plot a way towards reform of a traditionally sensitive area, similar advice from both outside experts and from within the department must have provided the necessary reassurance and confidence to proceed.

When it came to securing agreement to implement the new arrangements, Ó Raifeartaigh also played an important role. Perhaps not a reformer by nature, he had nonetheless overseen the development of new thinking within the department and was happy to allow his second-in-command, Mac Gearailt, to take an active role as events unfolded. The leader of the

Catholic Church in Ireland, Cardinal William Conway, was following the Vatican line that emerged under John XXIII, which encouraged religious authorities to co-operate with civic authorities. He possessed a 'wide view of education and a nuanced political sense', possibly not fully appreciated at the time (Andrews, 1997, p. 152). The heads of religious orders who actually controlled secondary schools (O'Donoghue and Harford, 2011) were not very well disposed to O'Malley's proposals and it fell to Conway to persuade them to agree. A possible source of opposition within the hierarchy was John Charles McQuaid, Archbishop of Dublin. A very committed Catholic, Ó Raifeartaigh enjoyed the trust of McQuaid. McQuaid's confidence in Ó Raifeartaigh was particularly valuable in ensuring that sensitive changes were introduced without undue difficulty. Like Ó Raifeartaigh, there is little evidence that Seán Mac Gearailt was an instinctive reformer. However, both were able and loyal civil servants who used their skills to ensure political priorities were implemented. Mac Gearailt recognized the exceptionally innovative mind and acute vision of Seán O'Connor and was wise enough to provide space and the necessary support to bring forward his ideas. Indeed, in promoting the reform agenda, O'Connor was the central figure. Tony Ó Dálaigh, who served as private secretary to the three ministers for education during this period, has described him as 'the intellectual powerhouse of the department' (Ó Dálaigh, 2012). In the history of independent Ireland, he was, arguably, the most outstanding official ever to serve in the Department of Education. There is no doubt that the roles played by Seán O'Connor, Bill Hyland, Finbarr O'Callaghan and Paddy Lynch were central to the introduction of free education. All were contrarians who were critical of the *status quo*. Their knowledge base, political and administrative acumen, commitment to the less well-off and perspicacity was critical to the final outcome. Thus, while numerous individuals made key contributions, essentially the credit for the education reform of the 1960s should go to seven individuals. The reform resulted from the coming-together of Lemass and his vision for a modernized Ireland, his support for Hillery as he laid the groundwork and his appointment of a policy-driven minister in O'Malley, who had a strong social conscience, together with the presence within the system of O'Connor, Hyland, O'Callaghan and Lynch, who shared his values.

Postscript

Although hugely significant, the reforms of the 1960s did not achieve the objective of bringing about equality of education opportunity. The fact that the grant for pupils from extremely poor families was never introduced undoubtedly contributed to this, but the reality is that the problem was more complex than had been initially envisaged. From his work on the *Investment in Education* team, Hyland was well aware of the challenge involved in opening up post-primary education to all. In 1971, in a paper delivered to the Statistical and Social Inquiry Society of Ireland, he addressed, among other items, the issue of equality of opportunity (Hyland, 1971). His analysis stemmed from his consideration of the educational statistics gathered as part of the 1966 census. Acknowledging that 'some significant steps in the direction of equality of opportunity (however defined)' had been taken, he argued that the impact on the less well-off had been minimal:

> It is clear that the problem is more intractable than has been previously envisaged. In addition it has now become evident that the system works in most countries in such a manner that more public money is spent on the education of persons who start life in reasonably favourable situations than on those who start life in very unfavourable circumstances. Thus even the much lower objective of equality of expenditure per student is not likely to be achieved in most European countries in the foreseeable future. Secondly, data that are just now becoming available on the situation subsequent on recent advances in this area indicate that when the general run of society moves ahead in response to better opportunities the failure of those who are not able to benefit from these opportunities becomes more evident and also of more concern. (Hyland, 1971, p. 74)

Paddy Lynch was one of the participants in the discussion that followed Hyland's presentation. He described it as 'timely' and noted that it raised some 'very important policy issues' (Hyland, 1971, p. 74). However, by that time, the window of opportunity in Irish education had closed. The government's attention was focused elsewhere and the voices of the contrarians in Irish education were being ignored. Lemass had retired, O'Malley had died at an early age in 1968, and the Department of Education had reverted to its highly conservative traditions. It would be fifteen years before a Minister for Education, Gemma Hussey, began to address the issue of educational disadvantage again. Her successors have followed suit and various useful schemes and initiatives have been introduced which have brought about significant improvements. Sadly, however, the vision articulated by Donogh O'Malley in 1966 has yet to be achieved over half a century later.

Bibliography

Andrews, P. (1997). 'Irish Education Transformed', *Studies*, 58:342, pp. 149–55.

Bonel-Elliot, I. (1996). 'The Role of the Duggan Report (1962) in the Reform of the Irish Education System', *Administration*, 44:3, pp. 42–60.

Brown, T. (1981). *Ireland: A Social and Cultural History, 1922–85* (London: Fontana).

Coolahan, J. (1981). *Irish Education: Its History and Structure* (Dublin: Institute of Public Administration).

Coolahan, J., with O'Donovan, P. F. (2009). *Ireland's School Inspectorate, 1831–2008* (Dublin: Four Courts Press).

Department of Education (1962). *Report of the Council of Education – The Curriculum of the Secondary School* (Dublin: Stationery Office).

Farrell, B. (1971). *Chairman or Chief? The Role of the Taoiseach in Irish Government* (Dublin: Gill & Macmillan).

Federation of Irish Secondary Schools (1962). *Investment in Education in the Republic of Ireland with Some Comparative Statistics* (Dublin: The Federation).

Fine Gael (1965). *Towards a Just Society* (Dublin: The Fine Gael Party).

Fleming, B., and Harford, J. (2014). 'Irish Education Policy in the 1960s: A Decade of Transformation', *History of Education*, 43:5, pp. 635–56.

Garvin, T. (2004). *Preventing the Future: Why was Ireland So Poor for So Long?* (Dublin: Gill & Macmillan).

Government of Ireland (1965). *Investment in Education: Report of the Survey Team Appointed by the Minister of Education in October 1962* (Dublin: Stationery Office).

Hall, P. A. (1993). 'Policy Paradigms, Social Learning and the State: The Case of Economic Policymaking in Britain', *Comparative Politics*, 25:3, pp. 275–96.

Horgan, J. (1997). *Seán Lemass: The Enigmatic Patriot* (Dublin: Gill & Macmillan).

Hyland, Á. (2014). 'The Investment in Education Report, 1965: Recollections and Reminiscences', *Irish Educational Studies*, 33:2, pp. 123–39.

Hyland, Á., and Milne, K. (1987). *Irish Educational Documents*, vol. 2 (Dublin: Church of Ireland College of Education).

Hyland, W. J. (1970). 'Education and Irish Society – With Special Reference to Informational Needs', *Journal of the Statistical and Social Inquiry Society of Ireland*, vol. xxii, no. iii (1970–1), pp. 74–83.

Kingdon, J. (2011). *Agendas, Alternatives and Public Policies* (London: Longman, 2nd edn).

Labour Party (1963). *Challenge and Change in Education* (Dublin: The Labour Party).

Lee, J. J. (1989). *Ireland, 1912–85: Politics and Society* (Cambridge: Cambridge University Press).

Nusight, 'Lemass: A Profile', December 1969, pp. 81–96.

Ó Buachalla, S. (1988). *Education Policy in Twentieth Century Ireland* (Dublin: Wolfhound).

O'Connor, S. (1986). *A Troubled Sky* (Dublin: Educational Research Centre, St Patrick's College Drumcondra).

Ó Dálaigh, T. (2012). Address at *Investment in Education* seminar, Trinity College Dublin.

O'Donoghue, T., and Harford, J. (2011). 'A Comparative History of Church-State Relations in Irish Education', *Comparative Education Review*, 55:3, pp. 315–41.

O'Dubhlaing, S. (1997). *Donogh O'Malley and the Free Post Primary Education Scheme* (MEd dissertation, Maynooth University).

O'Meara, J. J. (1958). *Reform in Education* (Dublin: Mount Salus Press).

Ó Nualláin, P. (2012). Address at *Investment in Education* seminar, Trinity College Dublin.

O'Sullivan, D. (2005). *Culture, Politics and Irish Education since the 1950s* (Dublin: Institute of Public Administration).

Randles, E. (1975). *Post-Primary Education in Ireland, 1957–70* (Dublin: Veritas).

Tuairim (1962). *Irish Education* (London: Tuairim Research Group).

Walsh, W. (2009). *The Politics of Expansion: The Transformation of Educational Policy in the Republic of Ireland, 1957–72* (Manchester: Manchester University Press).

Whitaker, T. K. (1983). *Interests* (Dublin: Institute of Public Administration).

Whitaker, T. K. (2006). *Protection or Free Trade: The Final Battle* (Dublin: Institute of Public Administration).

Whyte, J. H. (1980). *Church and State in Modern Ireland* (Dublin: Gill & Macmillan).

4 The Impact and Aftermath of the Free Education Policy Initiative

The Background Context

Following its establishment in 1924, the Department of Education adopted a blended policy of change and continuity with regard to post-primary education. It got rid of the 'payment by results' examinations framework which had been in operation since 1878. This was replaced by the new Intermediate and Leaving Certificate examinations, with a much more radical and open approach to syllabi up to 1942, when prescribed texts and traditional examination processes were reintroduced (Coolahan, 1986). In 1930, the Irish Vocational Education Act was passed, establishing the Vocational Education Committees, but their role was largely confined to providing two-year courses in technical and vocational courses, with the Church opposed to them having a broader role. It took some years to devise new salary structures and pension arrangements for post-primary teachers (Coolahan, 1984).

The policy of continuity related to the state's endorsement of the inherited structures of secondary schools, the vast majority of which were established by the Churches, particularly the Catholic Church, which was the Church of the majority. Apart from setting up a small number of preparatory colleges for Gaeltacht pupils to progress as national teachers, and facilitating the provision of 'secondary tops' for senior primary pupils in some primary schools, the state took no role in the provision of secondary schooling. Furthermore, its provision of scholarships at second level was very niggardly. A number of lay personnel established small secondary schools, but sometimes met with Church opposition. From 1935 to

1960, educational policy for post-primary education was moribund and passive, with no active government initiatives to extend its participation and duration. This was reflected in the complacency and lack of vision in the Council of Education report on the secondary school curriculum. The council took from 1955 to 1960 to present its report to the minister and the report was only published in 1962.

Towards a Change of Policy for Post-Primary Education

Shortly after taking over as Taoiseach in 1959, Seán Lemass signalled a significant change in policy direction. In October 1959, he put on the Dáil record that it was the government's 'immediate policy to increase the facilities for post-primary education' (*Dáil Éireann Proceedings*, vol. 177, cols 470–1, 28 October 1959). At senior levels of the Department of Education, new planning was underway and the *Investment in Education* investigative team was also formed. In 1961, improved scholarship schemes were introduced for post-primary entrants. In 1964, for the first time, the state gave grants for secondary school infrastructural expansion. In May 1963, Minister Patrick Hillery made a landmark speech on future policy. The most significant part of the speech was the revelation that the government was to undertake the building of post-primary schools of a new type, termed 'comprehensive schools'. These were to be co-educational, open to all classes and levels of ability, and would offer an academic and technical curriculum. Furthermore, the two-year course in vocational schools was to be extended to three years and the Intermediate Certificate examination could be taken by all pupils. It was also announced that a new Technical Leaving Certificate would be introduced for senior cycle. The fourth new policy in Hillery's address was that new regional colleges were to be established to boost technical education and manpower needs. When Minister Colley was appointed in 1966, he maintained this policy approach, and sought to promote co-operation and co-ordination between small post-primary schools in towns where a number of such schools existed.

By the mid-1960s, it was clear that improved provision for education was high on the public agenda and political parties were more conscious that there were votes to be won on education issues. In 1963, the Labour Party published its *Policy on Education* and in 1966 Fine Gael published its *Just Society: Education*. In July 1966, Taoiseach Lemass appointed Donogh O'Malley as Minister for Education. On 7 July 1966, in the debate on the adjournment of the Dáil, Lemass committed the government to giving priority to education over other desirable objectives. He went on to 'emphasise the need for a very considerable expansion of financial outlay on educational development' (*Dáil Report*, vol. 223, col. 2194 ff., 7 July 1966). Of course, 1966 was also the Golden Jubilee Year of the 1916 Rising, and the phrase 'cherish the children' was very much in evidence at commemorative events. This also coincided with the publication of the 1966 Census, which, happily, recorded the first increase in population since the Great Famine.

Minister O'Malley's Address to the National Union of Journalists (NUJ), 10 September 1966

Quite clearly, Minister O'Malley chose to address the NUJ to get maximum publicity for his policy plans. He formally referred back to the Taoiseach's statement of July 1966: 'I bring with me, as announced by the Taoiseach in Dáil Éireann, a Government assurance that education is to receive priority. Priority is going to mean exactly what it says – as I hope the events of the coming year will show' (*Sunday Press*, 11 September 1966). Boosted by the Taoiseach's commitment, Minister O'Malley announced a range of national policy changes in his speech. He bemoaned the inadequate provision of post-primary education in the past and referred to it as a 'dark stain on the national conscience'. He went on to state: 'I believe this is a situation which must be tackled with all speed and determination.' He announced that he was introducing a scheme of free post-primary education, up to the end of the junior cycle and he intended to make provisions whereby no pupil would, due to a lack of means, be prevented from continuing his or her education up to the end of the Leaving Certificate course. He also stated that there would be assistance towards the cost of books and accessories. He envisaged assistance being available for boarding school accommodation, in certain circumstances. In addition, he planned to prepare a scheme to assist participants to engage in higher education. O'Malley's speech incorporated a number of radical proposals, but it was the free education scheme that got most public attention, and the plan to introduce it from September 1967, with an associated free school transport scheme.

Direct Impact of the Free Education Scheme

The timing of the announcement in September 1966, and the use of the NUJ, ensured maximum publicity. There was a celebratory éclat in the reportage in the Sunday morning newspapers on 11 September. This was sustained by newspaper columnists and letter writers over subsequent weeks. Irish television had been introduced in 1961, and by 1966 had established a strong tradition of debate and political comment, from which educational policy issues benefitted. There were positive and enthusiastic reactions from public bodies. It was evident that the initiative engaged the public mood and whetted the traditional appetite of the Irish public for accessing education provision with assistance from public funds. The scheme had a significant psychological impact and led directly to raising social aspirations in the general public.

However, the scheme also encountered a significant degree of criticism. The plan was criticized for being rushed and for the element of surprise. It was criticized for having inadequate financial planning and for its lack of advance approval by the Department of Finance and the cabinet. Some key stakeholders resented what they regarded as inadequate advance consultation. In particular, the secondary school management associations and the Association of Secondary Teachers in Ireland (ASTI) were highly critical of the lack of consultation and the lack of detail regarding implementation. Implementation was to create real problems for schools, particularly in terms of accommodation and the provision of teachers. Fee-paying schools faced the dilemma of whether or not to join the scheme. In the event, the vast majority of schools joined the scheme, with some of them experiencing a drop in income as a result. The year from September 1966 to September 1967 proved to be a difficult one for the gestation and delivery of the free education and transport scheme, but it successfully got underway by September 1967.

One of the great societal driving forces for the change in educational policy was the multi-faceted findings and critiques of the existing system by the *Investment in Education* team. Other contributors have dealt with these in detail. Here, I wish to highlight one illustration of the problem set out by the *Investment* team. Taking the cohort of the 1958 primary school leavers, who numbered 55,000, it was shown that 17,500, almost a third, left school at primary level, and that 11,000 of these had not achieved the Primary Certificate. A further 13,500 dropped out in the early years of post-primary schooling. In 1960, 6,000 sat for the Group Certificate and in 1961, 16,000 took the Intermediate Certificate. Of the original cohort of 55,000, just 10,000, or 18.2 per cent, sat the Leaving Certificate examination in 1963; 2,000 of these went on to university in 1963, amounting to 3.6 per cent of the original cohort. The pattern of student engagement was also seen to be strongly linked to socio-economic conditions, with the better-off students much more favoured (Government of Ireland, 1965). Apart from what was a lamentable pattern of participation from the point of view of citizens' well-being, the government's drive for economic and social progress in the 1960s presented no alternative other than investment in education.

It did not take long for the impact of the free education scheme to radically change the inherited patterns outlined above. The pattern of student duration in post-primary education was also greatly altered, as indicated by the fact that, in 1979, 19,000 took the Group Certificate, 50,000 took the Intermediate Certificate, and 36,000 took the Leaving Certificate. It is also relevant to note that in 1968 a university grants scheme was introduced. This scheme nurtured an increase of 127 per cent in students engaged in full-time higher education from the year 1964–5 to 1978–9. Thus, it can be established that the free education scheme had a direct impact on a massive expansion in participation and duration of post-primary education by Irish students.

A further direct impact of the scheme was the associated and unprecedented free school transport scheme. O'Malley himself rated the scheme very highly, stating, 'I personally think that far more important than the decision on fees was the decision to give free transport, particularly in rural areas' (*Dáil Report*, vol. 227, col. 426, 9 March 1967). The yellow-topped buses traversing the roads of rural Ireland to transport teenagers to schools were an unprecedented example of the state reaching out to help the educational development of the young. The nationwide scheme was divided into catchment areas, with a radius of 15 miles from school centres. Pick-up points were devised, a minimum of 3 miles from the school. The scheme was co-educational and had an impact on local schools' organization. The scheme was warmly welcomed by the public, who valued the fact that their teenagers were being transported to schools dry, comfortably and safely.

Indirect Impact of the Free Education Scheme

As could be expected, such a significant educational policy initiative also had a range of indirect impacts on the system. The Department of Education was seriously engaging with the shaping of the post-primary education system and this was not appreciated by all existing agencies. For instance, Sister Eileen Randles, a major figure in Catholic education circles, complained that O'Malley's speech on 10 September 1966 had 'torn through every shred of red tape in the area of secondary education, ignoring rights, traditions and sensitivities' (Randles, 1975, p. 219).

The 'intrusion' of the department was resented, as if the department did not have national responsibility for education. As far as Lemass and O'Malley were concerned, action on education policy was important and urgent. Even though it was published as late as 1975, the hurt tone of Sister Randles' book about the department's approach is evident in remarks such as:

> Up to 1966, the acknowledged private nature of the Secondary Schools had put
> them virtually beyond interference by Department officials. It now began to emerge
> that the fortunes of all schools would in future lie in the hands of the Development
> Branch. (Randles, 1975, p. 239)

A further indirect impact of free education related to the planned restructuring of the post-primary school system. At the time, the vast majority of
post-primary schools were very small. As many as 64 per cent of secondary schools and 73 per cent of vocational schools had less than 150 pupils
enrolled, with consequent implications for the range of curriculum provision, particularly at senior cycle. The Development Branch of the department sought a rationalization of school provision, setting up post-primary
centres, catchment areas, junior and major centres, the promotion of comprehensive curricula and local co-operation between schools. However,
the 'pupil numbers bounce' following the introduction of free education
stymied this approach to a large extent. As Randles commented:

> The new importance of having sufficient numbers to be considered viable gradually
> outweighed real anxieties about possible loss of autonomy, and compelled many
> schools to accept the free scheme. The options had become simple: survival required
> numbers and numbers required free education. The O'Malley scheme should there-
> fore be accepted. (Randles, 1975, p. 242)

As a result, the school rationalization scheme lost momentum, but the
comprehensive curriculum policy made progress, albeit vocational schools
were at a disadvantage for a period. 'Secondary tops' were dropped and the
preparatory colleges were adapted to ordinary secondary schools. By the
early 1970s, post-primary education was provided in secondary, vocational,
comprehensive and community schools.

Integral to free education was the impact on teacher numbers. The huge
expansion in pupil numbers necessitated the employment of an increased
numbers of teachers. Accordingly, the number of teachers almost tripled
from 6,800 in 1964 to 17,200 by 1979. In turn, this put pressure on teacher-
education institutions, which were not well equipped to cope in the early
years. However, in the early 1970s, reform and expansion of teacher-educa-
tion departments in the universities took place and the quality of teacher
education was sustained. The enlarged pupil numbers in schools led to

the appointment of remedial teachers and guidance counsellors in some schools, and the schools' psychological service was established at that time. A further indirect impact of the scheme was the success and growth of the school transport system. As well as the manufacturing of buses, the transport system fostered regional employment for drivers and support personnel. The expanded grants for school extensions and pre-fabricated buildings throughout the national landscape also had a positive impact on regional employment.

With a much more heterogeneous student clientele participating in post-primary education, questions arose regarding the appropriateness of the inherited curricula. A great deal of work was done during the 1960s by representative syllabus committees to reform and update syllabus content for a large range of subjects. This led to syllabus reform for common Intermediate and Leaving Certificate courses, on modern lines. Appraisal of assessment/examination systems also took place, as evidenced by the Madaus and McNamara report on the Leaving Certificate in 1970 (Educational Research Centre, 1970) and the report on the Intermediate Certificate Examination (ICE) in 1975 (Committee on the Reform and Function of the Intermediate Certificate Examination). Many innovative curriculum development initiatives were undertaken in the early 1970s, some of which impacted on mainstream schooling. However, economic difficulties during the early to mid-1970s impeded planned progress.

O'Malley was deeply and genuinely committed to those who experienced great social inequality and exclusion from many aspects of the well-being of society. In an address to the Dáil on 30 November 1966, he expressed satisfaction at the provision of free fees, free transport and free school books, but he emphasized his concern about core background preventative factors impeding participation for the 'outsiders'. He stated:

> In the lower income groups there will always be a number of pupils whose family circumstances would be such that even with the provision of free tuition and free books, keeping them at school will still be a hardship on their parents. When my scheme is in operation and I have an opportunity to assess the extent of the problem, I shall have to see what special provision for such cases should be made. (Dáil Éireann Debate, 30 November 1966)

In the event, Minister O'Malley did not live long enough to carry out this intention. Yet, the issue was a real concern for him. He returned to it during a Senate debate on 2 February 1967. He stated:

> It is the background of the underprivileged of the children we want to get in – that is the family background, the environmental background – which is the great problem in Ireland today. (Senate Reports, vol. 62, no. 1, col. 1086, 2 February 1967)

In conclusion, while the free education scheme did not resolve inequalities in post-primary education provision, which would have required more multi-faceted action, it left a landmark reform legacy, from which succeeding generations have greatly benefitted.

Bibliography

Coolahan, J. (1984). *The ASTI and Post-Primary Education in Ireland, 1909–84* (Dublin: Association of Secondary Teachers Ireland).

Coolahan, J. (1986). 'The Secondary School Curriculum Experiment, 1924–42', in V. Greaney and B. Molloy (eds), *Dimensions of Reading* (Dublin: The Educational Company), pp. 42–62.

Government of Ireland (1965). *Investment in Education: Annexes and Appendices* (Dublin: Stationery Office).

Government of Ireland (1965). *Investment in Education: Report of the Survey Team Appointed by the Minister of Education in October 1962* (Dublin: Stationery Office).

Randles, E. (1975). *Post-Primary Education in Ireland, 1957–70* (Dublin: Veritas).

D. G. MULCAHY

5 Responding to the Neglect of Aims in Irish Post-Primary Education[1]

Introduction

Imagine the bewilderment of an airline attendant if you turned up at the airport and all you asked for was a return ticket and an aisle seat far forward in the aircraft. As you searched for your passport, the attendant may well have wondered if you had any idea where you were headed. Now imagine a system of schooling that didn't know where it was going either, but was adamant on how it would get there, that is, by teaching the subjects it had already chosen, using methods of assessment it had adopted from an earlier century. Struck by the odd logic of this scenario, in the late 1970s and early 1980s I began to study the particular form this system took in Ireland as I examined the evolution of curriculum and policy in Irish post-primary education throughout much of the twentieth century. Now, from a different point in time, I am taking the opportunity to look at it again.

When I was invited to participate in marking the fiftieth anniversary of the roll-out of the free education scheme at the Royal Irish Academy in April 2017, I was asked to address the aims of education and Irish post-primary school education between 1922 and 1967. Keeping the historical dimension of the question in mind, I also range beyond it here by reflecting

1   I wish to express my thanks to Professor Ciaran Sugrue and Professor Mary O'Sullivan for their helpful comments on the earlier version of this chapter presented at the symposium held in the Royal Irish Academy, Dublin, on 19 April 2017, marking the fiftieth anniversary of the roll-out of the free education scheme. I would also like to thank Professor Joe Lee and Professor Judith Harford for their interest and support.

on how the neglect of aims in educational discourse can be detrimental to practice in the present day and how we might respond.[2] So, here is my four-part plan of approach. First I will review the extent and manner in which attention was given to aims in the expression of policy regarding post-primary education in Ireland from the founding of the Irish Free State in 1922 up until 1967 and some years beyond. Next I will consider weaknesses arising from the evident neglect of aims in this time frame. Because of its instructive potential going forward (and because I previously discussed limitations of this negligence from the standpoint of the late 1970s and 1980s), in doing so here, I take into account scholarly literature on curriculum and related areas that in some cases did not exist back in the 1970s and 1980s. I will then look at a number of subject areas in Irish post-primary education that were misunderstood or largely overlooked for much of the period from 1967 up to the present. These are subject areas which, because they deal with practical forms of education involving personal engagement and possible social action, resonate well with emerging directions in the discussion of general education in recent years. In conclusion I will address possible directions for future developments.

Lastly, by way of introduction and for clarification, by 'post-primary' (or 'second-level') education, I mean essentially education as offered in secondary, vocational, comprehensive and community schools in the Republic of Ireland. Without getting into all the complexities involved, in discussing theoretical and practical knowledge, I draw upon the widely debated distinction introduced by Gilbert Ryle (1949) between 'knowing that' or propositional knowledge, such as knowing that it is raining, and 'knowing how' or procedural knowledge, such as knowing how to ride a bicycle.[3] As indicated already, I pay particular attention to practical knowledge or practical education that has a personal or social orientation as distinct from an economic one. In addition, in treating the neglect of aims in education, I

2   For a recent discussion of the pitfalls associated with the articulation of aims in education, see Hardarson (2017). While I clearly accept the necessity of aims, avoiding undue specificity guards against such pitfalls.

3   For further discussion, see, for example, Ryle (1949) and Martin (1958). For a helpful summary overview, see Fantl (2012).

shall consider the related idea of a general education that was highlighted in Ireland during the period from 1922 to 1967 and beyond and which was intended to enable students to qualify for entry largely into higher education and employment. I shall also advert to the very different conceptions of general education espoused by two of the main sectors of second-level schooling in Ireland, namely, the secondary and the vocational.

The Neglect of Aims, 1922–67

In attempting to discern whatever aims existed or were relied upon during the period from 1922 to 1967, I shall draw from earlier and more extended accounts that I have provided elsewhere (Mulcahy, 1981, pp. 51–72 and Mulcahy, 1989, pp. 7–97). To put this in context, it will be helpful to refer to how the aims of education were dealt with in the years immediately preceding and following 1922. Especially important is the light this throws on the role of Eoin MacNeill, the first Minister for Education in the Irish Free State, and his reluctance to pay attention to aims in the consideration of secondary education (O'Donoghue, 1988, pp. 102–13). This was so despite the urgings of T. J. O'Connell of the Irish National Teachers' Organisation and of the Labour Party at the time of the introduction of the new programme for secondary education in 1924. It is a reluctance that was to live on long after MacNeill, as is detailed by Gleeson (2010, pp. 12–23), for example.

To my knowledge, between 1922 and 1967 (and even later) there were just two official documents that to some degree considered the question of aims in Irish post-primary education. The first was *Memorandum V. 40*, or *Memo V. 40*, as it was known (Department of Education, c. 1942), which was published in 1941/2 or thereabouts. This served as a guiding document for continuation education in vocational schools. The second was the *Report of the Council of Education – The Curriculum of the Secondary School* (Department of Education, 1962). The *Rules and Programme for Secondary Schools* (Department of Education, *Rules*, 1924–81), which was published each year, also provided a clue about intent. In these annual publications, statements of the purpose or aim of the Intermediate and Leaving Certificate courses and of the certificates were presented, as were the aims of many of the recognized subjects of study. Although this was so, there is little evidence that the courses were drawn up in response to careful deliberations regarding aims or purpose.

In the first place, the wordings of the statements were ambiguous. In some cases, what was being referred to were the certificate courses; in others cases, it was the certificates themselves. For example, in the original wording in the *Rules* for 1924–5, regarding the Intermediate Certificate, it was stated that 'the purpose of the Intermediate Certificate is to *testify* to the completion of a well-balanced course of general education ...'; as regards the Leaving Certificate, it was stated that 'the aim of the Leaving Certificate is to *testify* to the completion of a good secondary education ...' (Department of Education, *Rules*, 1924–5, pp. 8–9, italics added). No explanation was given as to how the one aim differed from the other. Without any further significant alteration of the overall wording, moreover, these statements were subsequently modified to state that it was the aims or purpose of the Intermediate and Leaving Certificate courses that were being presented (see Mulcahy, 1981, pp. 53–8). In the same vein, statements of aims of various subjects often left much to be desired. In the case of history at the Intermediate Certificate level, for example, a relatively substantial statement of the aims for that subject was introduced in 1980–1 where none previously existed, although there was no corresponding alteration in the content itself. By contrast, the statement of content consisting of a few skimpy sentences for history for the Leaving Certificate in 1980–1 remained unchanged, and there was no reference to aims. To magnify the inconsistency, there was a fairly extensive statement of content for economic history for the Leaving Certificate (Department of Education, *Rules*, 1974–5, pp. 78–94; Department of Education, *Rules*, 1980–1, pp. 74–7, pp. 291–6).

Lack of clarity was also a feature of the statements of aims for secondary education set forth in *Report of the Council of Education*. Even if this report had little impact on existing practice, it did reflect how secondary education was understood by those accustomed to wielding influence leading up to the time of its publication. Central to the lack of clarity was the vagueness and ambiguity of the report regarding what it deemed the 'immediate objective' of secondary education, namely, 'liberal or general education'. Although this notion constituted a guiding principle of sorts for the council, it was defined by it in two different ways. In the first place, a general or liberal education was defined as 'an all-round formation, aimed at the development and enrichment of the faculties of the human person rather than any specialised preparation for a particular skill or profession'. With attention focused on outcomes rather than curriculum content, it went on to say that anyone completing a secondary or general education would 'popularly be regarded' as 'educated', a person of character and knowledge 'who would be capable of taking a responsible place in society' (Department of Education, 1960, p. 90). In the second place, general education was conceived in terms of what 'in practice constitutes a "general education"'. Understood here as subjects or curriculum content, what is viewed as acceptable practice in the traditional schools of Europe fills out the definition of general education. These subjects are 'religion and/or moral instruction; command of the native language in speech, writing, literature; a reasonable outline of history and geography; elementary mathematics; drawing, singing and some initiation into science' (Department of Education, 1960, p. 92).

Even as these subjects corresponded largely to those already on the programme, a problem remained. This was the confusion of means and ends reflected in the two definitions. That is to say, used interchangeably, these two quite different definitions allowed the council to forego the task of determining which school subjects (as well as other potential curriculum content) were actually best suited to promoting a general education that provided 'an all-round formation'. Clearly, this begged the question of what subjects can best serve this purpose. The position of the council also exposed a serious disagreement between the thinking behind the *Report of the Council of Education* and that found in *Memo V. 40*. The view taken of general education in *Memo V. 40* emphasized the need to provide students with a preparation for practical engagements in their working world on leaving school. This would be supplemented by the study of some academic subjects that also had a contribution to make to all-round formation.

Adding an element of irony to this disagreement is the fact that, for some time before the introduction of the free education scheme, the views of the *Report of the Council of Education* regarding the aims of secondary education took a back seat as a new view of the role of second-level education in the economic development of the country began to take hold. If the view expressed by Dr Hillery in 1964, while he was Minister for Education, is to be accepted, the views of the council were on the verge of being rejected. Reportedly, he said then that if you gave 'a secondary grammar, academic type education' (the kind envisioned by the council) to everybody, you would be wasting your money in two ways: 'you would be getting too many people taking a course which is no use to most of them – we haven't jobs for them, we haven't need for them' (Hillery, 1964, p. 8, quoted in Randles, 1976, p. 147). Yet, if the emerging thrust towards education for economic development indicated by Dr Hillery was about to become the new order, it, too, would be set forth without any more substantial an articulation of the aims of education than the old order. It is some measure of the reluctance to engage in a serious debate regarding the aims of education evident in MacNeill that this is a point to which I thought it necessary to draw attention in 1989 in *In Our Schools* (Curriculum and Examinations Board, 1986; Mulcahy, 1989), twenty-five years after Dr Hillery's statement.

Consequences of the Neglect of Aims for Practical Education

Retaining the experience in Ireland from 1922 to 1967 as a point of reference, I shall now consider more broadly some consequences for aims of the lack of clarity regarding the idea of a general education and some alternative conceptions to the one that was once dominant – and possibly still is. Whatever else may be concluded from the limited discussion of the aims of second-level education in Ireland in the half-century or so from 1922 to 1967, there was some verbal consensus regarding the idea of a general education that was central to the debate. Even if there was disagreement on what it actually meant, as authorities in the secondary and vocational sectors viewed the idea very differently from each other, it was still thought to be a good idea. The wishes of the new order in government notwithstanding, moreover, in some important ways it is the view of the Council of Education that prevailed. It is a view that is on the wrong side of history.

While defining the idea of a general education in two different ways was likely to lead to trouble for the Council of Education, it was by no means unique to it or to the conduct of post-primary education in Ireland. In fact, it was commonplace for centuries in the theory and practice of general education in schools and universities everywhere. Long before the *Report of the Council of Education*, and even since then, prominent writers on second- and third-level education have spoken of liberal or general education in broadly similar terms. Dominating the discussion, the protagonists of this mainstream thinking defined its ends or aims as narrowly intellectual in scope and its curriculum as composed largely of a core of traditional academic subjects – or academic subjects as traditionally conceived (see, for example, Hirst, 1974; Adler, 1982; Tubbs, 2014). It is tempting fate to anticipate that many innovative approaches can be gained today from this perspective, although Tubbs (2014) bravely attempted to do so recently. But there are others – those who represent what I term the 'minorstream' – who have adopted different stances that may beneficially be drawn upon as we look to the future. Especially important here is the fairly new attention given to practical education or education for action among those engaged in the debate on general education. This is a matter to which I have drawn attention outside of the Irish context, as well as in that context (Mulcahy, 2008; Mulcahy, 2009, pp. 465–86; Mulcahy, 2012b, pp. 3–10; and Mulcahy, 2013, pp. 153–75). It is worth reflecting on this here again, given the rather limited recognition of practical subjects on the curriculum of Irish secondary education in particular.

Of those in the mainstream since the time of the Council of Education, none expressed more fully than Paul Hirst what many considered to be the core intellectual values of general education fashioned after the ideal of a liberal education. These are the values reflected in the orientation of the *Report of the Council of Education* towards academic or theoretical studies and away from practical studies. Yet, a quarter of a century ago, Hirst retracted his position and declared 'practical knowledge to be more fundamental than theoretical knowledge, the former being basic to any clear grasp of the proper significance of the latter' (1993, p. 197; 2005, pp. 615–20). Coming after Hirst, another prominent English philosopher of education, John White, appears to go farther by highlighting what he calls 'the primacy of the practical' (White, 2004, p. 184). He argues that we ought to 'begin our thinking about the curriculum with the human being as agent, not the human being as knower' (White, 2004, p. 184). In what would surely have been music to the ears of those in the vocational sector and the authors of *Memo V. 40*, this, he believed, could lead us to 'a more practically-oriented curriculum' of general education. For her part, Noddings declared that 'liberal education is a false ideal for universal education' (1992, p. 28).

One of the consequences of the neglect of aims in education is a tendency to fall back on practice and, in doing so, inherit its failings along with its strengths. One of the failings in question is overlooking new thinking and the promise it may hold for improving the education of the young. In this regard, it is helpful to consider the positions of those such as White and Noddings (and even some within the Irish educational establishment, as we shall see below) both for their critical dimension and for their departure from conventional theory and practice. It may also serve to expose the distance between forward-looking discourse and entrenched positions that lie behind prevailing practice. None have succeeded better than Jane Roland Martin in addressing this matter. In 'The Disciplines and the Curriculum' (Martin, 1994, pp. 133–53; original work published in 1969), Martin argued that as valuable as discipline or academic knowledge may be, the school curriculum should not be constrained by it. For all their merits, academic disciplines largely downplay or dismiss practical knowledge. As presented in school programmes, academic disciplines also tend to overlook issues of concern to adolescents. These include matters such as friendship and relationships, civic well-being, war and peace. In 'Needed: A New Paradigm for Liberal Education' (Martin, 1994, pp. 170–86; original work published in 1981), Martin's most incisive critique of the traditional theory of a liberal education as expounded by Hirst, having chided Hirst for neglecting the place of purpose or aims in curriculum theorizing, she went on to state that this theory overlooks feelings and emotions, along with what she refers to as the three Cs of care, concern, and connection. According to Martin, this has serious adverse consequences for the curriculum because, on its own, and by separating thought from action, reason from emotion, and education from life, an exclusive focus upon theoretical knowledge leads to the formation of lopsided and incomplete human beings. As a result, such human beings may be both uncaring and inactive.[4]

Liberal education – or general education, as it is referred to in the *Report of the Council of Education* – may always have been a contested concept (Kimball, 1995). There can be little doubt, however, that in the more recent evolution of the idea, the notion of education for action or participation and not mere observation has gained particular attention. According to Ivan Marquez, for example, Western philosophy has described well desirable states of being, but it has failed miserably 'at providing a framework for understanding, effecting, and affecting the process of becoming' (Marquez, 2006, p. 152). He believes that this is a deficiency that we need to remedy. This challenge is taken up by William Sullivan and Matthew Rosin (2008), who advocate for the education of practical reason. This can be achieved, they argue, by recognizing the interdependence of liberal education and professional education. Especially pertinent here is Richard Pring's distinction between practical knowledge and vocational knowledge, which makes practical knowledge eligible for inclusion in a programme of liberal education (Pring 1993).[5] In emphasizing the importance of intellectual and practical skills and urging an end to what it calls the artificial

---

4   In saying this, Martin makes clear that she is speaking strictly of Hirst's account of liberal education as a theory and does not deny that in practice there may be unintended outcomes to obviate some of the shortcomings of the kind of education his theory entails (Martin 1994, p. 175). Martin added to her critique of Hirst by arguing that an education confined to the disciplines is biased against women. This is a critique which she elaborated further in *Coming of Age in Academe* (Martin, 2002). Of special importance is her view that in conventional theorizing not only are women devalued, but males are as a consequence deprived of an adequate education because the masculine ideal inherent in a discipline-based education may lead to people lacking emotions and feelings (Martin, 1994, pp. 170–86).

5   Pring's point is that the intent of a subject of study may be what determines whether the subject matter in question is to be deemed vocational or more broadly practical.

distinction between liberal and practical education, the Association of American Colleges and Universities (2002) essentially concurs.

Practical Education

Agreeing with this general view, I welcome the increased willingness in recent years to attend to the place of practical education in Leaving Certificate programmes. Arising from the historical reluctance to recognize and properly accommodate the place of practical knowledge in the secondary stream in Irish education throughout much of the twentieth century, however, I also want to advert to the tenuous nature of this willingness. To do so, I will now consider a small number of subjects, including home economics, physical education and politics and society, where efforts have been made at the level of the Leaving Certificate to promote a particularly important form of practical education and the challenges encountered in doing so. This is a form of practical education that is paid lip service but which – in contrast to practical subjects such as engineering and construction studies, for example – is then largely bypassed.

It recently came to my attention that such a form of practical education, one that seeks to go beyond 'knowledge that' or propositional knowledge and enables students to develop 'the skills needed to participate effectively', was recognized by the Department of Education and Science when it wrote some years ago that 'an active citizen':

> is someone who not only believes in the concept of a democratic society but who is *willing and able to translate that belief into action*. Active citizenship is a compound of knowledge, skills and attitudes: knowledge about how society works; the skills needed *to participate effectively*; and a conviction that active participation is the right of all citizens. (Government of Ireland/An Roinn Oideachais agus Eolaíochta/ Department of Education and Science, 1996, p. 19. Cited in Williams and Williams, 2016, p. 315, italics added)

This commitment to enable students to develop 'the skills needed to participate effectively' in civic life is reflected in the introduction of politics and society as a new Leaving Certificate subject that will be examined for certification for the first time in June 2018. So as to highlight the notion of practical education for social action and participation and not mere observation, to employ Martin's language, and that used in the excerpt just quoted from the Department of Education and Science, a note of clarification is in order. In the years since the establishment of the National Council for Curriculum and Assessment, school programmes have undeniably undergone change. Today, the Leaving Certificate (Established) programme includes practical subjects, including engineering, construction studies, technology, and design and communication graphics; the Leaving Certificate Vocational programme puts a special emphasis on such practical subjects; the Leaving Certificate Applied programme does likewise and even includes the subject 'social education', not included in the two other Leaving Certificate programmes. At the Junior Certificate level, practical subjects of the kind to which I draw special attention, such as social and environmental sciences, religious education, and civic, social and political education, are included, and the City of Dublin VEC (for one) has for decades done important work in this area. Yet, excepting physical education and home economics, and the recently introduced politics and society, the socially oriented practical subjects remain conspicuously outside the ambit of the Leaving Certificate (Established) programme. It is the omission of subjects such as these that is cause for particular concern.

Even if developments around physical education and home economics, and now politics and society, show a willingness to advance and demonstrate a sensitivity to the place of practical knowledge in general education not directly related to economic development, they also reveal a hesitancy to fully embrace it. This arises from an apparent difficulty in acknowledging how its particular requirements necessitate both a different mind-set regarding what constitutes legitimate knowledge or curriculum content and the ability to put it securely into practice. It is a mind-set that needs to be radically different from the one brought to bear on the treatment of home economics as a Leaving Certificate subject in the 1970s. To describe that mind-set as backward would be generous.[6]

In a case revealing the sometimes arbitrary and dubious nature of a dividing line believed to distinguish acceptable curriculum knowledge (i.e. theoretical or scientific knowledge) from unacceptable curriculum knowledge (i.e. practical knowledge), in 1977, the National University of Ireland introduced a sharp distinction between two forms of the subject home economics offered in Irish schools; 'home economics: social and scientific', as it was termed, was deemed acceptable as meeting requirements for university matriculation, whereas 'home economics: general' was not (see Mulcahy, 1981, pp. 102–5). The official difference between the two versions was that whereas the 'social and scientific' included elements of a scientific or theoretical nature, the 'general' included practical elements, such as cooking and sewing, along with some elements of a scientific or theoretical nature. It was because of its particular combination of omissions and inclusions that the general course was somehow considered unsuitable for matriculation. At least that was the justification. There was no explanation of how, in the social and scientific course, one could gain knowledge of a practical field of study without engaging in practical activities integral to it (even if, in practice, that sometimes occurred) or, even more simply, why there could not be recognition of the version combining practical elements and a scientific dimension. To be fair, no one went as far as to say that all of this was to keep girls and less able boys who were good cooks from going to college. One way or another, however, an obvious conclusion to be drawn was that there is something decidedly deficient and maybe offensive about the practical. Judging by a post dated 26 April 2017 on the website of the National University of Ireland, Galway, this is essentially the position it still maintains. The post reads as follows: 'Home Economics – General is not an acceptable matriculation subject for admission to NUI Galway. However, Leaving Cert Home Economics – Social and Scientific is an

6   Regarding higher education, Ed Walsh (2011) has also made a credible case that the promotion of practical forms of education of the kind implemented in NIHE Limerick around this time was also the target of uninformed obstruction.

acceptable matriculation subject for admission to NUI Galway' (National University of Ireland, Galway website).

How home economics was handled rightly makes one sensitive to the language now employed in dealing with the proposed introduction of physical education – or the treatment of any practical subject existing or proposed – as a subject in Leaving Certificate programmes. To my knowledge, the draft syllabus for physical education put out in 2011 by the National Council for Curriculum and Assessment (NCCA, 2011; see also Mulcahy, 2012a) remains the most recently available comprehensive official public statement on this matter. Although an updated version is reportedly on the way, it is on the 2011 draft that I shall rely here. In a number of places in the draft syllabus, varying but generally consistent statements regarding the aims or purpose for physical education are presented. One of these reads that the aim of Leaving Certificate physical education is 'to develop the learner's capacity to become informed, skilled, self-directed and reflective performers [*sic*] in physical education and physical activity in senior cycle and in their future life' (p. 10). In addition, the claim is made that 'Leaving Certificate physical education has the potential to make a significant contribution to enhancing learners' commitment to lifelong participation in physical activity' (p. 11). In general terms, the position adopted in the draft syllabus as regards aims or purpose and objectives in the Leaving Certificate physical education course is well informed by contemporary developments in the field. Although it would benefit from further elaboration and greater clarity, it does lay out the broad scope of the idea. The organization of the overall content of the course into two broad units of study is also well conceived. Including, as it does, knowledge, skills, and dispositions, alongside the range of physical activities and sporting activities identified, it captures physical activities of a kind suitable in a course in physical education.

The emphasis placed on knowledge, skill and understanding, along with physical activity and performance, in the draft syllabus is also to be commended. The attention paid to the relationship between physical education and recreation, and the inclusion of the activities, such as knowing the rules of games and standards of performance and excellence, is welcome too. But there are also deficiencies in the presentation. Greater attention could be paid to the social dimensions and to the place of enjoyment or satisfaction in being physically active throughout life. Without claiming too much on its behalf or being blind to downsides of sports, perhaps greater attention could be paid to how physical education can be of benefit to the character-building and emotional development of the student. The role of the student and the recognition of the experience, aptitudes, and interests of students, and how these would be relied upon in shaping a student's programme also need greater attention than they have been given. Of greatest concern, however, from the point of view of promoting practical knowledge, is an apparent, if unwitting, prioritizing of cognitive skills.

To elaborate: immediately following the statement of the aim of Leaving Certificate physical education presented above, there is a statement that the objectives of Leaving Certificate physical education are to develop:

> the learner's performance in physical activity, ability to *reflect* on performance in physical activity, *knowledge and understanding* of the factors which influence performance and participation in physical activity, *appreciation* of the benefits of physical activity for lifelong health and wellbeing, capacity to undertake different roles in physical activities, *understanding* of the principles underlying ethical participation in physical activity, *appreciation* of the role of physical activity and sport in the social and cultural life of Ireland. (p. 10, italics added)

Of these seven objectives, the five that I have italicized are primarily cognitive.

What is troubling about this is not the mere fact that five cognitive objectives are identified as opposed to two performance objectives. It is the ease with which the syllabus, and, as a likely consequence, practice, falls back on the conventional reliance on theoretical knowledge, thereby relegating the practical to a lesser status. It is not as if there are no other possible performance objectives beyond those identified. Other examples could include enabling students to commit to life-long engagement in physical activities, developing healthy-eating habits and other health-sustaining habits, developing the capacity to interpret nonverbal cues in social and environmental settings, and developing the capacity to behave as members of a team (which is commonplace in sports settings). It is this failure to identify other such objectives that suggests a mindset that is unwilling or unable – even if practitioners may think otherwise – to fully appreciate the richness and the promise of physical education and a consequent inability to give practical education its due.

On this general point, much the same may be said of the new politics and society course. The aspiration of the course, which 'aims to develop the learner's capacity to engage in reflective and active citizenship' (Department of Education and Skills, 2016, p. 7) is consistent with the thrust of my argument here and so is clearly welcome. Its conceptualization,[7] however, betrays the inablility to give practical education its due, that is, to recognize the legitimate claims of practical knowledge. Immediately following its statement of aims in the curriculum specification for the course, the first two objectives to be achieved completely overlook the significance of practical knowledge and skills and prioritize the cognitive objective of 'understanding'. They read as follows:

> The objectives of Leaving Certificate Politics and Society are to develop an understanding of the social systems within which people act: locally, nationally and more widely an understanding of concepts which underpin contemporary systems of government and of the diverse models for making these concepts operational. (Department of Education and Skills, 2016, p. 8)

Stated differently, although subsequent objectives do provide for learning practical skills, the conceptualization of the course relies heavily on the academic model. As stated in the curriculum specification itself:

> The focus of Politics and Society, in part, corresponds to that of other senior cycle subjects, notably geography, home economics, history, and religious education, and, to a lesser extent, economics (in the areas of economic systems and economic thought); English (in relation to social and media literacy); mathematics (in relation to the ability to interpret and analyse data) and technology (in relation to technology and society). (Department of Education and Skills, 2016, p. 9)

It is true that politics and society does provide a place for learning relevant practical skills, and it is also true that practical skills need to be 'informed

---

7   This is a topic that needs closer attention than I can give to it here, and I plan to return to it at a later time.

by the insights ... of social and political sciences' (Department of Education and Skills, 2016, p. 7). That said, the prioritizing of the theoretical over the practical seen here, as in the draft syllabus for physical education, and the clear suggestion that if it is to be considered fully acceptable (unlike home economics: general), 'the focus of politics and society' needs to correspond 'to that of other senior cycle subjects' of a more academic (or 'scientific') nature. This need not be so and, of course, it brings us back to the invidious treatment of the practical with regard to home economics. It also brings us back to the class distinction that existed between the secondary tradition and that of vocational or continuation education, as well as the questionable distinction between those students of 'academic ability' and those of 'practical ability' found in the Dr Hillery's (1963) landmark *Statement* regarding post-primary education. Regrettably, it also brings us forward to the present and the prospect of these distinctions being perpetuated by obvious lines drawn between the Leaving Certificate (Established) programme and both the Leaving Certificate Vocational programme and the Leaving Certificate Applied programme. The Leaving Certificate (Established) programme, which is the most widely followed of these programmes and which represents the continuing dominance of the secondary tradition, provides a straight-forward route to university. The other two Leaving Certificate programmes remain encumbered as hosts of vocational and applied subject matter (i.e. practical knowledge). On a more positive note, the commitment to equity of access for all citizens irrespective of their circumstances in the *National Plan for Equity of Access to Higher Education 2015–19* (Higher Education Authority, 2015) gives reason for some optimism.

Looking to the Future

In treating the neglect of aims in education, I have given special attention to its adverse effects on the place of practical education. By implication, I have raised the question of how one might better attend to aims and the promotion of practical education.

If the aims of education were considered independently of the academic subjects to which they were historically tied in the tradition of a liberal education, or if the idea of a general education had been conceived more broadly than in the *Report of the Council of Education*, the pronounced academic or theoretical character of the curriculum and of what it means to be an educated person could have been conceived very differently. That this was possible is evident in *Memo V. 40*, in which the influence of the historical ideal of a liberal education had little impact on the expression of what was meant by a general education. Yet, despite the value of the critique of rationalist approaches that fail to recognize the educational potential of practical knowledge and education for action, such a critique alone does not provide an alternative and fruitful conceptualization of general education. In looking to the future, and before drawing these remarks to a close, I point now to elements of such a conceptualization, one that accommodates both theoretical and practical knowledge and skills. In doing so, I shall keep in mind the implications for pedagogy.

Readers familiar with *Curriculum and Policy in Irish Post-Primary Education* will know that I have long viewed general education as grounded in a consideration of various activities of living – what Noddings subsequently referred to as human tasks or human activities (Noddings, 1992, pp. 45–6). The demands that these activities make require practical and theoretical knowledge, as well as skills and relevant dispositions, if we are to respond successfully to them (see Mulcahy, 2008 and Mulcahy, 2013). A pertinent feature of this way of looking at the matter is that it differs substantially from theories of liberal or general education where the nature and structure of knowledge is the organizing principle. Viewing human activities as the organizing principle of curriculum is less of an impediment to formulating a conceptualization of general education that aims to enable the young to engage in action and become proficient in practical forms of knowledge – even if these learnings pose challenges to existing assessment regimes. This being so, creating space for a conception of education promoting learning activities of a practical kind that can stand alongside, rather than in a subordinate position to, those of a theoretical kind becomes imperative. To modify White's position, to which reference was made earlier, this requires a focus upon the student as agent or actor as well as knower.

If the aims posited for education are freed of their association with the narrow concept of general education found in the *Report of the Council of Education*, and open to forms of knowledge, attitudes, and skills not previously associated with it, a wide range of new possibilities comes into view. What these possibilities might look like I have attempted to lay out in *The Educated Person*, in which I argued for an alternative concept of liberal or general education and of the educated person and introduced to both concepts the idea of many-sided development (Mulcahy, 2008). Without imposing undue preconceptions, in such a conceptualization, an educated person could deal with a wide range of the practical demands of living, such as civic engagement, participation in a range of work-related and recreational activities, and the development of a sense of guiding values.

General education intended for many-sided development would consist of academic disciplines and practical studies, and, sensitive to pedagogical considerations, it would be individualized for all students in accordance with their capacities and needs (for elaboration, see Mulcahy, Mulcahy and Mulcahy, 2015, pp. 65–7, 80–2, 171–8). As a consequence, it would constitute an important shift beyond the conventional view of a general education.

Conclusion

Reflection on the neglect of aims in education may take many forms. Beginning with a focus on the neglect of aims in Irish post-primary education, from 1922 to 1967, here I pointed to the close association between aims and the ideal of a general or liberal education that held sway at the time. Recognizing that this ideal was disputed by authorities outside the more dominant secondary sector, I examined the place of practical education favoured in vocational schools, linking it with the prominence increasingly accorded to it in contemporary curriculum theorizing. Exploring how forms of practical education in Ireland have been dealt with since 1967, and acknowledging that a variety of more practical subjects are now included in the post-primary school curriculum, I recognized the unique potential of a number of Leaving Certificate subjects, namely, home economics, physical education and politics and society. The aspirational dimension of the course in politics and society, namely, 'to develop the learner's capacity to engage in reflective and active citizenship', was especially welcomed. I also recognized the challenge that these subjects encounter in remaining true to the ideal of combining theoretical and practical knowledge. I concluded by indicating the need for a reconceived form of general education intended to provide a balanced blending of theoretical and practical knowledge conducive to the formation of a person of many-sided development. Such a form of general education may go some way towards rectifying harm caused by the neglect of aims in post-primary education in Ireland. For some, the worry is that by attempting to rectify the harm, politicians may exert undue influence on the open discussion of aims that this entails. Yet, while one ought to be cautious in this regard, and especially respectful of the views of parents and professional educators, in a democratic republic this is a matter for society at large. Proceeding with these understandings would be a fitting way to celebrate the introduction of the free education scheme these fifty or so years later.

Bibliography

Adler, M. J. (1982). *The Paideia Proposal: An Educational Manifesto* (New York: Macmillan).

Association of American Colleges and Universities (2002). *Greater Expectations: A New Vision for Learning as a Nation Goes to College* (Washington, DC: Association of American Colleges and Universities, National Panel Report).

Curriculum and Examinations Board (1986). *In Our Schools: A Framework for Curriculum and Assessment*. Report of the Interim Curriculum and Examinations Board to the Minister for Education (Dublin: Curriculum and Examinations Board).

Department of Education (annually from 1924–81). *Rules and Programme for Secondary Schools* (Dublin: Stationery Office).

Department of Education, Technical Instruction Branch (c. 1942). *Memorandum V. 40: Organization of Whole-Time Continuation Courses in Borough, Urban and County Areas.*

Department of Education (1960). *Report of the Council of Education on the Curriculum of the Secondary School* (Dublin: The Stationery Office).

Department of Education and Skills (2016). *Politics and Society: Curriculum Specification* < http://www.curriculumonline.ie/getmedia/e2a7eb28-ae06-4e52-97f8-d5c8fee9613b/13764-NCCA-Politics-and-Society-Specification-v2b.pdf > accessed 6 June 2017.

Fantl, J. (2012). 'Knowledge How', in *Stanford Encyclopedia of Philosophy* <https://plato.stanford.edu/entries/knowledge-how/> accessed 26 May 2017.

Gleeson, J. (2010). *Curriculum in Context: Partnership, Power and Praxis in Ireland* (Oxford: Peter Lang).

Hardarson, A. (2017). 'Aims of Education: How to Avoid the Temptation of Technocratic Models', *Journal of Philosophy of Education*, 51:1, pp. 59–72.

Higher Education Authority (2015). *National Plan for Equity of Access to Higher Education 2015–19* (Dublin: Higher Education Authority).

Hillery, P. J. (1963). *Statement* in Regard to Post-Primary Education. Press Conference, 20 May 1963. Reproduced in Randles (1976), pp. 328–37.

Hillery, P. J. (1964). Interview in *Hibernia*, 28 February.

Hirst, P. H. (1974). *Knowledge and the Curriculum* (London: Routledge and Kegan Paul).

Hirst, P. H. (1993). 'Education, Knowledge and Practices', in R. Barrow and P. White (eds), *Beyond Liberal Education: Essays in Honour of Paul H. Hirst* (London: Routledge), pp. 184–99.

Hirst, P. H. (2005). 'A Response to Wilfred Carr's "Philosophy and Education"', *Journal of Philosophy of Education*, 39:4, pp. 615–20.

Kimball, B. A. (1995). *Orators and Philosophers: A History of the Idea of Liberal Education* (New York: College Entrance Examinations Board).

Marquez, I. (2006). 'Knowledge of Being v. Practice of Becoming in Higher Education: Overcoming the Dichotomy in the Humanities', *Arts and Humanities in Higher Education*, 5:2, pp. 147–61.

Martin, J. R. [formerly J. Roland] (1958). 'On "Knowing How" and "Knowing That"', *The Philosophical Review*, 67:3, pp. 379–88.

Martin, J. R. (1994). *Changing the Educational Landscape: Philosophy, Women, and Curriculum* (New York: Routledge, 1994).

Martin, J. R. (2000). *Coming of Age in Academe: Rekindling Women's Hopes and Reforming the Academy* (New York: Routledge).

Mulcahy, C. M., Mulcahy, D. E., and Mulcahy, D. G. (2015). *Pedagogy, Praxis and Purpose in Education* (New York: Routledge).

Mulcahy, D. G. (1981). *Curriculum and Policy in Irish Post-Primary Education* (Dublin: Institute of Public Administration).

Mulcahy, D. G. (1989). 'Official Perceptions of Curriculum in Irish SecondLevel Education', in D. G. Mulcahy and D. O'Sullivan (eds), *Irish Educational Policy: Process and Substance* (Dublin: Institute of Public Administration), pp. 77–97.

Mulcahy, D. G. (2008). *The Educated Person: Toward a New Paradigm for Liberal Education* (Lanham, MD: Rowman and Littlefield).

Mulcahy, D. G. (2009). 'What Should it Mean to have a Liberal Education in the Twenty-First Century?', *Curriculum Inquiry*, 39:3, pp. 465–86.

Mulcahy, D. G. (2012a). 'Physical Education, Liberal Education and the Leaving Certificate Examination', *Irish Educational Studies*, 31:3, pp. 251–62.

Mulcahy, D. G. (2012b). 'Liberal Education', in J. Arthur and A. Peterson (eds), *The Routledge Companion to Education* (London: Routledge), pp. 3–10.

Mulcahy, D. G. (2013). 'Theory and Praxis in General Education', in D. G. Mulcahy (ed.), *Transforming Schools: Alternative Perspectives on School Reform* (Charlotte, NC: Information Age Publishing), pp. 153–75.

NCCA (National Council for Curriculum and Assessment) (2011). *Leaving Certificate, Physical Education: Draft Syllabus for Consultation* (Dublin: NCCA).

National University of Ireland, Galway website. 'Frequently Asked Questions' <http://www.nuigalway.ie/admissions/new_graduates_faq.html> accessed 30 May 2017.

Noddings, N. (1992). *The Challenge to Care in Schools* (New York: Teachers' College Press).

O'Donoghue, T. (1988). *The Irish Secondary School Curriculum and Curricular Policy in Ireland 1921–62* (unpublished PhD thesis, University College Dublin).

Pring, R. (1993). 'Liberal Education and Vocational Education', in R. Barrow and P. White (eds), *Beyond Liberal Education: Essays in Honour of Paul H. Hirst* (London: Routledge), pp. 49–78.

Randles, E. (1976). *Post-Primary Education in Ireland, 1957–70* (Dublin: Veritas Publications).

Ryle, G. (1949). *The Concept of Mind* (London: Hutchinson).

Sullivan, W. M., and Roisin, M. S. (2008). *A New Agenda for Higher Education: Shaping a Life of the Mind for Practice* (San Francisco: Jossey-Bass).

Tubbs, N. (2014). *Philosophy and Modern Liberal Arts Education: Freedom is to Learn* (Basingstoke: Palgrave Macmillan).

Walsh, E. (2011). *Upstart: Friends, Foes and Founding a University* (Cork: Collins Press).

White, J. (ed.) (2004). *Rethinking the School Curriculum: Values, Aims and Purposes* (London: Routledge Falmer).

Williams, K., and Williams, P. (2016). 'The Problematic Character of Critical Pedagogy', *Irish Educational Studies*, 35:3, pp. 307–18.

EMER SMYTH

6 Educational Inequality: Is 'Free Education' Enough?

Introduction

The joint OECD/Department of Education *Investment in Education* (1965) report presented the first systematic evidence on social inequality in educational participation in Ireland, documenting relatively low levels of full-time participation among fifteen- to nineteen-year-olds and rates that were highly socially structured. This endeavour represented a sea change in educational policy, given the lack of coherent strategy on equality of educational opportunity in previous decades (Ó Buachalla, 1988). As discussed in the other chapters of this book, the *Investment in Education* report provided the impetus for the introduction of free second-level education in Ireland. This chapter traces patterns of educational inequality in the subsequent period. The first section focuses on differences in educational outcomes by individual social background while the remainder of the chapter examines the extent to which unequal outcomes reflect differences in the social mix of students attending second-level schools.

Inequality in Educational Outcomes

Inequalities in outcomes have been documented for Irish children and young people at all stages of the educational career. The *Growing Up in Ireland* study has collected rich information on experiences among five-year-old children around the time of entry to primary education. Even at this early stage, significant differences are found the attitudes and dispositions of children from different social backgrounds towards school (including whether they are interested in classroom activities, maintain attention, etc.) and in their use of language for communication and thinking (how they listen and speak, and take turns interacting with others). These differences are determined both by parental social class (based on the highest occupation of the parents) and by mother's education, with the lowest language scores and least positive attitudes found among those from non-employed households, where parents have only lower secondary education or less (Smyth, 2016a). By the age of nine, clear differences are evident in reading and mathematics performance between social class groups and by parental education (Smyth et al., 2010). National Assessment data also show clear differences in English and maths test scores among children in second and sixth class of primary school using a composite measure of socio-economic status (Eivers et al., 2010). Similarly, analyses of reading, mathematics and science test results among fourth-class students show significant variation by mother's education and home educational resources (such as books) (Cosgrove and Creaven, 2013).

The *Investment in Education* report revealed substantial differences in educational participation prior to the introduction of free second-level education, with fifteen- to nineteen-year-olds from higher professional backgrounds 4.7 times more likely to be in full-time education than those from semi- and unskilled manual backgrounds. The period following the introduction of free education saw a rapid growth in educational participation among fourteen- to seventeen-year-olds (Tussing, 1978), but no data were available for quite some time on the extent to which there was a resulting reduction in inequality in participation. Information from the School Leavers' Survey, a nationally representative survey of those leaving full-time second-level education conducted from 1980 to 2007, allows us to examine the extent to which school completion varied by social background over this period (Figure 6.1). The categories used are based on the Central Statistics Office's (CSO) social class grouping; farmers are presented as a separate category because of their distinctive profile in relation to educational participation. At the beginning of the 1980s, Leaving Certificate completion continued to vary markedly by parental social class, with the vast majority (four-fifths) of those from higher professional backgrounds staying in school to the end of senior cycle, compared with a third of those from unskilled manual backgrounds. While these social class differences are sizable, differences are smaller than had been the case prior to the introduction of free second-level education (albeit using slightly different measures of social class). By 2006–7, Leaving Certificate completion rates had further increased across all social classes, with the exception of the higher professional group, who had already reached near-saturation in participation levels by 1980–1. Increases in participation were greatest among those from working-class (manual) backgrounds, but farm family participation also increased dramatically, matching the levels of the higher professional group by 2006–7. Given ongoing improvements in school retention levels to the point where 91 per cent of those entering second-level education now complete senior cycle (DES, 2015), it is likely that the social gap in Leaving Certificate completion has narrowed even further since 2007. However, this cannot be systematically assessed because of the lack of current data on the social background of school leavers.

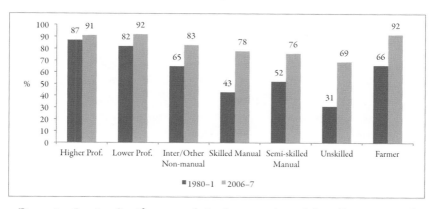

Figure 6.1: Leaving Certificate completion by parental social class. (Source: Annual School Leavers' Survey 1980–1 and 2006–7)

Social differentiation is also found in how well young people do within second-level education. Higher Junior Certificate grades are obtained by young people from higher professional backgrounds (Smyth et al., 2007) and by those whose mothers have degree-level qualifications (GUI, 2016). Figure 6.2 shows the proportion of Leaving Certificate leavers who achieved four or more 'honours' (that is, at least a C grade on a higher-level paper) in 2007. Over half of young people from higher professional backgrounds achieved this standard, but this was the case for only a fifth of those from skilled or semi-skilled backgrounds and fewer than one in six from unskilled backgrounds.

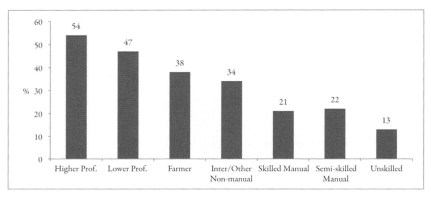

Figure 6.2: Proportion of Leaving Certificate leavers who achieved four or more C grades or higher at higher level, 2007. (Source: School Leavers' Survey, 2006–7)

In the Irish context, educational level and grades have a very significant impact throughout the life course, in terms of access to employment, the quality of employment and broader outcomes, such as health (Smyth and McCoy, 2009). Thus, educational inequality reinforces social inequality in adult life, with the resulting disparity in resources shaping outcomes for the future generation.

School Social Mix and Inequality in Outcomes

There is quite a remarkable degree of active selection of second-level schools on the part of families in Ireland, with almost half of junior cycle students not attending their nearest or most accessible school (Hannan et al., 1996;

Smyth et al., 2004). Parents in higher professional occupations are more likely to send their children to school outside the local area than those in other social groups. As a result, school selection processes, in conjunction with patterns of residential segregation, accentuate differences between individual schools in their social-class mix. The selection criteria used by over-subscribed schools also serve to reinforce social differentiation (Smyth et al., 2009), with fulfilling criteria such as being on a waiting list often requiring insider knowledge of the system and advance planning in relation to school options. There has been a good deal of debate internationally on the extent to which the school attended, and its social composition, matters for student outcomes. Many studies point to substantial variation between schools in levels of educational achievement (Teddlie and Reynolds, 2000), while others highlight constraints on the extent to which schools can (be expected to) make a difference in the context of wider social inequality (Thrupp, 1999). Scholars have also highlighted the importance of considering whether schools reproduce inequality or indeed exacerbate it (Downey and Condron, 2016). Findings from international research studies on the effect of the social composition of the student body, over and above the influence of individual social background, have been quite variable (see Nash, 2003; Teddlie and Reynolds, 2000). In contrast, research in Ireland has consistently shown significant variation by school social composition in relation to a range of outcomes, including student performance, rates of early school leaving and the proportion going on to higher education (Smyth, 1999; Smyth and Hannan, 2007; Smyth et al., 2011; Smyth, 2016b). Thus, young people attending schools with a concentration of working-class students obtain lower exam grades, are less likely to complete senior cycle and have lower rates of transition to higher education, even taking account their own family's socio-economic circumstances. Indeed, the existence of this contextual effect has underpinned Irish educational policy through the DEIS (Delivering Equality of Opportunity in Irish Schools) programme (and its predecessors), which targets additional resources at schools serving disadvantaged populations.

The remainder of this chapter draws on a mixed-methods longitudinal study of second-level students (the Post-Primary Longitudinal Study, for further details, see Smyth, 2016b). It seeks to unpack why this contextual effect is evident in Irish schools by exploring the ways in which school processes are related to the social mix of students. The analysis focuses on three factors in particular: ability grouping, the expectational climate of the school and the social climate of the school.

Ability Grouping and Inequality

Schools vary in the way in which they allocate students to base classes. They may employ streaming, whereby students of similar assessed ability are grouped into classes, ranked from 'higher' to 'lower'. They may use banding, a somewhat looser form of streaming, where students are divided into broad ability bands (for example, two higher and two lower classes). Alternatively, students may be placed in mixed-ability base classes, based on random (e.g. alphabetical) allocation or, more rarely, using test scores to achieve an intentional ability mix across classes. The use of rigid ability grouping (streaming) in Irish second-level schools has declined over time; survey data indicate that the proportion of schools using streaming for first-year students was 60 per cent in 1980, declining to 44 per cent by 1993, with a further decline to 30 per cent in the school year 2001–2 (Hannan et al., 1983, 1996; Smyth et al., 2004). At the same time, streaming has come to be disproportionately concentrated in schools serving working-class populations. Schools that are designated disadvantaged are more than twice as likely to use streaming as other similar-sized schools (Smyth, 2016b).

In interviews, staff in schools serving more disadvantaged populations emphasize the way in which streaming allows additional teaching resources to be targeted at the lower stream class:

> Our weaker students are in smaller classes and get the benefit of more individual teaching. I think certain do better than if they were mixed in with the better students. (Staff, Lang Street,[1] boys, working-class)

In contrast, other disadvantaged schools emphasize the need to provide opportunities for the 'brighter' students by having one 'good class':

> The advantage I suppose is that the better group can advance without being held back ... and the group which has difficulties then is a smaller group, so it gets easier then. From the teacher's point of view to deal with a smaller group of students is better. (Staff, Dawes Point, boys, working-class)

Working-class young people, especially boys, are more likely to attend schools that use streaming. Within these schools, there are also social-class differences in allocation, with working-class young people found to be under-represented in higher-stream classes; a third of those in higher-stream classes in the case-study schools were from professional backgrounds, compared with 14 per cent of those in lower-stream classes. Thus, if the use of streaming affects student outcomes, it will especially impact on working-class boys.

Among the study cohort, significant differences were found in student outcomes depending on the streamed class to which they were allocated. A majority (60 per cent) of those who were allocated to lower-stream classes did not complete senior cycle, compared with a fifth to a quarter of those in higher- and middle-stream classes and just 7 per cent of students in mixed-ability base classes. Variation is evident not just in retention but in exam performance at a given level. Figure 6.3 shows the difference in Junior Certificate achievement levels across ability groups, controlling for a range of factors including gender, social background and reading and maths achievement on entry to second-level education. Achievement levels are measured in terms of grade point average, with a minimum value of zero and a maximum value of 10, which is calculated on the basis of subject level and grade received and averaged across all exam subjects taken. There is

---

1   Schools in the study are identified on the basis of pseudonyms, with additional descriptors given on the social and gender mix of the school.

a very substantial difference in performance between higher- and lower-stream classes, a difference of over two grade points per subject. This pattern indicates that those assigned to lower-stream classes underperform relative to their initial ability levels compared to those allocated to other types of classes. It is also worth noting that higher-stream classes actually achieve a lower grade point average than those in schools with mixed-ability base classes so no educational benefit is evident for the higher-stream group. Among the minority of lower-stream students who remained on in school to Leaving Certificate level, a significant gap in grades was also evident. Even taking account of their lower Junior Certificate grades, those who had been in a lower-stream class scored 4.7 grade points per subject (out of a maximum of 28) less than those who had been in mixed-ability or higher-stream classes.

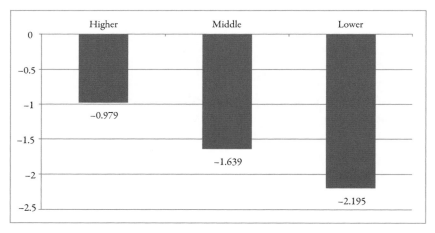

Figure 6.3: Net differences in Junior Certificate grade point average between streamed and mixed-ability classes. (Source: Smyth, 2016b)

What factors account for this pattern? One of the key drivers is the strong relationship between access to different subject levels[2] and class allocation.

2   For the Junior Certificate exam, students could take subjects at higher or ordinary level, with an additional foundation level available in Irish, English and maths.

Lower-stream classes were most commonly allocated to ordinary or foundation level while higher-stream classes were more likely to be able to access higher-level subjects. Thus, students in higher-stream classes took an average of 5.9 higher level subjects in the Junior Certificate exam, compared with 4.7 for those in middle-stream classes and just 0.2 in lower-stream classes. This set a ceiling on potential achievement for those in the lower-stream groups and had longer-term implications for access to higher-level subjects at senior cycle and therefore for potential entry to higher education. A more fundamental influence related to the way in which day-to-day classroom processes contributed to the construction of difference among learners. Students quickly became acutely aware of their place in the pecking order, applying labels such as 'dumb' and 'smart' to the different class groups. This labelling was reinforced by a number of processes, including the pace of instruction, the workload expected of students and the quality of interaction between teachers and students. On entry to second-level education, lower-stream classes were more likely to report covering much of the same material as in primary school. Over half of those in lower-stream classes felt that their teachers went too slowly with the class, with this lack of challenge often fuelling disruptive behaviour. As students in lower-stream classes progressed into second and third year, they were more likely to report that schoolwork was 'about the same', compared with higher stream and mixed-ability groups, who reported more demanding work. The gap in time spent on homework and study between the lower stream and the top and middle streams grew over time, with lower-stream groups actually spending less time on homework in their Junior Certificate exam year than they had on entry to first year. Student accounts point to the mutually reinforcing role of teacher expectations and student behaviour, with one class stating:

> We don't do our homework so we don't get it. Teachers know we don't do it so they don't bother checking it.
> We don't get homework.
> We never did get homework.
> We're sort of the thick class. (Lower/middle stream, Dixon Street, coeducational, working-class)

The influence of labelling and teacher expectations is also reflected in the quality of teacher-student interaction over the course of lower secondary education. All class groups report similar average levels of negative interaction with teachers, being reprimanded or scolded, at the beginning of first year. For lower-stream classes, the level of negative interaction increases progressively, with the gap between ability groups in the quality of interaction with teachers widening over time. Thus, a cycle of being reprimanded by teachers and 'acting up' in response appeared to emerge in lower-stream (and, to some extent, middle-stream) classes:

> School drives you mad, it actually would, the teachers, if you'd better teachers there would be no one getting in trouble.
> When you come back at the start of the year you're alright for a while.
> You calm down but then it starts building up through the year because you're so bored of school and you want to get out of it. (Middle stream, Dawes Point, boys, working-class)

This pattern is all the more important in a context where negative relations with teachers were a dominant feature in the accounts of early school leavers (Byrne and Smyth, 2010) and influence a range of other educational outcomes (see below). In summary, the evidence indicates that the use of streaming reinforces disengagement, underperformance and early school leaving among those assigned to lower-stream classes, without any educational benefits for higher-stream groups. Given the disproportionate use of streaming in working-class schools, ability grouping thus serves to reinforce social inequalities in educational outcomes.

The Expectational Climate of the School

Research in a number of European countries (Iannelli, 2004; Pustjens et al., 2004) has shown that schools differ in the proportion of students going on to higher education, even taking account of factors such as gender, social background and prior academic performance. This pattern has been explained in terms of the institutional habitus of the school, that is, the way in which social class is embedded in day-to-day school processes in such a way that going or not going on to higher education assumes a taken-for-granted quality (McDonough, 1997; Reay et al., 2001, 2005). This concept sheds light on the way in which the expectational climate of the school is shaped by the social composition of the student body and the concrete ways in which this habitus is reflected in school organization and process. This section highlights two aspects of this process in particular: school practice in relation to the take-up of higher-level subjects, and guidance regarding post-school options.

The previous section has described the way in which allocation to middle- and lower-stream class groups can serve to constrain access to higher-level subjects and thus longer-term options. Even within mixed ability schools, variation was found in the way in which schools framed the choice of subject levels. In middle-class and socially mixed schools in the study, high expectations for students were reflected in teacher encouragement to take higher-level subjects, at least for as long as possible:

> It is assumed straight off that most of them are going to do honours level at Junior Cert cycle. But then through the years you'll obviously find children who are struggling and they will do pass. But the vast majority of children here take honours in most of their junior cycle subjects unless there's a very obvious weakness, except ... in Irish ... and ... Maths. (Teacher, Harris Street, girls, middle-class)

In contrast, in working-class schools, there was a sharp decline in the proportion taking higher level in subjects such as maths and Irish as young people approached the Junior Certificate State exam. Thus, 65 per cent of students in working-class schools dropped from higher-level Irish compared with 12 per cent in mixed/middle-class schools. Furthermore, just over half of students in working-class schools dropped higher-level maths compared with just over a tenth of those in socially mixed or middle-class schools. Over the transition from lower to upper secondary education, students rarely, if ever, were allowed to move 'upwards' from ordinary to higher level in a subject. Thus, patterns of subject level take-up at junior cycle set limits on what was possible at senior cycle (and subsequently access to certain courses within higher education). Figure 6.4 shows considerable variation across the case-study schools in the average number of higher-level subjects taken for the Leaving Certificate, ranging from a low of 0.9 in Hay Street, a working-class coeducational school, to a high of 4.6 in Fig Lane, a middle-class coeducational school. There is a clear difference between working-class schools and those of socially mixed or middle-class intake, with students in working-class schools taking far fewer higher-level subjects than those in other schools. The average number of higher-level subjects taken is higher in the two middle-class schools, Fig Lane and Harris Street, but the average among students in Belmore Street, a mixed-intake girls' school, is comparable in level to these middle-class schools, showing that school organization and process can also play a role in shaping student outcomes.

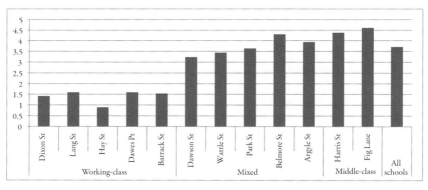

Figure 6.4: Average number of higher-level subjects taken in the Leaving Certificate exam by school and school social mix.

The expectational climate of the school was also expressed through the nature of formal guidance regarding post-school options. Access to formal guidance sessions was largely restricted to the final year of second-level education and was strongly focused on helping students complete applications for higher education. However, expectations about the likelihood of students going on to higher education were expressed in more indirect and subtle ways as they moved through the school system. In more middle-class schools, going on to higher education was taken for granted ('There was never any question of anything else', Fig Lane, middle-class, coeducational), so student decision making focused on which institution and which course rather than whether to progress (Smyth and Banks, 2012). In the case of this latter school, regular guidance sessions were scheduled for final-year students and the school social networks were mobilized to secure university visits for students outside the regular open day slots (Smyth and Banks, 2012). In contrast, in one of the working-class schools, Barrack Street, over half of the cohort intended to go on to higher education, but many felt that their guidance counsellor was discouraging these ambitions, suggesting instead that a further education course would be more 'appropriate':

> I can't even talk to my guidance counsellor. Just, she just puts me off every time I go to her like so I'll do it myself.
> And she shouldn't be doing that, she should be encouraging you. Like when we were doing the CAO she was like 'this is a joke I haven't seen this many people filling out CAOs in all my life'... you know ... in the room.
> Basically putting you down like. (Barrack Street, girls, working-class)

Teacher expectations are found to be highly predictive of the likelihood of young people applying for higher education, all else being equal (Smyth and Hannan, 2007). Young people's educational aspirations are formed as early as lower secondary education, remaining relatively stable thereafter, and strongly affect the actual routes taken after leaving school (McCoy et al., 2014). These aspirations are not only influenced by parental aspirations for their children but by the way in which expectations of students are expressed through formal and informal guidance within the school and through encouragement to take higher-level subjects, factors which are strongly related to the social mix of the school.

The Social Climate of the School

Young people in the Post-Primary Longitudinal Study cohort were asked a number of questions about the nature of their interaction with teachers in each year of their second-level education. These questions formed two scales, which were used as indicators of the school social climate: positive interaction, which assessed the frequency with which students received praise or positive feedback from teachers, and negative interaction, which measured the frequency with which students were given out to or reprimanded by teachers either in relation to their schoolwork or for misbehaviour. Figure 6.5 shows the way in which the quality of interaction changes as students move through the system. The beginning of first year represents somewhat of a 'honeymoon' period, with students receiving much more praise than censure from teachers. As students move through junior cycle, the frequency of praise and positive feedback declines while the incidence of negative interaction increases. These patterns are related to the structure and phasing of the school system. By second year, a pattern of drift and disengagement sets in for some students, with a resulting decline in the quality of teacher-student relationships. This pattern is further reinforced in third year, with the focus on exam preparation and the necessity to 'cover the course' for teachers and students putting pressure on the relationship. The transition to upper secondary education marks a period of change in teacher-student relations. While praise and positive feedback are on the whole less frequent than at lower secondary level, levels of reprimand are much lower, as teachers allow greater independence for (at least some) young people as learners.

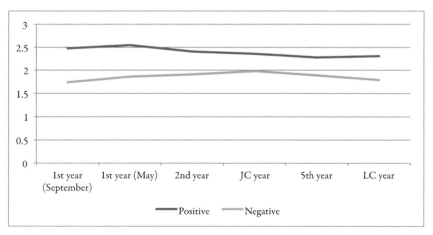

Figure 6.5: Frequency of positive and negative teacher-student interaction by year group.

Individual social class background and school social mix play an important part in shaping school climate. Social-class differences are not evident in levels of positive interaction with teachers. However, young people from working-class and non-employed backgrounds experience much higher levels of negative feedback from their teachers than their middle-class peers. Furthermore, schools with a concentration of working-class students have quite different school climates than other schools, having greater levels of both positive and negative interaction, suggesting greater surveillance, positive and negative, in working-class schools. Unfair treatment by teachers emerged as a dominant theme in group interviews with students. This was especially evident in schools with a concentration of working-class students, where many students felt that teachers held low expectations for them and consequently did not treat them with a great deal of respect. Thus, some students in Barrack Street, a working-class girls' school, reported that their teachers expected them 'to be pregnant when you're 16', while boys in another working-class school (Hay Street) felt their teachers expected them to have 'no lives and we're going to be on the dole when we're 18 ... out on the streets'. These young people saw criticism by teachers as rooted in a lack of esteem among teachers for students in the school, which in turn fed a lack of respect for teachers on the part of students:

> They say in order to get what you want you have to give what you want, respect and stuff, and some of them [teachers] don't do that. You give respect to them but they don't give it to you. (Barrack Street, girls, working-class)

This process appeared to result in a mutually reinforcing dynamic of 'giving out' (reprimanding) on the part of teachers and 'acting up' on the part of students, which in turn led to further reprimands:

> Picking on every single detail like.
> Small bit of noise and they make a big deal.
> ... Yeah, you'd make even more noise then like.
> It's like they are living in the past or something, you know. (Lang Street, boys, working-class)

I'd be nice to the teachers if they'd be nice to be but if they are not going to be nice to me I'm not going to be nice to them, you know what I mean. (Barrack Street, girls, working-class)

The nature of the school climate was also reflected in the application of disciplinary measures within the school. The use of sanctions was found to differ significantly by the social mix of the school. Middle-class schools were much less likely to give 'lines' or extra homework as punishment than mixed or working-class schools. The use of harsher sanctions such as detention and even suspension (temporary exclusion) were much more common in working-class schools. For example, two-thirds of young people in working-class schools received at least one detention period in second year, compared with a third of those in mixed or middle-class schools. Furthermore, a sizeable proportion, one fifth to one quarter, of young people in working-class schools were suspended from school each year over their second-level school careers. In one lower-stream class, boys reported that 'there's nearly one out [on suspension] every day' (Dawes Point, boys, working-class). While differences in school discipline partly reflected greater levels of misbehaviour in working-class schools, harsher sanctions such as detention or suspension were more likely to be used in working-class schools, even controlling for levels of student misbehaviour (Smyth, 2016b).

The school climate, that is, the quality of interaction between teachers and students, was found to have a significant effect on a range of student outcomes. All else being equal, young people who had experienced more negative interaction with their teachers were more likely to drop out of school. Negative interaction with teachers contributed to early school leaving in large part because students disengaged from investment in study and lowered their aspirations for the future. In follow-up interviews with the cohort of young people who dropped out of school (see Byrne and Smyth, 2010), negative relations with teachers was a dominant theme in their account of why they left school. A negative dynamic of feeling they were treated unfairly, acting out in response and receiving further sanctions from teachers culminated in early school leaving for several young people:

> I hit third year and I just started not getting on with the teachers and all. I kept getting thrown out of classes and suspended all and I just hated it and I hate that school. (Dixon Street, coeducational, working-class)
>
> I'd never cooperate with any of the teachers in the class or anything and once they came into the classroom they'd be like 'sit down the back', and I'd sit down the back with nobody, on my own, so, and then that made me worse. So I just started hating them. Then I wanted to leave. (Barrack Street, girls, working-class)

Others felt that they had been labelled as 'troublemakers' at a certain stage in their school career and that label had persisted despite any of their efforts:

> If you got into trouble say a couple of times, that would stick to you like, you know no second chances like, forget him if he doesn't want to learn, leave him do you know that kind of way. You either wanted to learn or you didn't, you know that kind of way, the way they put it, you get out of it what you put into it like. (Hay Street, coeducational, working-class)

Among young people who stayed on in school, those who had experienced negative interaction with their teachers in second year received lower grades in the Junior Certificate exam, all else being equal. Negative teacher-student interaction in second year is also found to have a significant impact on Leaving Certificate performance. This influence operates indirectly through lower secondary performance. Thus, young people with negative relationships with their teachers achieve lower exam grades at the end of lower secondary education and these grades are associated with lower exam performance two to three years later. Given the importance of Leaving Certificate performance for access to higher education and employment, the findings highlight the long-term consequences of a negative school climate for young people's life chances.

Similarly, final-year students who had experienced negative interaction with their teachers at lower secondary level were significantly less likely to go on to higher education than their peers, even taking account of their lower Junior Certificate exam performance. Thus, a negative experience of relationships with teachers served to discourage young people from pursuing other educational opportunities. A follow-up study of this cohort of young people (McCoy et al., 2014) confirmed that those who had experienced negative interaction with their teachers were much less likely to actually go on to any form of post-school education or training. The school climate shaped other aspects of young people's development, with positive teacher-student interaction contributing to reduced feelings of stress and isolation (Banks and Smyth, 2015).

Conclusions: Is 'Free Education' Enough?

The introduction of free second-level education led to a significant increase in educational participation and a reduction in inequality in the proportion of young people staying on in school until Leaving Certificate level. Despite this policy development, inequalities remain evident at all stages of young people's educational career, with persistent social differentiation in educational participation and performance. There has been a good deal of discussion internationally about the extent to which schools reproduce or counter inequalities resulting from the unequal distribution of economic, social and cultural resources in the wider society. This chapter considers the way in which certain school practices reflect the social-class mix of the school population and therefore serve to reinforce social inequality in educational outcomes. The discussion in the chapter focuses on three sets of processes: ability grouping, the expectational climate of the school and the school social climate. The use of rigid ability grouping (streaming) has declined over time in Irish second-level schools but is disproportionately concentrated in schools serving working-class populations. Streaming is found to enhance disengagement, underperformance and early school leaving among those assigned to lower-stream classes, without any educational benefits for higher-stream groups. These outcomes reflect differential access to higher-level subjects and, more importantly, to the way in which the identity of lower-stream students is shaped by lower teacher expectations, fewer academic demands and a slower pace of instruction. Thus, ability grouping serves to reinforce social inequalities in educational outcomes. Expectations of students are expressed through formal and informal processes, through encouragement to take higher-level subjects and through the kinds of guidance given regarding post-school opportunities. In more middle-class schools, going on to higher education assumes a taken-for-granted quality, while in working-class schools, students report lower expectations and more constrained prospects. The social climate of the school, that is, the quality of interaction between teachers and students, varies significantly by school social mix, a pattern that is all the more important given its significant effect on a range of student outcomes, including retention and exam performance. The chapter shows the complex way in which individual social-class background and school social mix can interact to shape unequal outcomes for young people, depending on the school they attend, and highlights the challenges in creating equitable schools even where there is 'free' education.

Bibliography

Banks, J., and Smyth, E. (2015). 'Your whole life depends on it: academic stress and high-stakes testing in Ireland', *Journal of Youth Studies*, 18:5, 598–616.

Byrne, D., and Smyth, E. (2010). *No Way Back? The Dynamics of Early School Leaving* (Dublin: Liffey Press/ESRI).

Cosgrove, J., and Creaven, A.-M. (2013). 'Understanding achievement in PIRLS and TIMSS 2011', in E. Eivers and A. Clerkin (eds), *National Schools, International Contexts: Beyond the PIRLS and TIMSS Test Results* (Dublin: Educational Research Centre), 201–39.

Department of Education and Skills [DES] (2015). *Retention Rates of Pupils in Second Level Schools: 2008 Entry Cohort* (Dublin: DES).

Downey, D. B., and Condron, D. J. (2016). 'Fifty years since the Coleman Report: Rethinking the relationship between schools and inequality', *Sociology of Education*, 89:3, 207–20.

Eivers, E., Clerkin, A., Millar, D., and Close, S. (2010). *The 2009 National Assessments technical report* (Dublin: Educational Research Centre).

Government of Ireland (1965). *Investment in Education: Report of the Survey Team Appointed by the Minister of Education in October 1962* (Dublin: Stationery Office).

Hannan, D. F., Breen, R., Murray, B., Hardiman, N., Watson, D., and O'Higgins, K. (1983). *Schooling and Sex Roles: Sex Differences in Subject Provision and Student Choice in Irish Post-Primary Schools* (Dublin: ESRI).

Hannan, D. F., Smyth, E., McCullagh, J., O'Leary, R., and McMahon, D. (1996). *Coeducation and Gender Equality: Exam Performance, Stress and Personal Development* (Dublin: Oak Tree Press/ESRI).

Iannelli, C. (2004). 'School variation in youth transitions in Ireland, Scotland and the Netherlands', *Comparative Education*, 40:3, 401–25.

McCoy, S., Smyth, E., Watson, D., and Darmody, M. (2014). *Leaving School in Ireland: A Longitudinal Study of Post-School Transitions* (Dublin: ESRI, 2014).

McDonough, P. M. (1997). *Choosing Colleges: How Social Class and Schools Structure Opportunity* (New York: SUNY Press).

Nash, R. (2003). 'Is the School Composition Effect Real?: A Discussion with Evidence from the UK PISA Data', *School Effectiveness and School Improvement*, 14:4, 441–57.

Ó Buachalla, S. (1988). *Education Policy in Twentieth Century Ireland* (Dublin: Wolfhound Press).

Pustjens, H., Van de gaer, E., Van Damme, J., and Onghena, P. (2004). 'Effect of secondary schools on academic choices and on success in higher education', *School Effectiveness and School Improvement*, 15:3–4, 281–311.

Reay, D., David, M. E., and Ball, S. (2001). 'Making a difference? Institutional habituses and higher education choice', *Sociological Research Online*, 5:4 <http:\\www.socresonline.org.uk/5/4/reay.html>.

Reay, D., David, M. E., and Ball, S. (2005). *Degrees of Choice: Social Class, Race and Gender in Higher Education* (Stoke on Trent: Trentham Books).

Smyth, E. (1999). *Do Schools Differ? Academic and Personal Development among Pupils in the Second-Level Sector* (Dublin: Oak Tree Press/ESRI).

Smyth, E. (2016a). 'Inequalities from the Start? Children's integration into primary school', in J. Williams, E. Nixon, E. Smyth and D. Watson (eds), *Cherishing All the Children Equally? Children in Ireland 100 Years on from the Easter Rising* (Dublin: Liffey Press).

Smyth, E. (2016b). *Students' Experiences and Perspectives on Secondary Education: Institutions, Transitions and Policy* (Basingstoke: Palgrave Macmillan).

Smyth, E., and Banks, J. (2012). '"There was never really any question of anything else": young people's agency, institutional habitus and the transition to higher education', *British Journal of Sociology of Education*, 33:2, 263–81.

Smyth, E., Banks, J., and Calvert, E. (2011). *From Leaving Certificate to Leaving School: A Longitudinal Study of Sixth Year Students* (Dublin: Liffey Press).

Smyth, E., Darmody, M., McGinnity, F., and Byrne, D. (2009). *Adapting to Diversity: Irish Schools and Newcomer Students* (Dublin: ESRI).

Smyth, E., Dunne, A., Darmody, M., and McCoy, S. (2007). *Gearing Up for the Exam? The Experiences of Junior Certificate Students* (Dublin: Liffey Press/ESRI).

Smyth, E., and Hannan, C. (2007). 'School Processes and the Transition to Higher Education', *Oxford Review of Education*, 33:2, 175–94.

Smyth, E., and McCoy, S. (2009). *Investing in Education: Combating Educational Disadvantage* (Dublin: ESRI/Barnardos).

Smyth, E., McCoy, S., and Darmody, M. (2004). *Moving Up: The Experiences of First Year Students in Post-primary Education* (Dublin: Liffey Press/ESRI).

Smyth, E., Whelan, C. T., McCoy, S., Quail, A., and Doyle, E. (2010). 'Understanding parental influence on educational outcomes among 9 year olds in Ireland: the mediating role of resources, attitudes and children's own resources', *Child Indicators Research*, 3:1, 85–104.

Teddlie, C., and Reynolds, D. (eds) (2000). *The International Handbook of School Effectiveness Research* (London: Falmer Press).

Thrupp, M. (1999). *Schools Making a Difference: Let's be Realistic!: School Mix, School Effectiveness, and the Social Limits of Reform* (Buckingham: Open University Press).

Tussing, D. (1978). *Irish educational Expenditure – Past, Present and Future* (Dublin: ESRI).

7 Economic Inequality and Class Privilege in Education: Why Equality of Economic Condition Is Essential for Equality of Opportunity

Introduction

Mindful of the political and cultural context preceding the introduction of free education, this chapter engages reflexively with the contemporary educational 'common sense' that equalizing opportunities in education is an effective means of overcoming social class inequalities and promoting a meritocratic society more generally in Ireland. In doing so, it is conscious of the fact that no view comes from nowhere in academic life: academics, including the authors, do not stand on neutral intellectual ground; their personal and intellectual premises and values underpin their theoretical positions (Crean and Lynch, 2011; Gouldner, 1970; Lynch and Ivancheva, 2015).

The following statement from the 'experts' in the Irish Council of Education (1960) is salutary, and a reminder of how 'educated' people at a given time in history are bound by what Alvin Gouldner (1970) termed their 'domain and paradigmatic assumptions', that is to say, by their own values and assumptions emanating from their biography, professional interests, academic backgrounds and experiences.

> An unqualified scheme of 'secondary education for all' would be both financially impractical and educationally unsound. Only a minority would be capable of benefiting from such education and standards would fall. The voluntary system has worked well and preserves a sense of the value of education. Better State grants and more scholarships are needed to further stimulate it. (Department of Education, Ireland, 1960)

The experts serving on the Council of Education in the 1950s were people who genuinely believed that a selective and exclusive secondary education should be retained; they thought that most people were not capable of being educated to secondary level. While this may seem extraordinary, given what we now know from the history of education, sociology, developmental psychology and other disciplines, council members were merely reflecting the 'common sense', the received and unquestioned 'wisdom' of that time in Ireland. Though respected educators, the council was also limited by the lack of diversity and reflexivity within their own ranks. They were overwhelmingly male religious drawn from the secondary school sector. The domain assumptions and values of their social backgrounds, and the narrow paradigmatic assumptions of their academic education, framed their educational and social imaginary. As respected 'experts', they were not required to be reflexive about how their *domain* assumptions may have framed their *paradigmatic* assumptions regarding what was educationally possible.

This chapter suggests that we may be suffering from an equally constrained educational and social imaginary in our current thinking about equality in education. The 'common sense' of our time, enshrined in both EU and Irish law, is that equality of opportunity is a reasonable and tenable principle for promoting equality in education and in society more generally. It is also widely believed that the educational system is itself meritocratic. Using empirical evidence from a range of international studies, this chapter claims that equality of opportunity needs to be underpinned by the principle of equality of condition, especially equality of economic condition, if it is to be meaningful. As the principle of equality of opportunity is operationalized in education through the practice of meritocratic selection in schools and colleges, the chapter demonstrates how meritocracy is an unrealizable myth in an economically unequal society.

Why Equal Opportunities Policies in Education Cannot Undo Social Class Inequalities

Ireland's educational achievements over the last fifty years have been remarkable in aggregate terms. Ireland is among an elite group of countries with relatively high rates of educational attainment, a low rate of early school leaving and a high proportion of graduates from second-level schools entering higher education (Byrne and McCoy, 2017). Moreover, Clancy's analysis of EUROSTUDENT surveys (2005–11) shows that access rates to higher education for blue-collar (working-class) students is higher in Ireland than in several other European countries, including Germany, France and Austria (Clancy, 2013).

However, as with all aggregated data, the general picture does not tell the complete story. Educational expansion, while raising the national standards of education, has not led to the kind of reduction in *relative* social class inequalities that many believed it could or would. The relative class advantage of the upper and upper middle classes only tapered off in a given sector of education when their participation rates reached saturation point, in other words when they had maximized their social class advantages at that level (Raftery and Hout, 1993; McCoy and Smyth, 2011). Social class background exercises a direct influence on educational opportunities including school choice (Cahill and Hall, 2014); it also interfaces with ethnicity and race in determining educational opportunities for Traveller and immigrant children (Devine, 2011; Darmody, Byrne and McGinnity, 2014). The educational advantages of the Irish professional and business elite are also aided financially through the state funding of elite schools (Courtois, 2015). Although there is little known about how social class and disability[1] classifications and inequalities are operating in Ireland, due to the lack of attention given to these issues in research (McDonnell, 2003), there is ample international research showing that access to disability support services and disability classifications are also classed and raced in ways that advantage those who are privileged (Blanchett, 2010; Riddel and Weedon, 2016).

While international evidence confirms that the relatively privileged have maintained their social class advantages within and without education for many decades (Blossfeld and Shavit, 1993; Marsh, 2011; Reardon, 2011), this is not to suggest that the quality of education in schools is

---

[1]	The word 'disability' needs to be challenged as a category of identification. 'Dis–' is a negative prefix in English, so to define any person or group as 'disabled' or having a 'disability' is to implicitly suggest they are lacking something in human ability terms. Perhaps the word should change to 'diffability', thereby recognizing the enormous diversity in abilities within the human condition.

inconsequential in challenging inequality. Irish research shows that the quality of teaching, the inclusiveness of the curriculum and assessment procedures, and school organizational arrangements are important for mitigating the impact of social class, ethnic, racial and gendered injustices in society (Banks et al., 2014; Devine, Kenny and McNeela, 2008; Darmody and McCoy, 2011). However, while education can significantly enhance a given *individual's* capabilities and life chances, it cannot overcome structural (group-based) injustices arising from economic inequalities as the generative site of those injustices is not located within the education system in the first instance (Lynch and O'Neill, 1994; Lynch and Lodge, 2002; Lynch and Baker, 2005; Marsh, 2011).

What has remained largely unappreciated in Ireland and elsewhere is that the expansion of education and liberal equal opportunities policies cannot have a significant impact on relative social class dis/advantages, for reasons arising from the dynamic relationship between the structures of a capitalist economy and formal education (Marsh, 2011). The false promise of meritocratic individualism in a hierarchically organized society needs to be recognized. While a small minority from working-class households can and do succeed relative to their upper-class peers, this is not feasible for the majority. Educational credentials are competitively acquired positional goods, and those who are collectively and individually best-resourced are at a competitive advantage in attaining the most valuable educational credentials. A major study in the US (involving a meta-analysis of nineteen national studies over a fifty-year period) has confirmed this. Reardon (2011) found that social class-based inequalities in educational attainment have risen in the US since the 1970s and these inequalities are directly related to income inequalities; those who own and control private wealth are always in a position to use this wealth to advantage their own children, especially by buying extra educational resources outside the formal educational system. Kaushal, Magnusson and Waldfogel's (2011) research in the US shows that families in the top income quintile (richest 20 per cent) are spending almost seven times as much per child each year compared with the poorest 20 per cent: they paid $9,000 per child for 'enrichment' activities such as out-of-school tutoring, athletic activities, test preparation, summer camps, second-language learning and cultural activities, compared with the $1,300 per child that families in the bottom quintile (20 per cent) spent. Private, out-of-school financial investment is advantaging children in high-income households in terms of educational attainment (Duncan and Murnane, 2011). There is every reason to believe that private family investment is also advantaging children from privileged backgrounds in Ireland. The data from the *Growing Up in Ireland* study shows that most structured, out-of-school cultural activities are only fully accessible on a paid basis. The net effect is that 'those in the higher income families are much more likely to attend' (Smyth, 2016, p. 96).

Even though the Irish state has invested much in making education more egalitarian in terms of standardizing the quality of schools and teaching, this work is undermined by what is happening in other fields of fiscal and public policy. Economic inequalities in Ireland are among the highest in the OECD *prior to social transfers* (TASC, 2015, 2016a); inequality has remained consistent over time, and was exacerbated during austerity from 2008 to 2014 (Lynch, Cantillon and Crean, 2017). Rising economic inequalities means that children from poorer households cannot participate on equal terms with others within education as they do not have equal resources. The way poverty impacts on returning to school each year exemplifies this: the average cost of returning to school varied from €340 (primary) to €775 (second level) for a given child in 2017 (Barnardos, 2017). Yet, the government back-to-school allowance for low-income families was €125 for a child up to the age of eleven, and €250 per child after that age. The allowance does not meet even half the costs involved, forcing poorer parents into debt (Ibid.). This reflects the general underinvestment in public education in Ireland, and the disinvestment in public goods and services during and since the financial crisis (Lynch, Cantillon and Crean, 2017; Murphy and Dukelow, 2016). The lack of political commitment to equality in education is evident from cuts to educational services for children with learning disabilities, Travellers, and language supports for immigrant children over the last ten years. The latter cutbacks exemplify in particular the ways in which race and disability interface with social class in undermining equal opportunities: lower-income households (and low-income immigrant families are among them) rely most heavily on public services; the lack of investment in public services impacts most severely on them (TASC, 2015, 2016a).

As public schools in Ireland are not adequately funded, the majority are required to supplement their income by requesting 'voluntary contributions' from parents, a policy that is deeply inequitable given parental differences in ability to pay: schools with the poorest parents have the lowest voluntary contributions even though they are the ones that need it most. Moreover, the costs of school books, computers and extracurricular activities require considerable parental investment even in the so-called free educational system (Barnardos, 2017). Social class advantage comes into play through differential economic power. Ireland has a long-established 'educational market': the middle and upper classes are free to migrate to semi-private and private service provision to make up any deficits in the public education system (Tormey, 2007). They can also supplement public schooling with private investment. The use of private tuition (grinds) is a prime example of this. It is 'common sense' among those who are educational 'insiders' (Lyons, Lynch, Close, Sheerin and Boland, 2003, pp. 329–56) to get private tuition for their children prior to the Leaving Certificate in particular (Lynch and O'Riordan, 1998). While Smyth's (2009) analysis of School Leaver Survey data suggests that grinds *per se* may not boost grades, grinds are only one of the panoply of market services available for those who can pay for them. Summer camps, language travel and educationally relevant extracurricular activities are widely available for those who can pay.

The market for out-of-school tuition in Irish and music reflects the longevity (and widespread acceptance) of privately funded education. Private tuition in Irish and music is so well established that it is rarely if ever framed as a grind. Given that 40 per cent of the overall grade for Leaving Certificate Irish is now given for oral Irish, parents who can afford to send children to the Gaeltacht[2] are at a distinct advantage in the Leaving Certificate Examination. Almost 50 per cent of the overall grade in Leaving Certificate music can be given for performance; yet, it is extremely difficult to excel in performance in the Leaving Certificate without undertaking private tuition over an extended period of time and the costs are very high: in 2017, one-to-one instrumental music classes were advertised on the internet

2   While a small minority get scholarships, the average basic cost for a standard three-week course in 2017 was €950.

at €25 for half an hour. The costs are prohibitive for low-income families (Conaghan, 2015). The introduction of the Higher Professional Aptitude Test (HPAT) assessment for medicine is a more recent example of a class-biased selection criterion; both preparation for the test and taking it has to be privately funded.[3]

The link between economic and educational inequality is reflected in the fact that at the age of thirteen, a 1 per cent increase in household income predicts a 6.5 per cent increase in verbal scores, a 5.2 per cent increase in numerical scores and a 5.8 per cent increase in the total Drumcondra Test scores (TASC 2016b). Moreover, data from the *Growing up in Ireland* survey shows that classed inequality in educational attainment literally increases with age (TASC, 2016b). Entry to higher education is also highly class-stratified, and while the proportion of students attending higher education has increased for all classes since free education was introduced, 50 per cent of students from Ireland's most affluent areas study at one of the most elite universities in Ireland, four times the rate of those from disadvantaged areas (TASC, 2016b). As is true internationally (Reay, 2017), higher education has become an increasingly important site for social class stratification. What is clear from the above is that there is a circular relationship between economic inequality and educational attainment: the relative lack of economic resources disables those seeking competitive advantage; lower rates of attainment at key educational transition stages limit people's opportunities to outcompete others in the quest for valuable educational credentials.

The Generative Sites of Economic Inequality

Although the quality of public education can significantly enhance an individual's capabilities and life chances relative to others, especially in a labour-migratory globalized economy, it cannot overcome economic

---

3   It cost €130 to do the HPAT test in 2017 and a basic preparation course cost €250.

injustices directly when the generative site of those injustices is not located within the education system in the first instance. Education can enable people to develop individually; however, as it is not the generative site of economically led social class inequality, it must not be held accountable for its persistence. It was the restructuring of the economies and occupational structures in Western capitalist states in the post-Second World War period that enabled absolute rates of social mobility to rise, not changes in education *per se* (Goldthorpe, 2007). In the post-1980 period, it was the deregulation and geopolitics of taxation and finance that contributed significantly to the rise of economic inequality (Piketty, 2014, p. 20). The rise of precarious work, zero-hour contracts and the proliferation of low-waged economies in the services sector in Western capitalist economies (Standing, 2011) is not the direct outcome of actions in the education sector; education cannot prevent powerful employers creating low-paid jobs, or failing to provide pensions for their workers; it cannot alter the structure of the capitalist economy that creates the inequality that contributes to unequal access to and participation in education (Marsh, 2011). The new oligarchic rich are global citizens and increasingly detached from nation states and their policies (Streeck, 2016, p. 28); *noblesse oblige* does not apply. It is not the educational institutions that enable them to maintain their class advantage through inheritance, low taxes on wealth, deregulated financial markets and the free movement of capital across borders. The latter is a function of mobilized class power, be it in international law, military spending, fiscal policy and/or the legislative and political infrastructures of global capitalist economies. This applies in Ireland as elsewhere (Allen, 2007). The super-rich can block wealth taxes and buy political majorities through campaign contributions, while maintaining social legitimacy through philanthropy (Streeck, 2016, pp. 28–30). In determining levels of inequality, 'inherited wealth comes close to being as decisive at the beginning of the twenty-first century as it was in the age of Balzac's Père Goriot' (Piketty, 2014, p. 22). As major class inequalities are not a product of educational policy *per se*, it is not appropriate to hold them responsible for them. It is equally unacceptable to promote the idea that education can alter the class structures of society through meritocratic means, selecting the academically capable and creating a class-fair system of social selection in an economically unequal society. Yet, blaming schools for failing to resolve social inequalities has become a powerful narrative in recent decades in a number of countries, including the United States (Kantor and Lowe, 2013). Education has been given the responsibility to challenge class inequality, something it cannot do alone.

The Myth of Meritocracy and Equality of Opportunity in an Economically Unequal Society

It would be very difficult for educational (and economic) inequality to be sustained over time in democratic societies unless it was deemed morally justifiable. The moral justification for unequal outcomes in education is provided through widespread allegiance to a liberal code of equality of opportunity (EO).[4] There is a belief that the EO principle is an acceptable guide to policy in the distribution of social goods: it is encoded in EU treaties, and advanced within member states by a variety of legally binding directives. Its legal status adds to its legitimacy as a mechanism for distributing social goods, including education.

The principle of equality of opportunity is formally operationalized in education through the practice of meritocratic selection; competition for advantage is regulated by rewarding those who achieve highly. The most

---

4   Equality of opportunity is a liberal concept. Liberal egalitarians typically define equality in terms of individuals rather than groups; while they vary between conservative liberal and left-leaning liberals, they all subscribe to the view that equality of opportunity means that people should in some sense have an equal chance to compete for social advantages. As they assume that inequality is endemic to society, equality of opportunity is about equalizing the distribution of educational (and life) chances within an unequal society. For a discussion on the difference between liberal ideas of equality and equality of condition, see Chapter 2 of *Equality: From Theory to Action* (Baker, Lynch et al., 2004).

'meritorious', where IQ+Effort=Merit[5] (Young, 1958), are given high grades and the least 'meritorious' are awarded lower grades. On the basis of these classifications, education and social selection for each stage of education and, ultimately, for the labour market is determined. There is widespread allegiance to the fairness of this 'meritocratic' system in Ireland (Kennedy and Power, 2010). Given the relationship between educational success, income, wealth and other forms of social and cultural capital outlined above, meritocratic selection is simply unattainable in an economically unequal society (Brown, Lauder and Ashton, 2011; Brown, 2013; Mijs, 2016). There is a false promise of methodological individualism underpinning equal-opportunities thinking: the selection of the few cannot become the pattern for the many, not least due to the limited number of elite positions within a hierarchical system. Also, because credentialized education is a positional good, its value is always relative: to succeed one must have more of the valued credentials than one's competitors. In an economically unequal society the competition is never a fair one as competitors are not equally resourced, and that includes being resourced in terms of social networks (Kennedy and Power, 2010). A study involving Ireland and a number of other Western European countries by Frazini and Raitano (2013) highlights this point. It shows how, even when people have comparable college degrees and grades, the class position of their social origins impacts on the prestige and income of their jobs, to the advantage of the already privileged. They hypothesize that class-based social networks and social skills contribute to these class-biased labour market differentials.

Meritocratic policies are also unrealizable for other reasons. The abilities and opportunities to be meritorious are based on non-meritocratic factors, including inheritance and the circumstances of birth; in addition, what is defined as worthy of merit recognition at a given time and in a given culture is quite arbitrary and, by definition, excludes some groups (Mijs, 2016).

---

5   For Michael Young (1958), this formula was not a principle to be lauded as a fair means of operating social selection; quite the contrary, his book is an ironic critique of the idea, and of the moral judgement that would ensue from its implementation. To fail due to bad luck would be forgivable but to fail because you did not deserve to do well (lacked merit) is be held accountable for failure and not so easily forgiven.

The key question always remains: who has the power to define which abilities are of merit and how does a society know and measure abilities (intelligences) and/or effort? There is no clear formula for measuring these that is not deeply subjective and numerous studies show that meritocratic traits vary across societies and over time (Mijs, 2016). Unfortunately, although it is known that many tests of 'abilities', such as aptitude and IQ-type tests like the SAT, are both social class and racially biased (Lemann, 1995) (and inherently disablist, given their reliance on online equivalents of pencil-and-paper tests), they remain in widespread use across the world. Karabel's (2005) study of how the definitions of merit changed in Harvard, Yale and Princeton over the twentieth century in ways that enabled them to exclude unwanted outsiders, be these non-whites, Jews, Catholics or women, is proof of the arbitrariness of merit. The inclusion of large numbers of students within contemporary universities who have dyslexia or other disabilities is also proof of how arbitrary exclusions 'on merit' have been historically. The problem remains that those who have the power to define 'merit' will always do so in a way that will ensure their own children are meritorious (Mijs, 2016, p. 21). The principle of meritocracy is an ideology that justifies inequality not a means of overcoming it.

A further problem with the principle of meritocracy is that it 'crowds out' debates about equality and need (Mijs, 2016, 23–6). This is perhaps its most dangerous characteristic. The belief that one can select and find the meritorious creates a widespread political and educational culture focused on finding 'the talented few'. It fosters a belief in a neoliberal era that only a minority of talented (market-valuable) people exist, propelling the so-called 'global war for talent' (Brown and Tannock, 2009) and the self-righteousness of the 'successful'. Meritocracy has a moral as well as a market message: the educationally successful are of value while the relatively unsuccessful are not. The moral code implicit in meritocratic thinking, focusing on the prioritization of the few at the expense of the many, overrides and weakens other values in education: nurturing, trust, integrity, care and solidarity are subordinated to regulation, control and competition. Investment in 'elite' scholars, athletes, leaders, musicians, actors (the so-called 'bright', 'gifted', 'smart', 'able' students) is prioritized over investment in those with greatest educational needs, who could be equally 'bright, smart, gifted and able' if given the opportunity. As the amoral principle of competition becomes necessitous in a meritocratic system, documenting scores, educational attainments and ranks becomes an industry in itself. Student and staff idealism to work in 'the public interest' is diminished as energy and time must be devoted to documenting institutional and/or personal achievements (Lynch, 2015). Moreover, educating those who are most disadvantaged ceases to be a priority as the vulnerable are a threat to a good performance appraisal. What emerges is a twenty-first-century manifestation of essentialist, eugenics-related logic, declaring that only a minority are worthy of investment. Educational resources are redirected to policies and practices that will ensure the selection of the meritorious few rather than enabling the socially disadvantaged to gain parity (Brown and Tannock, 2009). The rise of elite academies, centres for so-called gifted children in schools and merit scholarships in universities are all indicative of this trend. Claims of 'giftedness' are mirrored in parallel systems of disability labelling. Much of the latter is class-biased and racialized and does not lead to better services for those who most need them, although it may well advantage the better-off (Blanchett, 2010; Riddell, 2009; Riddell and Weedon, 2016).

A further danger of deploying meritocracy as a principle of justice for the allocation of rewards (including educational awards) is that it individualizes the problem of relative educational failure. What are effectively structural injustices become defined as personal troubles; they manifest themselves in feelings of guilt, anxiety, failure and, at times, hopelessness. Over time this creates cynicism and anger, individually and politically, as people realize that their 'failure' was the inevitable outcome of an unfair competition (Liu, 2011). Arlie Hochschild's (2016) five-year study with supporters of the Tea Party in the Southern States of the US shows how the meritocratic myth has exploded into political agitation and anger in America. What is also dangerous about relying on liberal equality-of-opportunity policies, and their moral ally meritocracy, to address injustices is that they foster an illusion of manageable and achievable success. They provide a moral legitimation for failure that depoliticizes the debate about social injustice. Meritocratic thinking is literally a smokescreen behind which privilege is normalized (Kennedy and Power, 2010). It focuses attention on the self, the actuarial self who has to manage her or his own risk and opportunities and blinds us to the need for solidarity and co-operation to overcome group-based injustices. It propels people to be more and more individually competitive and to ignore and out-compete others rather than stand by them in collective action.

Why Equality of Condition Matters

In educational terms, equalizing opportunity is about promoting fairness in the competition for advantage. It implies that there will be winners and losers, people who do well and people who do badly. An 'opportunity' in this context is the right to compete, not the right to choose among alternatives of equal value. So two people, or two different groups, can have formal equal opportunities even if one of them has no real prospect of achieving anything of value. For example, a society that allows only 20 per cent of the population to attend third-level education could, in this liberal sense, give everyone an equal opportunity to do so, even though in a stronger sense it would clearly be denying the opportunity for third-level education to 80 per cent of the population. Under an equal-opportunities framework, the purpose of having a principle of equality in public policymaking is to provide a fair basis for managing these inequalities, by strengthening the minimum to which everyone is entitled and by using equality of opportunity to regulate the competition for advantage. The most ambitious liberal equality principle is Rawls's 'difference principle', which states that 'social and economic inequalities' should work 'to the greatest benefit of the least advantaged' members of society (Rawls, 1971, p. 83; 2001, pp. 42–3). Rawls also argues that people should not be advantaged or hampered by their social background and that their prospects in life should depend entirely on their own effort and abilities. Rawls calls this principle 'fair equal opportunity' (1971, p. 73; 2001, pp. 43–4).

   The problem with the concept of equality of opportunity is that it pre-supposes the persistence of structural inequalities; it assumes that there will always be major inequalities between people in their status, resources, relationships and power. It is implied, if not stated, that the fundamental structures of modern welfare capitalist states (with the Nordic countries in Europe frequently cited as the ideal cases) are, at least in broad outline, the best humanity is capable of at this time in history. This is not to say that promoters of equality of opportunity in the liberal egalitarian tradition think that we live in the best of all possible worlds or that there is little we can do to improve the way we manage education or societies generally to make them fairer. However, there is an assumption that a mixed economy of capitalism and voluntary effort, a developed system of social welfare, a meritocratic educational system, and a specialized and hierarchical division of labour define the institutional framework within which any progress towards equality can be made. The task for egalitarians is to make adjustments to these structures rather than to alter them in fundamental ways.

In contrast to liberal equality of opportunists, promoters of equality of condition claim that inequality is rooted in changing and changeable social structures, and particularly in structures of domination and oppression. Equality of condition refers to the belief that people, individually and collectively, should be as equal as possible in relation to the central conditions of their lives, particularly in terms of their material conditions and the exercise of power. It is not about trying to make inequalities fairer, nor is it about giving people a more equal opportunity to become unequal; it is about ensuring that all of humanity have roughly equal prospects for a good and decent life. In education, it is not about just giving groups of people a formal right to education which in reality is unrealizable given pre-existing structural inequalities (e.g. due to lack of transport, money, books, or other cultural resources). Equality of condition recognizes the categorical and highly institutionalized character of social inequality that Tilly (1998) has identified. Because deep inequalities between peoples are encoded in laws and public policies in the form of property rights, relational and communication rights, and cultural and participatory rights and practices, equality of condition is focused on achieving changes in the organization of institutions, be these economic, political, cultural or affective.

What liberal egalitarians see as inevitable, promoters of equality of condition regard as changeable. Because social structures have changed in the past, they can be changed in the future. Exactly which structures need to change is a matter of debate, but they clearly include structures of capitalism (a predominantly market-based economy in which the means of production are privately owned and controlled, resulting in deeply exploitative work relations for the majority of humanity), patriarchy (systems of gender relationships that privilege men over women worldwide), racism (social systems that divide people into 'races' and privilege some 'races' over others, with enormous human cost in terms of life and livelihoods) and disablism (social systems that define people in terms of abilities they lack rather than those that they possess, thereby denying millions of people the right to education and autonomy).

Focusing on social structures when explaining inequality focuses policy attention on changing the structures and regulations protecting privilege. It recognizes the long, slow processes involved in unravelling centuries of privilege that are encoded in laws of ownership and control, in hegemonic modes of thinking and in language itself. In contrast to the tendency of liberal egalitarians to focus on the rights and advantages of individuals in particular, equality of condition pays equal attention to the rights and advantages of groups; it recognizes the intersectionality of injustices on life's positioning within (Gillborn, 2015) and without education (Anthias, 2012). In contrast to liberal egalitarians' tendency to concentrate on how resources can be redistributed, it focuses on the structures and relations of unequal ownership, control and distribution in the first instance and how these can be changed (Baker, Lynch, Cantillon and Walsh, 2004). It argues that pre-distributional inequalities of wealth and income need to be examined, not just the means for redistributing wealth and incomes after the fact. Equality of condition also means paying more attention to how people are related, how the wealth of some is at the cost of the poverty of others, and how unequal power relations interface with inequalities of wealth, status, and other resources. In contrast to the tendency of liberal egalitarians to hold individuals responsible for their successes and failures in education, equality of condition emphasizes the influence of social class, race, disability, care responsibilities, sexuality, gender, regional location, and other factors affecting people's choices and actions. It presents a holistic framework for social change in education, arguing that inequality in education is not only about issues of equality of access, but is also about *parity of respect and recognition* within education, *parity of participation* in the exercise of power and *the realization of love, care and solidarity* within the organization of schools and colleges (Lynch and Baker, 2005). While it has only been possible to focus on the significance of equality of economic condition in this chapter, similar issues arise for the realization of equality of condition in relation to achieving parity of respect and recognition and parity in the exercise of power in relation to race, gender, disability, ethnicity, sexuality, age, etc. There is also a profound need to rethink education in terms of its core care responsibility (*educare*) to nurture and enable people to grow and develop in a way that is not simply directed by the market economy.

Concluding Remarks

The equality principle governing Irish public policy, and particularly educational policy, is that of equality of opportunity based on merit. Those who adhere to the meritocratic position claim that those who work hard and are academically capable will do well in school regardless of their social background. The evidence does not support this claim: major social and economic inequalities inevitably undermine all but the thinnest forms of equality of opportunity in education because privileged parents will always find ways of advantaging their children in an economically unequal society. The inability of formal education to overcome social class inequalities is a reflection of the general inability of liberal equal-opportunities policies to deliver social justice in an economically unjust society, something Tawney (1931) predicted almost 100 years ago. Speaking of promoting equality of opportunity in a capitalist society, he stated: 'Equality meant not the absence of violent contrasts in income and condition, but equal opportunities to become unequal … equality is encouraged to reign provided it does not attempt to rule' (Tawney, 1931, p. 103). This presents a major dilemma for educators; even when schools do their best to overcome the many class (and increasingly ethnic/racial/disability-related) disadvantages that students experience within schools and colleges, they cannot eliminate the competitive advantage of the most advantaged. Yes, there are individual exceptions, but the exceptions are deceptive and dangerous when taken as examples (role models) of what is possible for the majority; they prolong the meritocratic myth that hard work and academic ability are all that is required to succeed relative to others. Unless we address social class inequality outside of school, and create a more economically equal society in Ireland more generally, we cannot have any meaningful equality of opportunity in education. We need to have a significantly more equal distribution of wealth and income to have substantive equality of opportunity in education. And for this to happen, both fiscal and educational policy need to be framed in an egalitarian way. This means dealing with pre-distributional and post-distributional injustices in the taxation system, and increasing taxes in a fair and equitable manner, something that is not the case currently as Ireland relies heavily on indirect systems of taxation that are highly regressive (Collins, 2014). Ireland visibly fails to tax profits and unearned wealth in an equitable manner. Given the relational nature of injustice, an unjust taxation system has a direct impact on the quality of the public education services and on the abilities of those who are most in need to maximize the benefits of education.

A number of questions arise from this chapter. Are we deceiving young people in working-class areas, and inadvertently promoting cynicism among them, by telling them they can compete on equal terms with those whose out-of-school resources are vastly superior to theirs, and who are able to activate these resources as required to maintain their educational advantage? Do our unspoken domain and paradigmatic assumptions about the efficacy of equal opportunities and meritocratic policies prevent us from documenting and highlighting the whole truth about equality in education in Ireland? In an educational competition where both the definition of merit and the resources to achieve it are already controlled by the upper middle and upper classes of Irish society, are we deceiving those who are working class and/or underprivileged for reasons of ethnicity or race or differences in abilities about what education can offer them? In other words, are we any different to the authors of the Council of Education Report in 1960 when we congratulate ourselves on what we have achieved while ignoring the perpetuation of inequalities in education and society more generally under a new coda? Equality of condition is possible, even if it takes time, but does it challenge too many vested interests? And if it does, who will take up the challenge?

Bibliography

Allen, K. (2007). *The Corporate Takeover of Ireland* (Dublin: Irish Academic Press).

Anthias, F. (2013). 'Moving Beyond the Janus face of Integration and Diversity Discourse: towards and intersectional framing', *The Sociological Review*, 61:2, pp. 323–43.

Baker, J., Lynch, K., Cantillon, S., and Walsh, J. (2004). *Equality: From Theory to Action* (Basingstoke: Palgrave Macmillan).

Banks, J., Byrne, D., McCoy, S., and Smyth, E. (2014). 'Bottom of the Class? The Leaving Certificate Applied Programme and Track Placement in the Republic of Ireland', *Irish Educational Studies*, 33:4, pp. 367–81.

Barnardos (2017). 'School Costs 2017' <https://www.barnardos.ie/media-centre/news/latest-news/school-costs-2017-infographic.htm> accessed 18 September 2017.

Blanchett, W. J. (2010). 'Telling It like It Is: The Role of Race, Class, & Culture in the Perpetuation of Learning Disability as a Privileged Category for the White Middle Class', *Disability Studies Quarterly*, 30:2 <http://dx.doi.org/10.18061/dsq.v30i2.1233>.

Blossfeld, H., and Shavit, Y. (eds) (1993). *Persistent Inequality* (Oxford: Westview Press).

Brown, P. (2013). 'Education, Opportunity and the Prospects for Social Mobility', *British Journal of Sociology of Education*, 34:5–6, pp. 678–700.

Brown, P., Lauder, H., and Ashton, F. (2011). *The Global Auction: The Broken Promises of Education, Jobs, and Incomes* (Oxford: Oxford University Press).

Brown, P., and Tannock, S. (2009). 'Education, Meritocracy and the Global War for Talent', *Journal of Education Policy*, 24:4, pp. 377–92.

Byrne, D., and McCoy, S. (2017). 'Effectively Maintained Inequality in Educational Transitions in the Republic of Ireland', *American Behavioral Scientist*, 61:1, pp. 49–73.

Cahill, K., and Hall, K. (2014). 'Choosing Schools: Explorations in Post-Primary School Choice in an Urban Irish Working Class Community', *Irish Educational Studies*, 33:4, pp. 383–97.

Clancy, P. (2013). 'Differentials in Inequality of Access to Higher Education in European Countries: Triangulation of Findings from EUROSTUDENT and Other Comparative Surveys', 26th Consortium of Higher Education Researchers (CHER) Annual Conference, 9–11 September 2013 <http://hdl.handle.net/10197/6367>.

Collins, M. L. (2014). *Total Direct and Indirect Tax Contributions of Households in Ireland*, Nevin Research Institute Dublin NERI WP 2014/No 18.

Conaghan, D. (2015). 'Instrumental Music Education in Ireland: The Canary in the Coalmine of Educational Equality'. Paper presented at the School of Social Justice Annual Conference at UCD, Belfield, 3 October.

Courtois, A. (2015). '"Thousands waiting at our Gates": Moral Character, Legitimacy and Social Justice in Irish Elite Schools', *British Journal of Sociology of Education*, 36:1, pp. 53–70.

Crean, M., and Lynch, K. (2011). 'Resistance, Struggle and Survival: The University as a Site for Transformative Education', in A. O'Shea and M. O'Brien (eds), *Pedagogy, Oppression and Transformation in a 'Post-Critical' Climate* (London: Continuum International Publishing Group), pp. 51–68.

Darmody, M., Byrne, D., and McGinnity, F. (2014). 'Cumulative Disadvantage? Educational Careers of Migrant Students in Irish Secondary Schools', *Race Ethnicity and Education*, 17:1, pp. 129–51.

Darmody, M., and McCoy, S. (2011). 'Barriers to School Involvement: Immigrant Parents in Ireland', in M. Darmody, N. Tyrrell and S. Song (eds), *Changing Faces of Ireland, Exploring Lives of Immigrant and Ethnic Minority Children* (Rotterdam: Sense), pp. 145–67.

Department of Education (1960). *The Curriculum of the Secondary School: Report of the Council of Education as presented to the Minister for Education* (Dublin: Stationery Office)

Devine, D. (2011). *Immigration and Schooling in the Republic of Ireland – Making a Difference?* (Manchester: Manchester University Press).

Devine, D., Kenny, M., and MacNeela, E. (2008). 'Naming the "Other": Children's Construction and Experience of Racism in Irish Primary Schools', *Race Ethnicity and Education*, 11:4, pp. 369–85.

Duncan, G. J., and Murname, R. J. (2011). *Whither Opportunity? Rising Inequality, Schools and Children's Life Chances* (New York: Russell Sage Foundation).

Frazini, M., and Raitano, M. (2013). 'Economic Inequality and Its Impact on Intergenerational Mobility', *Intereconomics*, vol. 6, pp. 328–34.

Gillborn, D. (2015). 'Intersectionality, Critical Race Theory, and the Primacy of Racism: Race, Class, Gender, and Disability in Education', *Qualitative Inquiry*, 21:3, pp. 277–87.

Goldthorpe, J. H. (2007). *On Sociology: Volume Two – Illustrations and Retrospect* (Stanford, CA: Stanford University Press, 2nd edn).

Gouldner, A. (1970). *The Coming Crisis of Western Sociology* (London: Heinmann).

Hochschild, A. (2016). *Strangers in their Own Land: Anger and Mourning on the American Right* (New York: The New Press).

Kantor, H., and Lowe, R. (2013). 'Educationalizing the Welfare State and Privatizing Education: The Evolution of Social Policy since the New Deal', in Prudence and L. Carter (eds), *Closing the Opportunity Gap* (New York: Oxford University Press), pp. 25–39.

Karabel, J. (2005). *The Chosen: The Hidden History of Admission and Exclusion at Harvard, Yale, and Princeton* (Boston, MA: Houghton Mifflin Harcourt).

Kaushal, N., Magnusson, K., and Waldfogel, J. (2011). 'How Is Family Income Related to Investments in Children's Learning?', in Richard Murnane and Greg Duncan (eds), *Whither Opportunity* (Chicago, IL: Russell Sage Foundation), pp. 187–206.

Kennedy, M., and Power, M. (2010). 'The Smokescreen of Meritocracy: Elite Education in Ireland and the Reproduction of Class Privilege', *Journal for Critical Education Policy Studies*, 8:2, pp. 222–48.

Lemann, N. (1995). 'The Great Sorting', *Atlantic Monthly*, September, pp. 84–8.

Liu, A. (2011). 'Unravelling the Myth of Meritocracy within the Context of the US', *Higher Education*, 62:4, pp. 383–97.

Lynch, K. (2015). 'Control by Numbers: New Managerialism and Ranking in Higher Education', *Critical Studies in Education*, 56:2, pp. 190–207.

Lynch, K., and Baker, J. (2005). 'Equality in Education: An Equality of Condition Perspective', *Theory and Research in Education*, 3:2, pp. 131–64.

Lynch, K., Cantillon, S., and Crean, M. (2017). 'Inequality', in William K. Roche and Philip O'Connell (eds), *Austerity's Poster Child? Ireland's Experience of the Great Recession and Recovery* (Oxford: Oxford University Press), pp. 252–71.

Lynch, K., and Ivancheva, M. (2015). 'Academic freedom and the commercialisation of universities: a critical ethical analysis', *Ethics in Science and Environmental Politics*, 16:1, pp. 1–15.

Lynch, K., and Lodge, A. (2002). *Equality and Power in Schools: Redistribution, Recognition and Representation* (London: Routledge Falmer).

Lynch, K., and O'Neill, C. (1994). 'The Colonisation of Social Class in Education', *British Journal of Sociology of Education*, 15:3, pp. 307–24.

Lynch, K., and O'Riordan, C. (1998). 'Inequality in Higher Education: A Study of Class Barriers', *British Journal of Sociology of Education*, 19:4, pp. 445–78.

Lyons, M., Lynch, K., Close, S., Sheerin, E., and Boland, P. (2003). *Inside Classrooms: The Teaching and Learning of Mathematics in Social Context* (Dublin: IPA).

McCoy, S., and Smyth, E. (2011). 'Higher Education Expansion and Differentiation in the Republic of Ireland', *Higher Education*, 61:3, pp. 243–60.

McDonnell, P. (2003). 'Developments in Special Education in Ireland: Deep Structures and Policy Making', *International Journal of Inclusive Education*, 7:3, pp. 259–69.

Marsh, J. (2011). *Class Dismissed: Why We Cannot Teach and Learn our Way out of Inequality* (New York: Monthly Review Press).

Mijs, J. J. B. (2016). 'The Unfulfillable Promise of Meritocracy: Three Lessons and Their Implications for Justice in Education', *Social Justice Research*, 29:1, pp. 14–34.

Murphy, M. P., and Dukelow, F. (eds) (2016). *The Irish Welfare State in the 21st Century: Challenges and Change* (London: Palgrave Macmillan).

Piketty, T. (2014). *Capital in the Twenty-First Century* (Cambridge, MA: Harvard University Press).

Raftery, A. E., and Hout, M. (1993). 'Maximally Maintained Inequality', *Sociology of Education*, 66:1, pp. 41–62.

Rawls, J. (1971). *A Theory of Justice* (Oxford: Oxford University Press).

Rawls, J. (2001). *Justice as Fairness: A Restatement* (Cambridge, MA: Harvard University Press).

Reardon, S. (2011). 'The Widening Academic Achievement Gap between the Rich and the Poor: New Evidence and Possible Explanations', in Richard Murnane and Greg Duncan (eds), *Whither Opportunity* (New York: Spencer Foundation and Russell Sage Press), pp. 91–116.

Reay, D. (2017). *Miseducation* (Bristol: Policy Press).

Riddell, S. (2009). 'Social Justice, Equality and Inclusion in Scottish Education', *Discourse*, 30:3, pp. 283–97.

Riddell, S., and Weedon, E. (2016). 'Additional Support Needs Policy in Scotland: Challenging or Reinforcing Social Inequality?', *Discourse*, 37:4, pp. 496–512.

Smyth, E. (2009). 'Buying your Way into College? Private Tuition and the Transition to Higher Education in Ireland', *Oxford Review of Education*, 35:1, pp. 1–22.

Smyth, E. (2016). *Arts and Cultural Participation Among Children and Young People* (Dublin: The Arts Council and the ESRI).

Standing, G. (2011). *The Precariat: The New Dangerous Class* (London: Bloomsbury Academic).

Streeck, W. (2016). *How Will Capitalism End?* (Brooklyn, NY: Verso Books).

TASC (2015). *Cherishing All Equally: Economic Inequality in Ireland* (Dublin: TASC: Think-tank for Action on Social Change).

TASC (2016a). *Cherishing All Equally 2016: Economic Inequality in Ireland* (Dublin: TASC: Think-tank for Action on Social Change).

TASC (2016b). *Cherishing All Equally 2016: Children and Economic Inequality in Ireland* (Dublin: TASC: Think-tank for Action on Social Change).

Tawney, R. H. (1931). *Equality* (London: Harper Collins).

Tilly, C. (1998). *Durable Inequality* (Berkeley: University of California Press).

Tormey, R. (2007). 'Education and Poverty in Combat Poverty Agency', *Welfare Policy and Poverty* (Dublin: Institute of Public Administration and Combat Poverty), pp. 169–200.

Young, M. (1958). *The Rise of the Meritocracy 1870–2033: An essay on education and society* (London: Thames and Hudson).

TOM BOLAND

8 The Development of the Institutes of Technology as a Key Part of the Higher Education Sector since Free Second-Level Education

Introduction

The decision to provide free second-level education was, by common agreement, a pivotal decision in the development of Ireland, socially and economically (Fleming and Harford, 2014; Walsh, 2009). In this chapter, I will focus on the inter-connectedness of that decision and its implementation with the implementation of another pivotal decision – the decision to establish a new kind of higher education institution, the regional technical colleges, now known as institutes of technology. These two policy developments have had a profound effect on Ireland and on its people, on its society, culture and economy.

But first, more general comment on the impact of the introduction of free second-level education itself. Professor John Fitzgerald recently wrote an article titled 'In Ireland, free education has more than proved its worth', the essence of which is in the headline (*The Irish Times*, 24 March 2017). Fitzgerald noted that Ireland was one of the last countries in northern Europe to wake up to the importance of investing in the education of its youth and points to the following outcomes of the introduction of free second-level education:

- A transformation of the rate of participation in second level, along with rising numbers completing the senior cycle, with Ireland joining the top of the class for participation and completion internationally within thirty years;

- Participation in third level also rose significantly, with Ireland now having one of the highest progression rates from second level to higher education in Europe;
- A transformative impact on employment opportunities and economic activity due to the higher skills now available;
- A particularly transformative impact for women in the labour force.

Fitzgerald makes the point that 'wiser policies' should have delivered these outcomes decades earlier. If only!

On another level, the introduction of free second-level education had a significant impact on the influence of religious denominations, especially the Catholic Church, on secondary education and in consequence on Irish society (O'Donoghue and Harford, 2011). The denominational aspect to our education system at primary and post-primary levels is constitutionally underpinned (Article 44.2.4–6). The Constitution was also so drafted to deny the state control over education (*Crowley v. Ireland* [1980], IR 102). While this brought some benefits, it also cemented the dominance of the Catholic Church, in particular, in social policy development in Ireland. The opening-up of education to the population as a whole, the rising levels of educational achievement, the accompanying growth in confidence and reduction in intellectual servility has done much to weaken the influence of a religious elite on social development in Ireland. Without universal access to free second-level education, it is hard to imagine that we would now live in a society that has not merely legislated for, but embraced, divorce, birth control and same-sex marriage. Would the outlawing of discrimination on grounds such as religion, sexual orientation and membership of the Traveller community have been possible if Irish people had not shaken off the paternalism fostered by the Catholic Church and, through the power of education, been given the confidence to inquire and make up our own minds?

These are some of the broader impacts of the introduction of free second-level education. But access to second-level education also had a direct impact on access to, and participation in, higher education. Once the barrier of second level had been crossed, students and their parents increasingly set their ambitions on higher education. The rest of this chapter is focused on the inter-connectedness of the decision to introduce free second-level education and the rise of the institute of technology sector as a key component of a higher education system that, without the institutes, would have continued to be an impediment to people's ambitions and the development of Ireland.

The Link between Free Second-Level Education and Access to Higher Education

The fifteen to twenty years previous to the onset of the recent deep economic problems saw unprecedented economic growth and success in Ireland. There were several factors that led to this economic success, but our supply of skilled labour is widely regarded as a key underpinning factor. Without a supply of skilled labour, the country would not have been able to support the levels of economic development that occurred. And without the institutes of technology, we would not have an adequate supply of skilled labour either in terms of quality or actual skills.

While much of our economic progress appeared to happen in a short space of time, it is important to acknowledge that the building blocks of this transformation were in place for a much longer period. The groundwork for the success of the 1990s was laid, in many ways, amid the ruins of an earlier economy. The late 1950s and 1960s saw a growing awareness in Ireland of the connectivity between education and economic development. This growth in awareness of the role of education in economic development mirrored a change in economic policy that saw the decades-long failed policy of protectionism ditched in favour of free trade and a deliberate effort to attract foreign direct investment. This awareness was also accompanied by a realization of a lacuna in our education and training provision as regards technological education, for which there was very limited provision, as the universities exercised a monopoly on higher education and training, but with an academic bias.

Decision to Establish Regional Technical Colleges

On 20 May 1963, the Minister for Education, Patrick Hillery, announced the setting-up of regional technical colleges (RTCs) as part of a major policy initiative. However, change had already long been in the air and the concept of higher education institutions regionally dispersed and with a vocational and technological focus had for some time been the focus of discussion among politicians and policymakers. An important milestone in the development of regional technical colleges came through the participation by Department of Education officials in an OECD policy conference on 'Economic Growth and Investment in Education', held in Washington in October 1961 (Coolahan, 1981). The OECD sounded out countries that might be willing to undertake a survey of their education system in its entirety. Ireland and Austria volunteered. This was a brave decision at the time as there were clear political risks associated with undertaking such a public review. The report of the Survey Team, *Investment in Education* (Government of Ireland, 1965), had a wide-ranging influence on education policy for many years thereafter. However, in the context of the development of the RTC sector, a more directly impactful development was a request by Ireland to the OECD to undertake a review of the supply and training of technicians in Ireland. An OECD report was published in 1964, *Training of Technicians in Ireland* (OECD, 1964), which recommended action to improve the existing facilities for the education and training of technicians. Although it was Patrick Hillery who first raised, in a serious way, a new policy approach to technological education and training (Clancy, 2015), it was in fact Donogh O'Malley who brought the project to fruition and so there is a direct connection between two policy decisions that were to have a profound impact not just on the Irish economy, but on the lives of millions of Irish people and Irish society more generally over the next half century. A Steering Committee on Technical Education, established by Minister O'Malley, reported in April 1967 and recommended that the minister proceed with the provision of nine regional technical colleges (Hill, 2003). It pointed out the lack of opportunity for people to access technological education and training and the academic bias in the higher education system. Changing this situation, to produce more technologically skilled graduates, was seen as essential if the opportunities for economic development were to be realized. In their report, the committee outlined the role of the regional technical colleges as follows:

> We believe that the main long-term function of the Colleges will be to educate for trade and industry over a broad spectrum of occupations ranging from craft to professional level, notably in engineering and science but also in commercial, linguistic and other specialities. They will, however, be more immediately concerned with providing courses aimed at filling gaps in the industrial manpower structure, particularly in the technician area. (Steering Committee on Technical Education, 1967, p. 11)

They also recommended that:

> We do not foresee any final fixed pattern of courses in the Colleges. If they are to make their most effective contribution to the needs of society and the economy they must be capable of continuing adaptation to social, economic and technological changes. Initiative at local and national levels will largely determine how far this vital characteristic is developed. We are concerned that the progress of these Colleges should not be deterred by any artificial limitation of either the scope or the level of their educational achievements. (Steering Committee on Technical Education, 1967, p. 11)

In the subsequent development of the RTCs, this recommendation was profoundly important.

The Remit of the RTCs

Initially the RTCs were established under the vocational education committees (VECs). They offered higher education programmes of shorter duration than would be typical in the universities, with a limited range of subjects in the fields of engineering and business studies. The curricula had a practical orientation, designed to be responsive to the needs of local industry and business. This placing of the RTCs under the VECs suited the VECs well, but, increasingly, came to be seen as a major block to the development of the colleges. A particular problem was that the VECs had a predominantly second-level focus, with no practical experience, or appreciation, of the place of research and business linkages in their new higher education colleges. The VECs, however, were very well entrenched in the political system and it took the recommendations of several reports and strong lobbying by the colleges themselves before, in 1991, the then Minister Mary O'Rourke introduced two bills to establish the RTCs and Dublin Institute of Technology on a statutory basis. The legislation came into effect on 1 January 1993 and defined the function of the sector as:

> To provide vocational and technical education and training for the economic, technological, scientific, commercial, industrial, social and cultural development of the State with particular reference to the region served by the college. (Regional Technical Colleges Act, 1992)

The regional technical colleges became institutes of technology in 1997/8 and in 2007 the institutes of technology came under the aegis of the Higher Education Authority (previously they had been under the aegis of the Department of Education). This was an important step in the autonomy of colleges that had started out as colleges within the VEC system and brought an important sense of parity of esteem between the institutes and the universities, the perceived absence of which had long been a bugbear of the institutes.

The Role of the EU

The European Union has also played an important part in the story of the development of the institutes of technology. From 1975 until the late 1990s, Irish students in the institute of technology sector benefited from European Social Funding. The policy position adopted by the Irish government was to direct financial resources towards the expansion of short-cycle, higher education courses. A special European Social Fund provision was made in 1975 in order to facilitate employment growth and the geographical and professional mobility of young people. The Department of Education and Science made an application to this fund for investment to cover training in middle-level technician skills in the newly established regional technical colleges. This funding came in the form of grants for students. The result was that by 1986, almost 90 per cent of all new entrants to full-time courses at the RTCs were in receipt of European Social Fund grants (Barry, 2005). These students accounted for approximately 20 per cent of total new entrants to Irish third-level education at that time. Aided by this EU support for students, the institutes of technology have contributed significantly to the expansion of higher education in Ireland since the 1970s. The emphasis on sub-degree, higher education programmes helped to improve the accessibility of higher education in Ireland and complemented a substantial expansion of the university sector. Combined, this led to the increase in higher education participation rates from 20 per cent in 1980 to almost 60 per cent. It is estimated that 20 per cent of all new entrants to higher education during the 1980s and 1990s went to the institutes and they currently account for approximately 45 per cent of all undergraduate students in the higher education system (HEA, 2016).

Through a twin-track approach to higher education provision, the binary system, Ireland provided a suite of programmes to meet the diverse capacities of students and the diverse needs of the economy. While there has been some 'mission drift' across the sectors, the policy continues to be at the core of our higher education system and maintaining that diversity is a policy to which the Higher Education Authority and the government are strongly committed.

Concluding Thoughts

The growth in the participation rate in higher education noted earlier is phenomenal and is a pace of growth that is one of the highest among OECD countries. It is noteworthy that much of this growth happened at a time when the country did not have employment opportunities to offer higher education graduates (i.e. throughout the 1980s). In effect, Ireland was oversupplying the market with higher education graduates, with the result that a large proportion emigrated. In the years leading up to 1989, nearly half a million people did so; of the 50,000 people who left each year during this period, 70 per cent were under twenty-five years old. This might seem like colossal folly and a waste of public money, but viewing it in this way would be to overlook a widely held perception in Ireland of education, and in particular higher education, as a route out of poverty and disadvantage. Furthermore, when a turnaround in economic conditions began to occur, graduates returned to Ireland, providing the necessary skills for industry and fuelled further economic growth. They also brought energy and innovation to our developing economy. Without this historical, in effect, over-investment in higher education and over-supply of graduates, it is unlikely that industries would have been attracted to Ireland and doubtful whether we would have experienced the same levels of economic growth in the recent past. Let those who guard the public purse today take note!

The regional technical colleges, and their successors the institutes of technology, are a well-recognized success story in modern Irish higher education and in the creation of contemporary Ireland. Their development on a regional basis throughout the country greatly expanded the opportunities for educational attainment. This, in turn, broadened access to higher education, as well as providing a local and technologically oriented alternative to the traditional universities. This was particularly important in providing Ireland with the labour-market skills necessary for the development of the scientific, technological and pharmaceutical sectors. These sectors continue to play a significant role in the Irish economy. The institutes explicitly aim to exploit knowledge in the interests of regional development. Their vocational and scientific orientation, as well as their mission to promote regional economic development, has contributed substantially to the economic success experienced in Ireland since the mid-1990s. and the story has not ended. In keeping with the National Strategy for Higher Education (Department of Education and Skills, 2011), the stage is set for some institutes to take a further step in their development by becoming 'Technological Universities'. They will be a feature of our higher education system for decades as they continue to make their unique contribution to their students and their communities.

Bibliography

Barry, F. (2005). *Third-Level Education, Foreign Direct Investment and Economic Boom in Ireland*, Centre for Economic Research Working Papers, WP05/09, University College Dublin.

Clancy, P. (2015). *Irish Higher Education: A Comparative Perspective* (Dublin: Institute of Public Administration).

Coolahan, J. (1981). *Irish Education: Its History and Structure* (Dublin: Institute of Public Administration).

Fleming, B., and Harford, J. (2014). 'Irish Education Policy in the 1960s: A Decade of Transformation', *History of Education*, 43:5, pp. 635–56.

Government of Ireland (1965). *Investment in Education: Report of the Survey Team Appointed by the Minister of Education in October 1962* (Dublin: Stationery Office).

Higher Education Authority (2016). *Higher Education System Performance Institutional and Sectoral Profiles 2013/14* (Dublin: HEA).

Higher Education Strategy Group (2011). *National Strategy for Higher Education to 2030: Report of the Strategy Group* (Dublin: The Department of Education and Skills).

Hill, J. R. (ed.) (2003). *A New History of Ireland Vol. VII: Ireland 1921–84* (Oxford: Oxford University Press).

O'Donoghue, T., and Harford, J. (2011). 'A Comparative History of Church-State Relations in Irish Education', *Comparative Education Review*, 55:3, pp. 315–41.

OECD (1964). *Training of Technicians in Ireland* (Paris: OECD).

Steering Committee on Technical Education (1967). *Report to the Minister for Education on Regional Technical Colleges* (Dublin: Stationery Office).

Walsh, J. (2008). *Patrick Hillery: The Official Biography* (Dublin: New Island).

Walsh, J. (2009). *The Politics of Expansion: The Transformation of Educational Policy in the Republic of Ireland, 1957–72* (Manchester: Manchester University Press).

JIM GLEESON

9 The Curriculum Response to 'Free Education' and the Raising of the School-Leaving Age

Introduction

As other authors in this volume have explained, Minister O'Malley unilaterally announced the introduction of so-called 'free' secondary education and the raising of the school-leaving age (ROSLA) to fifteen without prior notice or planning. This meant that, whereas the UK Schools Council had 'funded an unprecedented programme of research and development in support of teachers and local authorities' (Norris, 2007, p. 471) in preparation for their ROSLA (Stenhouse, 1971), Irish post-primary curriculum would remain essentially unchanged for more than twenty years after O'Malley's 1967 announcement.

The first section of this chapter locates the ROSLA announcement in its wider educational and curriculum policy contexts and considers post-primary curriculum prior to the 1983 establishment of the Interim Curriculum and Examinations Board (CEB) and its successor, the National Council for Curriculum and Assessment (NCCA). Younger readers will be less familiar with these historical antecedents which provide important context for subsequent curriculum policy and practice. The second section deals with the work of the CEB and the NCCA, including the introduction of the Junior Certificate, as well as subsequent developments under the statutory NCCA. The chapter concludes with some general observations.

Education Planning and Curriculum Context

Explanations for the tardy curriculum response to ROSLA are considered here. These include the *ad hoc* nature of educational planning, the neglect of macro curriculum issues, official attitudes to curriculum reform, as reflected, for example, in the experiences of the curriculum development agencies, and inattention to teacher and school development.

Educational planning

The culture of the Department of Education[1] over most of the twentieth century has been variously described as compartmentalized (Lynch, 1979), secretive (Lee, 1982) and hierarchical (OECD, 1991). Constitutionally, the Department is the 'handmaiden of the Minister' (OECD, p. 40), who is 'deemed responsible for all acts and actions of the civil servants working within the Department' (Harris, 1989, p. 7). This environment was well illustrated by Minister O'Rourke's performance at the 1989 Paris Review Meeting held in advance of the publication of the OECD (1991) report, where she dominated proceedings to the total exclusion of the senior Department members (Gleeson, 2010, p. 84). Educational administrators and policymakers must 'protect the minister of the day from controversy in view of his/her position as corporate sole', resulting in 'an unwillingness to take risks' (Coolahan, 1995, p. 20).

Many commentators have expressed concerns regarding the failure of the Irish education authorities to take planning seriously in a context in which education policy was communicated through a poorly coordinated succession of official circulars and the Department was concerned with 'all things great and small'. The Department's Planning and Development Unit,

---

1   The title of the National Education Ministry has changed three times over the period under consideration – Department of Education up until 1997, Department of Education and Science from 1997, and Department of Education and Skills since 2010. To facilitate reader-friendliness, it is simply referred to as 'the Department' throughout this chapter.

established after the *Investment in Education* review (Government of Ireland, 1965) had, with the exception of the Building Unit, been abolished in 1973. Lynch (1979, p. 21) noted the prevailing compartmentalization and identified the need for generalists to 'make the right connections between scientific, humanistic and socio-cultural concerns'. Ryan (1988, p. 6) remarked that the Department 'made fewer concessions to change than any other institution in society [while the government] has reacted like a frightened child at the controls of a runaway train, pushing all sorts of levers and knobs in the hope that something will work'. The OECD (1991, 36ff) noted 'the dearth of policy-related research' and identified 'in-built resistance to creating any permanent machinery for facilitating the policy-making process'. In his review, Cromien (2000, p. 4), former secretary of the Department of Finance, noted a 'certain passivity in the Department in relation to new developments'. He described the Department's approach as haphazard and lacking in coherence, with 'detailed day-to-day work [being] given priority over long-term strategic thinking' (Cromien, 2000, p. 2). The abiding picture is of an *ad hoc* approach where policy was expanding 'in piecemeal fashion [resulting in a] patchwork of structures and processes' (OECD, 1991, p. 36). As a former Senior Inspector and Principal Officer recalled (Gleeson, 2010, p. 79):

> The administrative decisions get taken because they're urgent. The professional ones can be put on the long finger ... the quality of the service doesn't cause government to fall or TDs to lose their seats, but it's different if a school is threatened with closure or can't afford the heating oil.

This *ad hoc* approach was greatly facilitated by public complacency, with education barely featuring during successive Irish General Elections (Gleeson, 2010, 131ff). As Sean Flynn (*The Irish Times*, 6 May 2002) noted, while 'education may have dominated recent British elections, it rarely figures in Irish electoral battles ... because most voters appear generally satisfied with the education service ... and the political parties are not anxious to rock the boat'. Education was a rather junior ministry up until the 1980s and the portfolio was not unduly onerous, with officeholders free to decamp for the summer (Logan and O'Reilly, 1985, p. 476).

Meanwhile, the Department of Finance had 'notable clout [and] enormous influence' (OECD, 1991, p. 38) and economists could 'get away with playing the philosopher king because there is so little challenge to the dominant orthodoxy' (Lee, 1989, p. 583). For example, Hussey (1990, p. 52) recounts in her diary entry for 14 August 1983 that the 'Department of Finance demanded that we take £68 million off our [budget] figures, which seems to be total nonsense considering both the rising numbers at all levels and pay deals that the Government has already entered into'.

Contrasting attitudes to primary and post-primary curriculum

O'Malley's announcement coincided with preparations for the introduction of the new primary curriculum, *Curaclam na Bunscoile*, heavily influenced by progressivist, child-centred curriculum ideology. This represented a major departure from the Primary Certificate examination, with its prevailing focus on the three Rs and narrowly focused school inspections (Walsh, 2012). The Irish National Teachers' Organisation, believing that both primary and post-primary curricula were too narrow and bookish (Hyland, 1988), had been calling for primary school curriculum reform since the 1940s and such concerns were reflected in the 1954 Council of Education Report. Members of the Primary Inspectorate were also influenced (Coolahan, 1981) by the publication of the Plowden Report in the UK (Central Advisory Council for England, 1967), with its 'emphasis on individual difference, on flexibility within the curriculum, the interaction of heredity and environmental influences, learning through activity and discovery and the integration of school subjects' (Walsh, 2012, p. 276).

   Curaclam na Bunscoile saw children as 'active constructors of knowledge and not simply "imbibers of information"' (Department of Education, 1971, p. 52), quoting Patrick Pearse's dictum that 'what the teacher should bring to his pupil is not a set of readymade opinions, or a stock of cut-and-dried information, but an inspiration and an example' (Department of Education, 1971, p. 15). Childhood was recognized as a unique cultural entity and there was a strong emphasis on recognition of individual differences and curriculum integration. The OECD Examiners (1991, p. 65) would later acknowledge that its 'very production marked a new direction for educational thought and practice in Ireland'.

Such progressivist thinking did not, however, carry any weight at secondary level. The 1962 Council of Education Report[2] for that sector expressed satisfaction with the existing curriculum, characterized as 'of the grammar school type, synonymous with general and humanist education and appropriate for the inculcation of religious beliefs and values which was the dominant purpose of the schools' (Coolahan, 1981, p. 81). As Ó Buachalla (1988, p. 68) remarks, the Council saw the notion of free secondary education as 'untenable, utopian, socially and pedagogically undesirable and economically impossible, [revealing] a sterility and an irrelevance which may have represented accurately the views of the educational establishment of the fifties'. That mood was indicative of the Catholic Church's opposition to the establishment of comprehensive schools in the early 1960s (O'Sullivan, 1989) and of its determination 'that a clerical manager, appointed by the local bishop, should control any new school, with the power to appoint staff and determine the curriculum in line with Catholic teaching' (Walsh, 2008, p. 115). While secondary school managers saw no need for increased levels of participation in secondary education or curriculum reform, O'Malley's shock announcement would require schools to cater for a huge influx of new students. The curriculum response would, however, take more than twenty years, and some 1.5 million Irish adolescents would experience a curriculum designed for the minority of mainly middle-class students who progressed beyond primary schooling.

Neglect of macro curriculum issues

Given the contextualized nature of curriculum (Cornbleth, 1992), it was inevitable that the prevailing anti-intellectual bias (Lee, 1989) spilled over into education (Gleeson, 2010). Minister Mulcahy declared in 1957 that he

---

2   The 1962 Council of Education, which focused on secondary as opposed to vocational education, consisted of twenty-nine ministerial nominees, of whom twenty-six were professional educators (including eleven clerics of various denominations) and three represented rural interests. There was no provision for the inclusion of parents *qua* parents.

did not have 'a duty to philosophise on educational matters' and Ministers
Colley and Hillery pronounced during the 1960s that comprehensive
schooling was not an ideological matter. As Crooks told the author, 'the
things that really mattered were control, structures, buildings, pension
rights, rather than curriculum ... for example, very few people outside
History teachers think of how important it is to teach people about our
culture and our past' (Gleeson, 2010, p. 95).

Curriculum policy was the exclusive prerogative of the Department
where curriculum was understood as an anthology of individual subjects
set out in *Rules and Programmes for Secondary Schools*.[3] Appointments to
the post-primary Inspectorate were made on the basis of subject expertise,
with 'the Inspectorate all staying in their subject boxes' (Gleeson, 2010,
p. 94). In his seminal book on whole curriculum, Mulcahy (1981, p. 56)
remarks that 'rarely is any attempt made to show how the aims of a particular subject tie up with the overall aims of the Intermediate and Leaving
Certificate syllabuses respectively'.

Treatment of curriculum in the 1980 Education White Paper was predominantly subject-based. Assistant Chief Inspector Seán Mac Cárthaigh[4]
(1983) prepared an important paper for his colleagues, calling for a new
departure in curricular thinking and planning that would keep pace with
technological and socio-economic change and the knowledge explosion.
Calling for a holistic approach to curriculum, he suggested that 'the first
task is to secure an overview that will enable us to relate all the stages and
aspects of education one to another, and to reconcile many ideals and interests' (Mac Cárthaigh, 1983, p. 35). However, money was simply not available
for curriculum development and Mac Cárthaigh's call went unanswered.

The OECD (1991, p. 67) would subsequently describe Irish post-primary curriculum as a 'derivation from the "classical humanist" tradition
with an overlay of technological/technical/vocational subjects'. Against that

3   The list of those subjects in which instruction is given to the pupils of the school
     in courses approved by the minister (*Rules and Programmes for Secondary Schools*
     published annually by the Department of Education).
4   Who had been active in the promotion of the Transition Year Programme and Irish
     studies.

background, the basic goals and values of Irish education have 'tended to be *tacit* rather than *explicit* during a period when major transformations in the society, economy and culture have been occurring [while] curriculum, assessment and examination changes have been continual but piecemeal' (OECD, 1991, p. 76, emphasis added). Callan (1995, p. 100) also highlights our tendency to make 'piecemeal adjustments or alignments to a host of social and cultural issues ... leading to an enlargement of curriculum contents with resultant pressures on schools to respond'.

The development of a coherent approach to curriculum reform was stymied by fragmentation, with the OECD (1991, p. 68) remarking that 'curriculum planning treats primary and secondary levels as quite distinctive and separate [so that] transition problems are an inevitable consequence'. Whereas the primary Inspectorate had been freed up to visit schools and classrooms following the abolition of the Primary Certificate Examination in 1968, post-primary Inspectors had little opportunity to do so prior to the establishment of the State Examinations Commission in 2003. Primary and post-primary Inspectors held separate annual conferences up until the early 1990s, as did secondary and vocational school Inspectors.[5]

Successive ministers were conservative regarding curriculum matters, with Minister John Wilson[6] asserting that his officials were 'fully conversant with the problems relating to curricula'. Such conservatism was often based on considerations of economic competitiveness and the safeguarding of a valuable national asset. As a former ministerial adviser put it, 'the bottom line at Cabinet was what's wrong that they want to change it? We have a credible examination system, don't start messing around' (Gleeson, 2010, p. 106). In this environment, the overarching concern within the Inspectorate was not to embarrass the minister by making public statements that he/ she would then have to defend in the Dáil.

5   The VEC sector had its legislative basis in the 1930 Vocational Education Act while the secondary Inspectorate did not have any such basis.
6   Dáil Reports, 1978, vol. 304, 1095–6.

Official attitudes towards curriculum reform including the experience
of the main curriculum development actors

Assistant Secretary of the Department, Sean O'Connor, established the
Intermediate Certificate Examination (ICE) Committee in 1970 'to break
down the system, abolish the Inter Cert and loosen the whole system up'
(Gleeson, 2010, p. 104). That Committee recommended reform of the
examination on the grounds that:

> ... with its emphasis on written examination, [it] was not a satisfactory mode of
> assessment of [students'] achievements ... it samples a narrow range of skills, leaving
> some important skills unrewarded [and] discourages innovation and curriculum
> development, and creates a sharp discontinuity with the integrated studies of the
> new Primary Curriculum. (Hyland and Milne, 1992, pp. 273–5)

However, following the 1977 change of government, the radical recommendations of the ICE Committee went unheeded and the state examinations continued to dominate the curriculum, with examination papers
receiving 'more scrutiny than notes in the Central Bank' (Gleeson, 2010,
p. 105). In such an environment, 'the Inspectorate had to do one job well,
that was to run the exams and if anything went wrong, the Inspector had
to carry the can' (Gleeson, 2010, p. 105).

The experiences of the curriculum development agencies provide a
unique insight into official attitudes towards curriculum reform. The City
of Dublin Vocational Education Committee's (CDVEC) Curriculum
Development Unit (CDU), of which Anton Trant was Director, and
Shannon Curriculum Development Centre (SCDC), directed by the principal of St Patrick's Comprehensive School, Diarmaid Ó Donnabháin, were
both established in 1972. Both directors had begun their teaching lives
outside of the Irish post-primary system, Trant in London and Malta and
Ó Donnabháin as a primary teacher in his native Cork. The Department
sponsored both men to investigate education systems in Europe and to participate in a six-week course on curriculum and school development at the
University of East Anglia, where Lawrence Stenhouse (1971) was leading
the Humanities Curriculum Project. Both agencies evolved at that excit-
ing time when Illich and Freire were challenging traditional pedagogies,

Counteshorpe College (Watts, 1977) was being established in the UK and Husen (1979) was asking fundamental questions about schools as institutions.

   With the exception of the Transition Year Project (Jeffers, 2011), Irish post-primary curriculum development has been primarily associated with schools serving disadvantaged students, arguably a case of 'necessity as the mother of invention'. The CDU was closely associated with the CDVEC, whose schools were bursting at the seams in the wake of ROSLA.[7] As captured in the title of his PhD thesis, 'The Power of the Provisional', Trant saw his role in terms of challenging the *status quo* and 'unfreezing' the system. The CDU was responsible for the establishment of the Irish Association for Curriculum Development (IACD) in 1972 and its continuation up until the mid-1990s.[8] That Association published two volumes of *Compass* annually[9] and encouraged school-based curriculum development, often supported by Teachers' Centres, through its conferences for primary and post-primary teachers.

   Shannon, Ireland's only 'new' town, with its international airport and tax-free industrial estate, was the location for one of Ireland's first comprehensive schools. As a strong proponent of curriculum reform, Assistant Secretary Sean O'Connor saw SCDC as a centre of experimentation to support the ideal of comprehensive education (Gleeson, 2010, p. 109).[10] Harris, principal of Newpark Comprehensive School for many years, also described the early comprehensive schools as 'experimental centres' (Gleeson, 2010, p. 109), while Barber (1989, p. 50) recalls how Minister Hillery saw 'curriculum reform as one of the major reasons for the establishment of the comprehensive schools' and teachers in that sector

---

7   The VEC sector generally has been heavily involved in the development of Post-Leaving and Adult Education courses. Other VECs, including North Tipperary and City of Galway, were also engaged in curriculum development during the 1980s.

8   The reasons for its demise included the increasing influence of the representational NCCA and the significant increase in educational discussion and debate following the publication of the Education Green Paper in 1992.

9   Edited by Dr Tony Crooks, Deputy Director of the Unit.

10   Following his promotion to the position of Department Secretary in 1973, the evolving third-level system would become O'Connor's primary focus.

received special salary allowances. However, the comprehensive experiment soon became embroiled in a power struggle between Church and state (O'Sullivan, 1989) and was subsequently overtaken by the establishment of Community schools.

The champions of curriculum development shared the aforementioned concerns of the ICE Committee (Gleeson, 2010, 95ff):

> Irish education is dominated by the culture of textbooks and exams with the result that nobody is asking serious questions. (Ó Donnabháin)
>
> Subjects and the public exams decide the whole bloody curriculum and the politics of the curriculum. (Trant)
>
> Curriculum policy-making is seen as playing around the edges. The dominance of the exams has reduced curriculum to a technical art, with exam papers to be proof-read and marked … they worry about exams because there will be Dáil questions if things go wrong … (Crooks)

Much like the Humanities Curriculum Project at the University of East Anglia (Stenhouse, 1971), the first CDU and SCDC curriculum development projects arose in response to the needs of post-ROSLA students coming from the new child-centred primary curriculum.[11] Both Ó Donnabháin and Trant recalled that official attitudes towards curriculum development were hostile and unhelpful at the time, with members of the Inspectorate wont to inquire when they would 'be finished developing the curriculum' (Gleeson, 2010, p. 110). When Ó Donnabháin brought the report on the pilot phase of SESP to the Department in 1977, the relevant official talked about 'getting back to normal … the project was now over and that was that. There was no question of any policy regarding innovation, evaluation, dissemination' (Gleeson, 2010, p. 101). In the absence of an official budget heading for curriculum development (Gleeson, p. 110):

> It was a case of going cap in hand looking for funding to continue work in hand. (Ó Donnabháin)

---

11 The CDU developed humanities and integrated science (ISCIP) programmes and Shannon developed social and environmental studies (SESP). The Junior Certificate subject social and environmental studies, formed out of SESP and humanities, will cease to exist under the Framework for the Junior Cycle (DES, 2015).

> The attitude was that there are these little pilot curriculum development projects and they are going to be very tightly controlled ... they are not mainstream curriculum, they will stay as pilot projects. (Harris)
>
> People were happy to see the pilot projects *as projects*. There was no mechanism for mainstreaming them apart from the Department's Curriculum Unit, which wasn't staffed. (Crooks)

Trant (1998, p. 24) recalls that 'the two centres grew up in a context of struggle, trying to survive and cope with difficulties, even with threats to their very existence'. While the Department representatives on the SCDC Steering Committee were enthusiastic, they appeared to be operating outside of the Department proper. Meanwhile the Assistant Secretary responsible for comprehensive schools appears to have been blissfully unaware of the existence of an associated Innovation Committee within the Department (Gleeson, 2010). Ó Donnabháin recalled that:

> We were seen as enthusiasts ... a rather cynical Department person told me that he saw curriculum development centres as places where you could send observers from other countries looking for examples of innovations. (Gleeson, 2010, p. 102)

These suspicions were confirmed by a former Department nominee on the SCDC Steering Committee:

> The curriculum development agencies were regarded as a nuisance ... while the Department was notionally spending 2 per cent of the total education budget on education and curriculum development, the reality was much less. Part of this strategy was to count the two curriculum agencies even though the money was largely coming from Europe rather than Ireland ...

The European Economic Community's (EEC) Transition from School to Work Projects (1978–88) (McNamara, Williams and Herron, 1990), which were quite well resourced in the context of that time, became a lifeline for the post-primary curriculum development movement, enabling both CDU and SCDC to develop teams of committed staff. However, Department Secretary, Lane, speaking at the 1983 Dissemination Conference for the first phase of these EEC Transition Projects, questioned the need for curriculum change, suggesting that students' lives after school were not the concern of the Department of Education and that the classical curriculum that had served the young Éamon de Valera well remained appropriate. It is little wonder that Browne (1985, p. 253) would sum up the post-ROSLA years as follows:

> [While] individual subject curricula have been reformed and reorganized ... overall secondary education has remained geared towards the attainment of a Leaving Certificate largely based on strictly academic assumptions, with vocational subjects enjoying less social esteem than traditional arts and sciences.

Following the austerity of the 1980s, both agencies encountered difficulties as the EEC wound down the Transition Projects:

> Year by year we had to make a case to the Department that the experiment should continue. It became a war of attrition ... In June 1987 ... the Department announced without warning that the CDU staff would be reduced to two people, and that henceforth the CDU programme would conform to the Department's wishes and be carried out according to the Department's guidelines. The Department had in fact stopped just short of closing down the CDU. (Trant, 1998, p. 31)

While the CDU continued to enjoy the support of its VEC, Shannon's influence waned significantly when the Department of Education disengaged from its Management Committee during the 1990s. In their efforts to survive, the poachers had little choice but to turn gamekeepers by providing support for Department-led initiatives through a 'proliferation of centres' model of dissemination (Schon, 1971), thus legitimating Department initiatives that were, in any event, often informed by the earlier work of the agencies themselves.

It is appropriate to note here the fate of the original curriculum prophets. The CDU continues to provide a range of valuable services that are of particular relevance to disadvantaged students and adult learners, particularly in the Education and Training Board (ETB) sector and in non-formal education settings (City of Dublin, Education and Training Board, 2016). The future of Shannon CDC became increasingly precarious in the changing environment of the 1990s and 2000s. However, given the key role of the first principal of St Patrick's Comprehensive School in the Centre's establishment, the manner of its termination in 2011 by the then school principal and the Secretary of the Board of Management was both insensitive and richly ironical. Suggesting either ignorance of the Centre's significant achievements, or contempt for its underlying beliefs and values, records and materials accumulated over forty years of curriculum development activity with hundreds of schools were summarily consigned to the rubbish bin. There is real pathos in the fact that the school website makes no reference to the existence of the Curriculum Development Centre, once a powerhouse of curriculum change in Ireland and highly respected across Europe (IFAPLAN, 1988).

Teacher and school development

The Intermediate Certificate, originally established pre-Independence in 1878, had been 'designed for a generation of teachers with inadequate training … keeping the responsibility for curricula and assessment in central control [and] discourag[ing] teacher development and initiative' (Hyland and Milne, 1992, p. 275). This was in sharp contrast with Stenhouse's (1975) notion of the teacher as researcher and extended professional, reflected in his axiom that 'there can be no educational development without teacher development' (Stenhouse, 1975, p. 83).

Provision for teacher development has been unsatisfactory in Ireland, particularly prior to the 1994 establishment of the Department's In-Career Development Unit.[12] For example, expenditure on In-Service Education was 0.05 per cent of total post-primary expenditure during 1986–8 and 0.15 per cent in 1989 (Gleeson, 1992). Irvine (1986, p. 122) concluded that, until the time when 'development activities for staff are not a luxury or an unwelcome addendum to an already overcrowded programme, INSET[13] will continue to play a marginal role'. The OECD (1991) examiners were critical of its narrow subject-based focus, while Sugrue, Morgan, Devine and Raftery (2001, p. 52) concluded that:

> Provision throughout the 1980s remained uncoordinated, consist[ing] of a very diverse range of activities involving numerous organisations, institutions and

12   Under the EU *Operational Programme for Human Resource Development.*
13   In-Service Education for Teachers.

individuals who operate independently and frequently without reference to each other [where] the overriding emphasis remains that of delivery, while issues of capacity building [and] the creation of appropriate infrastructure for sustaining on-going professional learning appear secondary ...

Granville (2005, p. 52) too notes the 'heavy leaning towards the technical adjustments of teaching' and suggests that teacher professional development is more concerned with *'teaching practice* than *mindset* change'. His worthwhile recommendation (Granville, 2005, p. 69) regarding the establishment of a national Centre 'whose brief should encompass curriculum support and innovation, school leadership and development, and continuing professional development' has not been progressed.

These problems are best understood in the context of the Teacher Registration Council (Government of Ireland, 1987)[14] regulations, which provided the framework for the University-based Higher Diploma (H. Dip.) programmes that all teachers in secondary schools were required to complete.[15] Studies in the foundations of education[16] were deemed essential, while there was also a requirement to incorporate professional studies, which *'must* include general methodology and specific methodology and should *normally* include studies in the areas of school organisation, audio-visual technology, evaluation and assessment and curriculum studies' (Department of Education, 1987, p. 8, author's italics). This attitude towards curriculum studies was in stark contrast with the situation in the UK, where, influenced by Stenhouse (1975), 'the theoretical tradition of education based on derivative disciplines began to give way to the new theorists of educational practice whose theory was based on the close observation of new curricula in action, grounded theory of school life' (McDonald, 1991, p. 6).

The theory/practice dichotomy is a recurring issue in teacher education (Cochran-Smith, 2005). While the CDU was associated with the Trinity College School of Education, Trant (1998, p. 29) believes that the work of the CDU 'was not properly understood within the academy [and that] the School

14   Drawn up in 1926 under the 1914 Intermediate Education Act.
15   But not teachers in vocational schools, who were only required to have the Ceard Teastas Gaeilge.
16   Philosophy, psychology, sociology and history of education.

of Education felt that what we were doing was not research [and] didn't deserve to be in a university at all'. This dichotomy surfaced at the Colloquium on Teacher Education (Ní Cheallaigh, Ó Dálaigh and O'Riordan, 1987) organized in conjunction with the EU Transition Projects. The colloquium concluded that 'the status quo cannot be allowed to continue' because 'the curriculum taught in schools, and reinforced through the Higher Diploma which trains students to teach a subject rather than a child, is unsuitable for many pupils in second-level schools' (Ní Cheallaigh, Ó Dálaigh and O'Riordan, 1987, pp. 2–7). A senior member of the Inspectorate recalled that 'the message for teacher educators was that the boat was leaving and they simply hadn't got their boarding passes ... the Department had a very low opinion of second level teacher education [and] the stereotypical H Dip people [were] acting as if only secondary schools existed' (Gleeson, 2010, 103ff). Rather ironically, although the Registration Council regulations were being revised around the time of the colloquium, the position regarding curriculum studies would remain unchanged until its inclusion among the Foundation Disciplines in the Teaching Council regulations of 2011.

In summary then, official attitudes towards curriculum development and reform were not conducive to an appropriate curriculum response to ROSLA for many years. While the curriculum development agencies were tolerated, they were not supported, and the main task of the teacher was to prepare students for state examinations. This inevitably resulted in a neglect of teacher and school development and an environment where curriculum debate, when it did occur, was narrow and technicist in nature (Gleeson, 2010).

Interim Curriculum and Examinations Board (CEB) and the National Council for Curriculum and Assessment (NCCA)

Against the background outlined above, there was a perceived need 'to broaden the social base of decision-making so that the process of selecting knowledge, skill or experience for inclusion on the national curriculum will address the common good' (Logan and O'Reilly, 1985, p. 475). Addressing Seanad Éireann regarding his proposal for an independent Curriculum and Examinations Board, the Minister for Education, John Boland, identified its purposes:

> Firstly, it would enable a re-evaluation of the role of schools, the courses on offer and the system of assessment. Secondly, it would allow for wider participation in the decision-making process; in particular it would allow for a greater input from teachers and other professional educators in the design of courses and assessment systems. Thirdly, it would allow for a closer look at the role of the school inspector who would have more time to spend in an advisory and supportive role, and in exercising their inspectorial role of monitoring standards. (Seanad Éireann Reports, 1981, vol. 96, col. 517)

General elections and changes of government were the order of the day in the early 1980s and the Interim CEB was eventually established by Minister Gemma Hussey in January 1984. Whereas the Department initially saw the Board as a 'talking shop' that would be run by a relatively low-grade civil servant, the minister made a clear statement of intent by appointing a Senior Inspector who was Head of the Department's Curriculum Unit as CEO and Dr Ed Walsh, then President of the National Institute for Higher Education, Limerick,[17] as Chair. The CEB immediately began to address urgent and fundamental curriculum issues, including junior cycle curriculum and the relationship between curriculum and culture. Their junior cycle discussion paper, *Issues and Structures* (CEB, 1984), which was predicated on Lawton's (1986) 'Areas of Experience' model, provided the basis for their innovative junior cycle curriculum framework, *In Our Schools* (CEB, 1986).

Political events intervened, however, and curriculum matters took a backseat yet again. When Patrick Cooney became Minister for Education in 1986, he was preoccupied with resolving the teachers' pay dispute and with the divorce and abortion referenda of the period. On returning to government in 1987, the Fianna Fáil government established the non-statutory NCCA with more restricted terms of reference. Whereas the CEB focused

---

17   Which became the University of Limerick in 1989.

on substantive curriculum issues such as breadth and balance, elements of learning and continuity between primary and post-primary schooling, the NCCA was charged, some twenty years after the ROSLA announcement, with the urgent development of a new junior cycle curriculum. Beginning with incoming first year students in September 1989, the Junior Certificate would replace the two existing junior cycle programmes, the Day Vocational Certificate (Group Cert)[18] and the Intermediate Certificate. The most significant post-primary curriculum reform since the foundation of the state was finally in train.

The NCCA, operating with the same core staff as the CEB, was immediately caught up in the development of new subject syllabi. Its representational Course Committees (Granville, 2004) worked at breakneck speed, in isolation from each other, and with little opportunity to engage with relevant research evidence. Seven subject syllabi were introduced in 1989 (Crooks, ed., 1990) with the remainder being introduced throughout the 1990s.[19] While continuity of staff facilitated the transfer of CEB thinking to the underpinning principles of the Junior Certificate, the Department did not incorporate these principles in its *Rules and Programmes* and it was left to the NCCA (1989) to promulgate them in *A Guide to the Junior Certificate.*

Granville's 2004 study of Junior Certificate Course Committee members found that 'one-third [reported that] curriculum development was their weakest or next-to-weakest contribution'[20] while they rated themselves highly on subject expertise, 'an existing format of knowledge content with its own integrity and conventions' (p. 76). He understandably concludes that 'a committee lacking in collective self-confidence in curriculum development will be unlikely to embark on major innovations' (Granville, 2004, p. 77).

18 Mainly offered in the VEC sector.
19 With the exception of mathematics, which had been revised just before the Junior Certificate was introduced. In this case, the revised Intermediate syllabus was simply renamed Junior Certificate.
20 The vast majority of Course Committee members were Teachers' Union nominees.

Based on his personal experience as NCCA Assistant Chief Executive Officer, Granville recalled that the relationship between the NCCA and the Department was fragmented and 'tense', characterized by a 'series of peaks and troughs' (Gleeson, 2010, p. 97). Whereas the NCCA was more or less 'the alternative Department of Education' during the programme development stage, that wave was replaced with the arrival of a new minister by a strategy of bringing 'the NCCA right back into the centre of the Department in an entirely seamless operation [where] the attitude was one of send over the [syllabus] documents and we'll take it from there ... Thanks very much, we really appreciate it' (Gleeson, 2010, p. 290).

A brief appraisal of the Junior Certificate

Some particularly salient aspects of the Junior Certificate are now briefly considered, including its subject-based design, assessment of student learning, provision for teacher professional development, and the streaming of students. Although the programme was informed by the CEB idea of pupil entitlements delivered through a curriculum framework, that framework was simply translated into 'course requirements', another name for traditional subject disciplines (NCCA, 1993). New wine into old wineskins! As noted by the OECD (1991, p. 68), the new Junior Certificate 'conceded a great deal to subject-centred teaching by claiming that existing subjects should be the "starting point"'. While the NCCA also aspired to introduce short courses in selected areas, with the exception of civic, social and political education, which became mandatory in 2000, that did not come to pass.

As noted by Richard Bruton TD,[21] the Department 'has insisted over the years that the only yardstick of success in education is examination results'. The CEB (1986) recommended that assessment procedures should serve rather than dictate the pedagogy of the curriculum and most Course Committees included a school-based assessment component in

21   Speaking at the Oireachtas Select Committee on Education, 7 December 1999.

the revised syllabi. A representative NCCA (1992, 9ff) Working Group[22] on Assessment subsequently recommended 'that school-based oral, aural, practical, project work and assignments should be an integral part of the final assessment process' under three conditions: school authorities would comply with DES guidelines; the assessments would be undertaken by the class teacher or by another teacher; cross-moderation of marking for purposes of objectivity and consistency.

The two post-primary teacher unions adopted different positions on the assessment of student learning for purposes of national certification. Having engaged with school-based assessment during the Humanities project (Trant, 1998), the Teachers' Union of Ireland (TUI, 1992, p. 4) called for 'the introduction of school-based assessment at Junior Certificate … and possibly at Leaving Certificate' on the grounds that the existing examination system 'puts a premium on regurgitation of facts learnt by rote, as opposed to stimulating initiative, enterprise and creative thinking'. However, the larger Association of Secondary Teachers in Ireland (ASTI, 1999, pp. 1–2) remained steadfast in its opposition to school-based assessment, arguing that '[just] because it is practised in other countries is not a sufficient argument to warrant its introduction [in] the Irish cultural tradition [which] is clientilist rather than judgmental'. Twenty years later, not a great deal has changed!

The subsequent review of the Junior Certificate (DES, 1999, p. 2), which was completely dominated by this question of assessment, reached the alarming conclusion that most students, due to the degree of dependency on terminal examinations, 'have never experienced the Junior Certificate as it was intended'. Concerns regarding the dominance of external assessment were also voiced at the National Education Convention (NEC) (Coolahan, ed., 1994, p. 74), while the Education White Paper called for 'assessment procedures [that are] comprehensive enough to … fully support the achievement of the full range of curricular objectives in the new Junior Certificate programme' (Department of Education, 1995, p. 61). Meanwhile, school principals were calling for the 'continuous assessment

---

22   This included three representatives of both ASTI and TUI and one representative
     of each of the post-primary school management bodies.

of [Junior Certificate] students by their teachers [including] more use of projects, orals, aurals and practicals' (NCCA, 1999, pp. 111–13).

Timing is a crucial factor in curriculum reform (Fullan, 1993) and when the curriculum response to ROSLA finally arrived, the 1980s recession was causing severe fiscal restraint with very high levels of unemployment and increasing birth rates (Crotty, 1986). The ministerial adviser of the day recalled (Gleeson, 2010, p. 113) that it was 'miraculous' to get IR£1million for Junior Certificate in-service at that time. This translated into one day's in-service per teacher in the form of monster meetings focused on information-giving. The NCCA found it particularly frustrating that the implementation of the programme they had developed was under the control of the Department from which they were separated by what their CEO called a 'bamboo curtain' (Gleeson, 2010, p. 290), and that resources did not allow teachers to experience active learning methodologies or have access to supplementary teaching materials.

The integration of the Intermediate and Group Certificates brought a welcome end to what the Education Minister referred to as the existing distinction between 'sheep and goats'. There was, however, a sting in the tail insofar as the new arrangements strongly encouraged the streaming of students by ability. Whereas most Intermediate Certificate subjects were offered at one common level,[23] the Junior Certificate provided for two levels in all subjects and three levels in Irish, English and mathematics. This meant that Ireland was 'unique in Europe in teaching mathematics (and English and Irish) at three levels for the junior phase of second-level education' (Lyons et al., 2003, p. 363). Furthermore, the ink was barely dry on Junior Certificate documentation when the Department announced the introduction of the Junior Certificate Schools Programme (JCSP),[24] originally and injudiciously called the Elementary Junior Certificate, for those unable to cope with the new programme.

23   Apart from Irish, English and mathematics, which had two levels each.
24   JCSP had its origins in the early school leavers' programme developed by the CDU as part of the EU Transition projects (Granville, 1982).

Senior cycle curriculum

ROSLA had the inevitable and positive impact of increasing school retention rates and O'Malley would surely have been thrilled to know that 82 per
cent of students were completing the Leaving Certificate by 1994 and that
Ireland has a completion rate of 90 per cent, one of the highest post-primary
in the EU, in 2017. Against that background, with the Junior Certificate 'in
place', the NCCA (1993) shifted its focus to senior cycle, with its four emerging strands – Leaving Certificate Established (LCE); Leaving Certificate
Vocational (LCVP); Leaving Certificate Applied (LCA), introduced in
1995 (Gleeson and Granville, 1996); and Transition Year, mainstreamed
in 1994. Given its enormous significance in the Irish psyche and its key
role in the allocation of higher education places, it was rather inevitable
that reform of the LCE would focus on syllabus review. It is regrettable,
however, that, more than twenty years after its introduction, the LCA has
not received the support and critical evaluation it deserves (Gleeson and
O'Flaherty, 2013).

NCCA becomes statutory

The NCCA became a statutory body under the terms of Section 40 of the
Education Act (Government of Ireland, 1998). Its consultative document on
senior cycle (NCCA, 2003), as an exercise in 'futures thinking', identified
certain goals for 2010, including changes to school culture, restructured
learning experiences, curriculum re-balancing and changed assessment and
certification arrangements. The focus was shifting away from topics to be
covered to learning outcomes and it was envisaged that the generic skills
of learning to learn, information processing, personal effectiveness, communication, critical thinking and working with others would be embedded
in subject disciplines. The NCCA School Network, established in 2006
to enable the inclusion of student and teacher voices in curriculum development, focused on the development of these key skills. Having worked
closely with twenty-eight volunteer teachers from this network, the NCCA
(2009, p. 6) reported that 'the five key skills are relevant to all subjects, [that]

their teaching became more learner-centred and less content-centred, [that key skills] contribute to effective learning [and that] embedding [them] requires curriculum and assessment change'.

Although Minister Hanafin acknowledged that the NCCA had come up with 'various imaginative [senior cycle] reforms', she saw them as a 'Rolls Royce option'[25] and repeated the familiar argument that the 'Leaving Cert is an independent, objective assessment that is well regarded internationally. People have great confidence in it and we should not undermine it'. LCE developments have subsequently been confined to the reform of individual subject specifications that include a coursework assessment component with a typical loading of 20 per cent.

The statutory NCCA enjoys significantly better resources than its predecessors, with the annual budget increasing from IR£230,000 (1988) to €2.9 million (2003) to €4.4 million (2006) to slightly over €5 million in 2016. This supports some forty full-time staff, including eight permanent directors and twenty-four education officers, as well as facilitating a range of consultation and deliberation strategies, including real engagement with teachers, parents and students in some fifty schools and with a wider audience on digital media. Such support remains modest, however, in comparison to sister agencies in other jurisdictions.

Increased resources have also enabled the Council to adopt a more research-informed approach, as exemplified by the longitudinal study of students' curriculum experiences over the first three years of post-primary schooling (2002–5). This study concluded that:

> ... the presence of the Junior Certificate exam influences the nature of teaching and learning, especially in third year [and that] schools can make a positive difference to student engagement and performance in a number of ways [including] a more flexible approach to ability grouping ... diverse teaching methods to actively engage students in learning ... and by promoting a positive climate with good relations between teachers and students. (Smyth, 2009, p. 5)

---

25   <https://www.irishtimes.com/newspaper/archive/2005/0118/Pg013.html#Ar01300>.

Armed with this evidence, and drawing on international best practice, the NCCA (2010) set out to re-think and re-imagine the whole junior cycle experience with its discussion paper, *Innovation and Identity*. In this paper, schools are seen as centres of innovation and change, with the freedom to be different and with the emphasis on learning rather than examinations.

The end result of this extensive consultation process, *The Framework for the Junior Cycle* (DES, 2015), represents a significant departure from the traditional focus on subject knowledge, one that is heavily influenced by current globalization trends (Biesta, 2013; Priestley and Sinnema, 2014). Consistent with the earlier senior cycle document, key skills are embedded in learning outcomes and in related statements of learning (DES, 2015, pp. 10–14) alongside assurances that 'subjects continue to play an important role as part of the new junior cycle programme' (DES, 2015, p. 17). The priority afforded to student learning is reflected in twenty-four statements of learning and the inclusion of 'a new area entitled Wellbeing' (DES, 2015, p. 22). In sharp contrast with the dependency on Course Committees when the Junior Certificate was introduced in 1989, the NCCA has worked collaboratively with teachers and students in some fifty schools during the development of the framework.[26]

Some General Reflections

The above historical backdrop provides important context for where we are. While the curriculum response to ROSLA took twenty-five years, the establishment of the Interim CEB and the NCCA has changed the Irish post-primary curriculum landscape considerably. The statutory NCCA is characterized by ongoing consultation with stakeholders and by an evidence-based approach to curriculum policy and review. Meanwhile, in a

---

26   ASTI members subsequently withdrew their co-operation as part of that union's industrial action.

fitting response to Cromien (2000), the DES is increasingly concerned with broad policy matters rather than minutiae. There is now a close working relationship between the DES and the NCCA, as evidenced in their collaboration around the Junior Cycle for Teachers (JCT) support agency.

Goodson (2001) identified three phases of curriculum change – the school-based internal phase, the external mandating phase and the 'new millennium' compromise between the internal and external phases. Irish curriculum policymaking missed out on school-based curriculum development and that situation is unlikely to change in an environment where the main function of Teachers' Centres, re-designated Education Centres, is to 'deliver' top-down reform (Lynch and McGarr, 2016). While Goodson's mandating phase has clearly characterized Irish post-primary curriculum for many years, the statutory NCCA's more consultative, evidence-based approach indicates a welcome move towards the 'new millennium' phase.

It is informative to revisit the four issues associated with the 1989 Junior Certificate –subject focus; assessment of student learning; teacher development and streaming. Whereas the 1989 programme was focused on knowledge, the Framework (DES, 2015) sets out 'to broaden students' learning and skill set [in response to] the changing nature of knowledge, the ease with which students have access to information, and the pace of change in the workplace and the world generally' (DES, 2015, p. 7). The minister, in her foreword, envisages a 'modernised curriculum [with] new ways of learning' (DES, 2015, p. 2), while the main document includes six times as many references to 'learning' as it does to 'teaching', although teaching, learning and assessment are used conjunctively in a number of places. Meanwhile, the Framework's twenty-four statements of learning have assumed the status of 'core curriculum' in place of the traditional list of subjects. This shift from knowledge to learning is indicative of the influence of 'cultural strangers' (O'Sullivan, 1992) on Irish education, with current international curriculum policy placing a heavy emphasis on the 'centrality of the learner' (Priestley and Sinnema, 2014, p. 51), what Biesta (2013, p. 29) calls:

> learnification ... a fairly recent development in which the language of education has been taken over by a language of learning [and] the emphasis ... has shifted from

questions about the content of education to questions about process, for example, the now ubiquitous idea of 'learning to learn' or ... so-called '21st skills.'

While the Framework (DES, 2015, p. 7) recognizes the importance of achieving balance between knowledge and skills, teachers who will implement that blueprint remain influenced by the contextual factors identified earlier, including a culture of knowledge reproduction for external state examinations that is indicative of classical humanist ideology.

The Framework identifies the need for 'a dual approach to assessment which will recognize and value the different types of learning and allow for a more rounded assessment of learning' (DES, p. 8) that combines classroom-based and external assessment. Notwithstanding endless hours of delicate negotiation, ASTI resistance to the involvement of their members in the assessment of their own students for purposes of national certification represents a significant impediment to the implementation of that Framework (Walshe, 2014, pp. 182ff; Travers, 2015). The sense of *déjà vu* elicited by the dominant place of classroom-based assessment in the latest junior cycle debate is as palpable as it is predictable. Resolution of this thorny dilemma demands recognition of the relationship between 'teacher professionalism' and 'curriculum control' (Helsby and McCulloch, 1986) and the development of extended forms of teacher professionalism (Hargreaves and Goodson, 1996, 14ff) that include 'opportunities and expectations to engage with ... major curriculum and assessment matters in which the [moral and social] purposes [of teaching] are embedded' (Hargreaves and Goodson, 1996, p. 20).

Teacher professional development also has a crucial role to play in achieving due balance between teaching and learning and between knowledge and skills. Irish levels of CPD provision and participation are mediocre by international standards (Shiel, Perkins and Gilleece, 2009). It is too early to gauge the impact of recent developments in that respect, while the effectiveness of initial continuing teacher education will continue to be tested by the impact of school-based socialization on student teachers' curriculum beliefs (Gleeson, O'Flaherty, Galvin and Hennessy, 2015). Finally, the invitation to stream students, a problematic feature of the 1989 programme, has been removed from the 2015 Framework, in which all subjects are to be assessed at a common level apart from English, Irish and mathematics, which will be assessed at higher and ordinary levels.

Looking ahead then, the well-documented backwash effect (Hyland, 2011) of the state examinations and the prevailing partnership approach to curriculum policymaking emerge as the most serious challenges. Irish teachers have lacked ownership of the curriculum for many years (Trant, 1998). While Minister Hussey wished to establish a broadly representative curriculum body, the teacher unions made the nomination of their own representatives a precondition of their co-operation with the CEB (Gleeson, 2010, 240ff). The constitution of the statutory NCCA is underpinned by the 1998 Education Act and curriculum policymakers must work within these parameters. Speaking, rather ironically, at the official launch of the statutory NCCA in 2003, Minister Noel Dempsey commented critically on the politics of partnership:

> ... agreement is easiest around the lowest common denominator, but harder to achieve when significant changes are proposed; consensus may make for easy implementation of change, but can it also lead to only the easy changes being proposed? In education, might it ensure that the *status quo* thrives at the expense of radical change, because radical proposals are harder to agree, because the radical is no friend of the comfortable.

On the one hand, our prevailing representational model of partnership has been very effective in terms of accountability, transparency and bringing the main partners on-side. On the other hand, Granville (2004, p. 94) expressed legitimate concerns that the NCCA:

> ... has moved from being a new and radical form of policy formulation to being an establishment body, a fixture in the educational landscape [with the result that it has] lost some of [its] cutting edge [and that] compromise and pragmatism tend to dominate [and] institutional power plays [and] conventions of practice [preclude treatment of] the broader or more fundamental issues of policy or the possibilities of alternative approaches.

One suspects that a similar fate is befalling the Teaching Council, a body that has the potential to play a strong leadership role in defining and mediating the relationship between meaningful curriculum reform and teacher professionalism.

Insofar as the progressive, student-centred nature of the *Framework for Junior Cycle* represents a significant advance from its 1989 precedent, it appears that some of Granville's (2004) concerns regarding curriculum design have been circumvented. However, the implementation of the blueprint document is invariably the real test. How will the quest for balance between knowledge and skills play out? Will the assessment tail continue to wag the curriculum dog? Will future junior cycle students actually experience the latest curriculum Framework any more than students had the intended experience of the 1989 Junior Certificate? Notwithstanding the increasing emphasis on research and evidence-based practice, the absence of a tradition of rigorous *independent* evaluation of curriculum policy and implementation remains a matter of concern.

Bibliography

ASTI (1999). *Policy on the Junior Certificate Examination.* Unpublished policy paper (Dublin: Association of Secondary Teachers of Ireland).

Barber, N. (1989). *Comprehensive Schooling in Ireland*, Paper 25 (Dublin: ESRI).

Biesta, G. J. J. (2013). *Responsive or Responsible? Education for the Global Networked* (Boulder, CO: Paradigm Publishers).

Browne, T. (1985). *Ireland: A Social and Cultural History 1922–85* (London: Fontana).

Callan, J. (1995). 'Equality of Learning in Quality Schooling: A Challenge for Curriculum Implementation', in J. Coolahan (ed.), *Issues and Strategies in the Implementation of Educational Policy* (Maynooth University: Education Department), pp. 92–117.

Central Advisory Council for England (1967). *Children and their Primary Schools* (England: DES).

City of Dublin, Education and Training Board (2016). *Curriculum Development Unit: Projects, Programmes and Services* (Dublin: Curriculum Development Unit).

Coolahan, J. (1981). *Irish Education: History and Structure* (Dublin: Institute of Public Administration).

Coolahan, J. (ed.) (1994). *Report on the National Education Convention* (Dublin: Convention Secretariat).

Coolahan, J. (1995). *Secondary Education in Ireland* (Strasbourg: Council of Europe).

Cornbleth, C. (1990). *Curriculum in Context* (London: Falmer).

Cromien, S. (2000). *Review of Department's Operations, Systems and Staffing Needs* (Dublin: DES).

Crooks, T. (ed.) (1990). *The Changing Curriculum, Perspectives on the Junior Certificate* (Dublin: O'Brien Educational).

Crotty, R. (1986). *Ireland in Crisis: A Study in Capitalist Colonial Underdevelopment* (Tralee: Brandon Books).

Department of Education (1971). *Primary School Curriculum: Teacher's Handbook, Part 1* (Dublin: Stationery Office).

Department of Education (1987). *Registration Council Regulations* (Dublin: Stationery Office).

Department of Education (1995). *Charting Our Education Future, White Paper on Education* (Dublin: Stationery Office).

Department of Education and Science (1999). *The Junior Certificate: Issues for Discussion* (Dublin: Department of Education and Science).

Department of Education and Science (2015). *Framework for Junior Cycle* (Dublin: DES).

Fullan, M. (1993). *Change Forces, Probing the Depths of Educational Reform* (London: Falmer).

Gleeson, J. (1992). *Gender Equality in Education in the Republic of Ireland* (Dublin: Stationery Office).

Gleeson, J. (2010). *Curriculum in Context: Partnership, Power and Praxis in Ireland* (Bern: Peter Lang).

Gleeson, J., and Granville, G. (1996). 'The Case of the Leaving Certificate Applied', *Irish Educational Studies*, 15, pp. 113–32.

Gleeson, J., and O'Flaherty, J. (2013). 'School-based initial vocational education in the Republic of Ireland: the parity of esteem and fitness for purpose of the Leaving Certificate Applied', *Journal of Vocational Education & Training*, 65:4, pp. 461–73, DOI: 10.1080/13636820.2013.838288.

Gleeson, J., O'Flaherty, J., Galvin, T., and Hennessy, J. (2015). 'Student teachers, socialisation, school placement and schizophrenia: the case of curriculum change', *Teachers and Teaching*, 21:4, pp. 437–58, DOI: 10.1080/13540602.2014.968895.

Goodson, I. (2001). Social Histories of Educational Change, *Journal of Educational Change* 2:1, pp. 45–63.

Government of Ireland (1965). *Investment in Education: Report of the Survey Team Appointed by the Minister of Education in October 1962* (Dublin: Stationery Office).

Government of Ireland (1987). *Registration Council Regulations* (Dublin: Stationery Office).

Government of Ireland (1998). *Education Act* (Dublin: Stationery Office).

Granville, G. (2004). 'Politics and Partnership in Curriculum Planning in Ireland', in C. Sugrue (ed.), *Curriculum and Ideology* (Dublin: Liffey Press), pp. 67–100.

Granville, G. (2005). *An Emergent Approach to Teacher Professional Development. Final Evaluation Report on the Experience and Impact of the Second Level Support Service* (Dublin: DES, Teacher Education Section).

Hargreaves, A., and Goodson, I. (1996). 'Teachers' Professional Lives: Aspirations and Actualities', in I. Goodson and A. Hargreaves (eds), *Teachers' Professional Lives* (London: Falmer), pp. 1–27.

Harris, J. (1989). 'The policy-making role of the Department of Education', in D. G. Mulcahy and D. O' Sullivan (eds), *Irish Educational Policy* (Dublin: Institute of Public Administration), pp. 7–26.

Helsby, G., and McCulloch, G. (1996). 'Teacher Professionalism and Curriculum Control', in I. Goodson and A. Hargreaves (eds), *Teachers' Professional Lives* (London: Falmer), pp. 86–100.

Husén, T. (1979). *The School in Question: A Comparative Study of the School and its Future in Western Societies* (London and New York: Oxford University Press).

Hussey, G. (1990). *At the Cutting Edge* (Dublin: Gill & Macmillan).

Hyland, Á. (1988). 'The Junior Cycle Curriculum: For all or some?', *Compass*, 17:2, pp. 31–46.

Hyland, Á. (2011). *Entry to Higher Education in Ireland in the 21st Century*. Discussion paper, NCCA/HEA Seminar, 21 September, University College Dublin.

Hyland, Á., and Milne, K. (eds) (1992). *Irish Educational Documents* II (Dublin: Church of Ireland College of Education).

IFAPLAN (1988). *Transition Education for the '90s: The Experience of the European Community Action Programme* (IFAPLAN: Brussels).

Interim CEB (1984). *Issues and Structures* (Dublin: Curriculum and Examinations Board).

Interim CEB (1986). *In Our Schools: A Framework for Curriculum and Assessment* (Dublin: Curriculum and Examinations Board).

Irvine, D. G. (1986). 'Initial and In-Service Training for Tutors of Adults: Some Implications for the Status of Adult Education', *Irish Educational Studies*, 9:1, pp. 88–102, DOI: 10.1080/0332331900090111.

Jeffers, G. (2011). 'The Transition Year Programme in Ireland: Embracing and Resisting a Curriculum Innovation', *Curriculum Journal*, 22:1, pp. 61–76.

Lawton, D. (1986). *School Curriculum Planning* (London: Hodder and Stoughton).

Lee, J. J. (1982). 'Society and Culture', in F. Litton (ed.), *Unequal Achievement: The Irish Experience 1957–82* (Dublin: Institute of Public Administration), pp. 1–18.

Lee, J. J. (1989). *Ireland 1912–85: Politics and Society* (Cambridge: Cambridge University Press).

Logan, J., and O'Reilly, B. (1985). 'Educational Decision-Making: the case of the Curriculum and Examinations Board', *Administration*, 33:4, pp. 472–80.

Lynch, P. (1979). 'Whither Science Policy?', *Administration*, 27:3, pp. 18–27.

Lynch, R., and McGarr, O. (2016). 'Negotiating Subject Hierarchies: Neo-Liberal Influences on the Comprehensive Curriculum in Ireland', *Educational Policy*, 30:5, pp. 721–39.

Lyons, M., Lynch, K., Close, S., Sheerin, E., and Boland, P. (2003). *Inside Classrooms: The Teaching and Learning of Mathematics in Social Context* (Dublin: Institute of Public Administration).

Mac Cárthaigh, S. (1983). *The Compulsory Secondary School: Adolescence and the Curriculum*. Unpublished paper prepared for the Department of Education.

McDonald, B. (1991). 'Introduction', in J. Rudduck, *Innovation and Change* (London: Falmer).

McNamara, G., Williams, K., and Herron, D. (1990). *Achievement and Aspiration: Curricular Initiatives in Irish Post-Primary Education in the 1980s* (Dublin: Drumcondra Teachers' Centre).

Mulcahy, D. G. (1981). *Curriculum and Policy in Irish Post-Primary Education* (Dublin: Institute of Public Administration).

NCCA (National Council for Curriculum and Assessment) (1989). *A Guide to the Junior Certificate* (Dublin: NCCA).

NCCA (1992). *Report of the Working Party on Assessment for the Junior Certificate*. Unpublished report (Dublin: NCCA).

NCCA (1993). *A Programme for Reform, Curriculum and Assessment Policy Towards the New Century* (Dublin: NCCA).

NCCA (1999). *The Junior Cycle Review: Progress Report: Issues and Options for Development* (Dublin: NCCA).

NCCA (2003). *Developing Senior Cycle Education: directions for development* (Dublin: NCCA).

NCCA (2009). *Key Skills Initiative: Report on Phase Two* (Dublin: NCCA).

NCCA (2010). *Innovation and Identity* (Dublin: NCCA).

Ní Cheallaigh, L., Ó Dálaigh, C., and O'Riordan, M. (1987). *Teacher Education – the Challenge of Change. Implications of the E.C. Transition Projects (1983–7) for*

Post-Primary Teacher Education (Department of Education/City of Galway VEC).

Norris, N. (2007). 'Raising the school leaving age', *Cambridge Journal of Education*, 37:4, pp. 471–2, DOI: 10.1080/03057640701733833.

Ó Buachalla, S. (1988). *Education Policy in Twentieth-Century Ireland* (Dublin: Wolfhound Press).

Ó Donnabháin, D. (1998). 'The Work-Related Curriculum', in A. Trant and D. Ó Donnabháin (eds), *The Future of the Curriculum* (Dublin: Curriculum Development Unit), pp. 39–56.

Organisation for Economic Co-operation and Development [OECD] (1991). *Reviews of National Policies for Education: Ireland* (Paris: OECD).

O'Sullivan, D. (1989). 'Ideational Base of Policy', in D. G. Mulcahy and D. O'Sullivan (eds), *Irish Educational Policy* (Dublin: Institute of Public Administration), pp. 219–74.

O'Sullivan, D. (1992). 'Cultural Strangers and educational change: The OECD Report Investment in Education and Irish Educational Policy', *Journal of Education Policy*, 7:5, pp. 445–69.

Priestley, M., and Sinnema, C. (2014). 'Downgraded curriculum? An analysis of knowledge in new curricula in Scotland and New Zealand', *The Curriculum Journal*, 25:1, pp. 50–75.

Ryan, L. (1988). *The Preservation of a Comprehensive Curriculum in an Age of Retrenchment.* Unpublished paper read at Annual Conference of Association of Community and Comprehensive Schools, Ennis.

Schon, D. A. (1971). *Beyond the Stable State* (London: Temple-Smith).

Shiel, G., Perkins, R., and Gilleece, L. (2009). *OECD Teaching and Learning International Study (TALIS). Summary Report for Ireland* (Dublin: Educational Research Centre).

Smyth, E. (2009). 'Junior Cycle Education: Insights from a longitudinal study of students', *ESRI Research Bulletin*, 4:1.

Stenhouse, L. (1971). 'The Humanities Curriculum Project: The Rationale', *Theory into Practice*, 10:3, pp. 154–62, DOI: 10.1080/00405847109542322.

Stenhouse, L. (1975). *An Introduction to Curriculum Research and Development* (London: Heinemann).

Sugrue, C., Morgan, M., Devine, D., and Raftery, D. (2001). *Policy and Practice of Professional Development for Primary and Post-Primary Teachers in Ireland: A Critical Analysis.* Unpublished report commissioned by the DES.

Teachers Union of Ireland (1992). *Response to Education Green Paper* (Dublin: TUI).

Teaching Council (2011). *Initial Teacher Education: Criteria and Guidelines for Programme Providers* (Maynooth: Teaching Council).

Trant, A. (1998). 'Giving the Curriculum Back to Teachers', in A. Trant and D. Ó Donnabháin (eds), *The Future of the Curriculum* (Dublin: Curriculum Development Unit), pp. 23–38.

Travers, P. (2015). *Junior Cycle Reform: A Way Forward* (Dublin: Department of Education and Skills).

Walsh, J. (2008). *Patrick Hillery. The Official Biography* (Dublin: New Island).

Walsh, T. (2012). *Primary Education in Ireland, 1897–1990, Curriculum and Context* (Bern: Peter Lang).

Walshe, J. (2014). *An Education – How an outsider became in insider – and learned what really goes on in Irish government* (Dublin: Penguin Ireland).

Watts, J. (1977). *The Countesthorpe Experience* (London: Unwin).

10 Changing the Educational Landscape: Transforming Teacher Professionalism?

Introduction

Radical reforms by their very nature ruffle feathers, particularly those soft, velvety, downy, comforting ones closest to the bosom of the *status quo*, the 'establishment' (Jones, 2015). Perhaps therefore, O'Connor's observations regarding Donogh O'Malley, Minister for Education for a mere two years (1966–8), provide some insight into the persona of this post-Independence politician who went against the advice of more cautious minds and temperaments, including O'Connor himself: 'He had a reputation as a "hell raiser", as being impetuous, and as having concern and sympathy for the underdog' (O'Connor, 1986, p. 139). The only straw in the wind as to what O'Malley might be like as minister was derived from a Dáil contribution some years earlier, when he expressed 'his support for free universal education' while otherwise senior civil servants 'had no idea where his interests lay' at the time of his appointment (O'Connor, 1986, p. 139).

Apart from a general cultural tendency towards retaining a 'soft spot' for the 'lovable rogue' as an endearing characteristic, O'Malley's major political 'stroke' or educational 'vision', depending on your point of view, has enabled him subsequently to be fast-tracked for secular sainthood. In the process, it is frequently forgotten just how pervasive opposition was to this 'brave new world' of 'free' education. To understand just how 'far out' O'Malley's decision was, it is necessary to position it within Hallin's spheres (Hallin, 1992). These may be imagined as three concentric circles with the circle at the centre being the 'sphere of consensus', the middle circle the 'sphere of legitimate controversy' and the outer circle understood as the 'sphere of deviance'. In a similar vein, and more recently, this phenomenon has been labelled the 'Overton Window', which deals with public opinion generally, and posits a sliding scale of public opinion on any given issue, ranging from conventional wisdom to unacceptable. By such established yardsticks, O'Malley's political decision was deviant and thus unacceptable to many. The internal consensus in the Department of Education at the time, carefully nurtured in preceding years by O'Malley's two predecessors – Hillery (1961–5) and Colley (1965–6) – along with senior civil servants, there was a general expectation that 'he [O'Malley] would adhere to the scheduled raising of the school-leaving age to 15 years by 1970, with, concurrently, a measure of free universal education at least for the term of compulsory schooling' (O'Connor, 1986, p. 139). Cautious incremental change was what the *status quo* had in its purview through its Olympian Overton window. As O'Connor himself recorded, 'I was dismayed at Mr O'Malley's insistence on bringing in free education from September 1967' (p. 152), while, with the benefit of hindsight, he acknowledged: 'I now believe that events proved ... O'Malley to be right', indicating that 'had free education been delayed until 1970 ... the scheme would have been applied only to students under 15 ... and that there would be no provision for students following the Leaving Certificate course' (pp. 152–3). This deviant endeavour therefore succeeded not because the establishment supported it enthusiastically, but because it was popular among 'those parents who hitherto would have not dreamed of sending their children to a secondary school' (p. 153). And, some contemporary members of the commentariat would have us believe that 'populism' is an entirely new politics! Nevertheless, it is important to recognize that some possible shifts in policy may be deviant and thus well beyond the consensus carefully crafted by the establishment. The aperture of the Overton window or the diameter of Hallin's spheres are not fixed entities and in this regard the wider context and 'timing' and 'generational turnover' (Schmidt, 2008) are of considerable import. Thus, O'Malley's decision fits comfortably within, and serves as a particularly good example of, populist politics defined as an ideology that 'pits a virtuous and homogeneous people against a set of elites and dangerous "others" who are together depicted as depriving (or attempting to deprive) the sovereign people of their rights, values, prosperity, identity, and voice' (Albertazzi and McDonnell, 2008, p. 3).

Investment in Education (1965) had been published, advocating major reform, while the 1960s more generally was a period of fresh ferment internationally. Similar, if somewhat jingoistic, sentiments surfaced due to the celebrations of the fiftieth anniversary of the 1916 rebellion and these too served as potent reminders of the revolutionary generation's commitment to 'cherish all the children of the nation equally', sentiments of some significance for O'Malley (O'Connor, 1986). From a policy and research perspective, these circumstances reinforce the view that context matters.

While it may be suggested that the birth pangs of 'free' education were considerable and did not 'come dropping slow' but overnight became a 'game changer', it is the legacies they have created for the educational system and for the much-expanded membership of the profession that are the primary focus and concern here. This chapter documents major changes in the topography of the post-primary education system over time and subsequently identifies the professional legacy issues that have emerged as significant shaping influences and challenges for the current and next generation of policymakers and practitioners, who are destined and privileged to have temporary custody of those onerous responsibilities. As a means of benchmarking the advent of this new era, and of marking the 'realities' of the system prior to O'Malley's political intervention, I quote at some length from O'Connor:

> In the school-year 1965/1966 ... At post primary level, there were 585 secondary schools with a student enrolment of 98,667 and a teacher complement of 6,795 of whom 1,897 were part-time teachers. There were 342 active schools in the vocational education system and these had 35,232 students in whole-time continuation courses, 2,288 students in whole-time technical courses and 8225 students in apprenticeships/ part-time courses.... In June 1966, the Intermediate Certificate Examinations were taken by 20,756 students (9,467 boys and 11,289 girls) ... The Leaving Certificate Examination was taken by 12,573 students ... and 11,309 passed. (O'Connor, 1986, p. 136)

In 2017, approximately 58,000 (*The Irish Times*, 16 August 2017) sat the Leaving Certificate Examination (LCE), almost a fivefold increase, while 61,654 sat the Junior Certificate (JCE) (*The Irish Times*, 13 September 2017), three times the number reported above. Even this cursory acquaintance with the educational landscape indicates that the reality painted above has 'changed utterly'. The following sections indicate major shifts in the post-primary landscape, from the introduction of 'free' second-level education to the present day.

The Socio-cultural Geography of 'Secondary' Schooling: Pre-'Free' Education

While a number of earlier chapters in this volume seek to explain and con-textualize the political decision made in 1967 to introduce 'free' education, it is important to situate the making of this decision in the context of wider socio-cultural forces. It is necessary to pay attention to population trends and the politics of 'location' and 'dislocation' that conspired to exacerbate the newly minted Republic's largely failed economic status; something of a 'labour camp' for post-war Britain or further afield, Boston, Chicago and Melbourne, to name but a few locations where there were family ties from earlier waves of emigration during the major crises of nineteenth-century Ireland. Such historical contextualization of population trends enables Mac Laughlin (1997, p. 137) to claim with considerable authority that 'with the exception of a brief downturn in emigration in the late 1960s and early 1970s, the country has continued to function as an emigrant nursery for entire sections of Irish society ever since'. I distinctly recall a contempo-rary in St Patrick's College, Drumcondra, in the early 1970s describing his primary-teaching father's conflict with successive school inspectors who decried the fact that he was not spending sufficient time teaching Irish in a Gaeltacht school to a pupil population, the majority of whom were des-tined for England or the US, when he was seeking to prepare them more adequately than the system then allowed for the realities of life 'abroad'. The conservatism of senior education policymakers and politicians is more easily understood against the assertion that 'while the process of decolonisation created in Ireland the semblance of political independence, the country still retained the status of peripheral state and was still highly dependent upon Britain for the export of agricultural produce and surplus labour' (Mac Laughlin, 1997, p. 137). The most recent census figures signal this wider perspective in which continuity and change in the education system benefits from being located within the wider sociohistorical context.

Table 10.1: Population, 1956–2016 (Table 1, CSO, 2016, p. 8)

Year	Population	Change	%
1956	2,898,264	−62,329	−2.1
1961	2,818,341	−79,923	−2.8
1966	2,884,002	65,661	2.3
1971	2,978,248	94,246	3.3
1979	3,368,217	89,969	13.1
1981	3,443,405	75,188	2.2
1986	3,540,643	97,238	2.8
1991	3,525,719	−14,924	−0.4
1996	3,626,087	100,368	2.8
2002	3,917,203	291,116	8.0
2006	4,239,848	322,645	8.2
2011	4,588,252	348,404	8.2
2016	4,761,865	173,613	3.8

The mid-1960s witnessed an increase in population for the first time in more than a decade, but this was arguably not sufficient to encourage educational policymakers to adopt a more radical, rather than a gradualist, incremental, approach to reform. More significantly, perhaps, population growth was the consequence of the reversal of the country's economic fortunes due to the First Programme for Economic Expansion (1958–63), the architect of which was T. K. Whitaker (1916–2017), placing a serious dent in the 'hegemonic status of the substantial rural bourgeoisie' (Mac Laughlin, 1997, p. 138) from which a considerable portion of the teachers in secondary schools, both lay and religious, were drawn. The landless rural labourer and his family, as well as the urban working class, were collateral damage to post-colonial policies pursued after Independence, patterns that had already been taking root in the nineteenth century. For these reasons, Miller concludes:

> ... emigration became a societal imperative of post-famine Ireland: in reality less a choice than a vital necessity both to secure the livelihoods of nearly all who left and most who stayed and to ensure the relative stability of a fundamentally 'sick' society which offered its lower classes and most of its young people 'equal opportunities' only for aimless poverty at home or menial labour and slum tenements abroad. (Miller, 1988, p. 362)

Of the 585 secondary schools mentioned above that were in existence in the mid-1960s, the vast majority were religious owned and run, with a small minority being entirely lay. The following figures regarding the employment of lay male and female teachers indicate clearly the hegemony of Church influence on the educational landscape at this time.

Diocesan Colleges	Christian Brothers	Protestant & Lay Schools	Other Religious Orders
12%	35%	16%	37%

Figure 10.1: Employers of Male Teachers, 1964. (Data from Cunningham, 2009, p. 112)

Mercy Sisters	Presentation Sisters	Protestant & Lay Schools	Thirty-Four Other Religious Orders
27%	11%	12%	50%

Figure 10.2: Employers of Female Teachers, 1964. (Data from Cunningham, 2009, p. 113)

Two issues of significance for the teaching profession are worth noting. Due to the fact that principalship was invariably in the hands of religious, and what we have subsequently come to know as 'posts of responsibility' were entirely 'abrogated by priests, nuns and brothers' (Cunningham, 2009, p, 112). Garret FitzGerald (later Taoiseach) wrote in 1966 'that the "downgrading of status" of the lay teacher, as well as the "absence of opportunities for promotion" has been very detrimental for Irish secondary education' (p. 112). As a secondary school teacher acquaintance remarked to me more than two decades ago, 'life was very simple when all the decisions were made in the convent, priest's house or monastery, and we knew our place was to serve and not to question'. A family member who worked in a religious school at this time frequently indicated a distinct lack of trust in lay teachers by the religious, with relationships being characterized, in many instances, by a mutual suspicion. At an earlier period in the 1940s and 1950s, the precariousness of the lay teacher was more evident when contracts were terminated in May (at the end of the school year) and were only renewed if a religious could not be found to take the place of the *spailpín* lay teacher. Such hegemonic control extended also to subject offerings whereby the curriculum 'was arranged to suit the minority of students who intended to proceed to Holy Orders' (Cunningham, 2009, p. 113). This controlling mind-set was captured comprehensively by Gleeson (2010) in an extended interview with Bishop McKiernan, who was the hierarchy's spokesperson on the Catholic Commission on Education (1974–91). He indicated:

> The Bishops were happy with the curriculum as it was ... it would be more correct to say that they weren't unhappy with what was there, to be taught within the atmosphere of Catholic schools ... we're a bit like the police, we come in after the deed has been done! (Gleeson, 2010, p. 255)

Control was paramount, intervention necessary only if some curricular 'crime' had been committed! From this and other evidence, Gleeson concluded: 'The managerial bodies weren't reformist, they were allowing the Department to set the agenda ...' (Gleeson, 2010, p. 255). Between Church control at school level, and Department of Education diktat at central level, the struggle for agency among secondary teachers in particular was a Sisyphean task. Arguably, the advent of 'free' education was a seminal moment for the secondary sector to grow, not only numerically, but to enhance potential leverage within the system, and to enhance the professional status and professionalism of teachers.

The glimpses into this educational landscape being sketched here are *terra incognita* to more recent generations of teachers, students and public alike, but these were the conditions that prevailed at the time of O'Malley's momentous decision. How has the system evolved subsequently, with particular focus on control, curricular reform and enhancing professionalism?

Schools, Teachers, Subject Provision: Patterns over Time

Another feature of the educational system at the time of the reform was a major apartheid between the secondary and vocational sectors, a segregation that was enshrined in the Vocational Education Act (1930), significantly influenced by the hierarchy of the day, to prevent vocational schools from competing directly with Church-controlled secondary schooling. In the data provided by O'Connor indicated above, in the mid-1960s there were 583 secondary schools and 343 vocational schools. Today the educational landscape is populated by the number and types of schools displayed in Table 10.2.

Table 10.2: Post-Primary School Types (Data extrapolated from Statistical Report 2015–16, Table 3.1)

Secondary	Vocational	Community	Comprehensive	Total
375	265	81	14	735

Particularly striking is the fact that in 1966 there was a total of 926 secondary and vocational schools, while that figure today stands at 735; 143 post-primary schools less for a vastly increased school population. Schools, therefore, are considerably larger than in previous decades, with important consequences for subject choice, as well as leadership, management structures, governance, etc.

A further remarkable feature of this transformation is that when traditional secondary and 'other' school provision in the sector is compared, the dominance enjoyed by religious run and owned schools has now all but evaporated: 375 'secondary' schools (religious owned, state-funded) as opposed to all other types totalling 360. As the decades have progressed, and amalgamations have been achieved in many towns between the vocational, convent and brothers' schools, or some variation thereof, it became necessary to coin the term 'post-primary' to put all such school provision on a par, perhaps an important symbolic gesture in terms of equality, but it simultaneously tends to hide class divisions and deep-rooted social prejudices. The merging and renaming of schools, as well as the provision of new entities such as multi-denominational schools, has transformed the educational landscape such that all schools provide students with access to the same state examinations, a parity of esteem denied to vocational schools by the 1930 Act, and only rectified with an amendment in 1970, in the wake of O'Malley's dramatic policy shift.

Allied to this transformation is the decline of religious as a presence in schools, to the extent that it is almost possible to assert that there are no religious principals, and a negligible presence of religious on school staffs. The lack of consistency in the manner in which annual statistics are reported by the DES makes change over time difficult to record. Nevertheless, a definitive pattern is evident. As a baseline, Table 10.3 is indicative of the dominance of religious in post-primary education at the time of O'Malley's decision, and against which subsequent decline may be measured.

Table 10.3: Religious as a Percentage of All Teachers, 1966–72 (Quoted in Fuller, 2004, p. 169. She indicates that the source of these figures is *Report on the Future Involvement of Religious in Education by a Working Party of the Education Commission of the Hierarchy and the Major Religious Superiors*, Dublin, 1973)

Year	Percentage (%)
1966	50
1968	45
1970	38
1972	34

This decline, already evident in terms of vocations in the early 1970s, accelerated as the decade of the 1980s advanced, evincing the following observation: 'Essentially what religious had to face up to was that their very *raison d'être* in education was being called into question and threatened in a changing socio-cultural context' (Fuller, 2004, p. 173). As part of this general trend, she remarks: 'The first appointment to the position of lay principalship of a religious secondary school was made on 9 November 1970' while 'the appointment of lay principals did not gather momentum until the late 1980s' (pp. 175–6). Nevertheless, apart from a post-Vatican II soul-searching within Catholic religious communities in general, those directly involved in education were asking 'more fundamental questions about their involvement in education – questions that went beyond the issue of control and maintenance of the status quo' (Fuller, 2004, p. 175–6).

While such trends were being established within the field of education, there continued to be a strong religious presence in classrooms and staffrooms. In the annual statistics for 1976–7, incremental salary was paid to 2,337 religious, while similar remuneration was paid to 7,839 lay teachers (Statistical Report 1976–7, Table 4a, p. 62). Nevertheless, there was an increasing awareness among the former that 'religious orders would no longer enjoy the same autonomy in the running of their schools, because teacher unions were becoming a force for change which it is significantly beyond the power of the secondary schools to shape' (Fuller, 2004, p. 175). Such sentiments certainly resonate with O'Connor's views, expressed in *Studies* in 1968, that 'no one wants to push the religious out of education ... but I want them in it as partners, not always as masters' (O'Connor, 1968). Undoubtedly, as the number of lay teachers increased, exclusion from the most senior leadership positions in schools was neither tenable nor attainable. These tell-tale patterns are very evident in the following: the number of religious teachers on probation in 1976–7 was 117, while the equivalent lay figure was 767. In the same annual statistics, the presence of fourteen comprehensive and twenty community schools was recorded (Table 1a, p. 66), while Table 10.4 indicates the number of lay and religious teachers in both.

Table 10.4: Total Number of Wholetime Teachers (Lay and Religious)

	Comprehensive	Community
Wholetime/Men		
Religious	17	20
Lay	239	311
Wholetime/Women		
Religious	8	36
Lay	194	240

Statistics for the vocational sector in that year do not discriminate on grounds of gender or religion. Twenty years later, while still registering a presence in schools, the proportion of lay teachers has dramatically increased.

Table 10.5: Number of Full-Time Religious and Lay Teachers in Secondary, Community and Comprehensive Schools (Table 3.14, p. 46 Statistical Report 1996–7)

School Type	Religious	Lay	Total
Secondary	663	12,031	12,649
Community	106	2,414	2,520
Comprehensive	15	512	527
Total	*784*	*14,957*	*15,741*

When I began my secondary schooling in the mid-1960s, apart from three lay teachers, the entire teaching staff (of more than twenty) was comprised of diocesan priests. What can be said with certainty is that the religious presence two decades ago, indicated above, has declined precipitously in the intervening years. Just how precipitous this decline has been may be gleaned from the figures immediately in Table 10.6.

Table 10.6: Number of Vocations, 1965–70 (Data from Fuller, 2004, p. 168, Table 12.1)

	1965	1966	1967	1968	1969	1970
Diocesan Clergy	282	254	291	219	221	164
Religious Orders	377	390	343	325	258	261
Brothers	179	173	166	119	79	98
Sisters	537	592	509	418	283	227
Totals	*1,375*	*1,409*	*1,309*	*1,081*	*841*	*750*

In sharp contrast to the religious presence in and ownership of schools at the introduction of 'free' education, reflected in the numbers above, in 2017 a total of six entered St Patrick's College, Maynooth, as potential diocesan clergy, 'believed to be the lowest number since its foundation in 1795' (McGarry, 2017, p. 5). Not surprisingly, therefore, as reported recently by Byrne and Devine (2017), there is also a marked decline in the attention to religious formation of students in the post-primary sector generally, even in private secondary schools. As evidence of what might be regarded as a gradual dilution of a Catholic ethos in schools, they identify faith-visible, faith-residual and faith-transition schools, as a form of categorization regarding the extent to which Catholic 'formation' is taken seriously, receives some residual attention, or is largely ignored or downplayed. Similarly, in an Australian context, though in a more advanced manner, Gleeson and O'Neill (2017) have made similar observations. There, Catholic school communities are composed of an ageing cohort of teachers who practise their faith and regard themselves as knowledgeable about it, a younger cohort who are nominally Catholic with little confidence in their 'theological literacy', but who have learned from older colleagues and religious, and those teachers who are non-Catholic and largely deficient in theological literacy and thus more limited in their capacity to exploit 'teachable moments' to imbue such opportunities with values rooted in theological tenets and social teachings of the Catholic Church. What is not recorded in annual statistics throughout this period is the number of ex-religious who were established in teaching and in several instances became principals and deputies as part of the first generation of lay leadership in post-primary schools, old and new. Nevertheless, there is considerable anecdotal evidence that as vocations declined, former religious were often appointed to the most senior leadership positions as a kind of ordered retreat in the face of declining vocations, re-evaluation of the role of religious and their contributions to society, as well as the rise of secularism and lay leadership in post-primary schooling. This is yet another under-researched area in Irish education and with significant consequences for school leadership.

Such creeping secularization, in a more globalized world characterized by competitiveness and individualism, and a more educated and demanding set of parents, who want their offspring to earn as many points as possible in the high-stakes testing that is the Leaving Certificate, and in the absence of commitment to more holistic formation, a 'grind' school culture can rather rapidly come to characterize school ethos, even if it is held at bay, barely below the surface, by ritual performance and symbolic actions on ethos; the 'characteristic spirit' of the school may not be conducive to inclusion, respect for diversity and the cultivation of a life-affirming learning environment in which to grow – psychologically, socially, culturally and individually – in a holistic, tolerant and open community. These new and emerging reference points on the educational landscape pose considerable challenges to the lay leadership in the teaching profession, for, as Maher (2017, p. 12) recently remarked, 'a post-Catholic society is one in which Catholicism still retains an influence in the people's personal lives and in the public sphere'.

Changing Patterns of Curricular Provision

Another feature worth noting, before turning our attention to issues of professional import to the teaching profession in a more focused manner, is the changing nature of subject provision, some of which continues to be reflective of greater apartheid in the system in previous decades. For example, while Latin and Greek were always a minority provision, more prevalent in all-male schools, Latin continues to be a notable absence in all vocational schools, as well as a large proportion of community and comprehensive schools. Table 10.7 captures in dramatic fashion just how precipitous the demise of Latin has been, thus contributing to a significant change in the educational landscape.

Table 10.7: Percentage of Leaving Certificate Students Taking Latin, 1955–89 (Fuller, 2004, p. 172; source: Department of Education Statistical Reports, 1995, 1965, 1969, 1979, 1989)

Year	Total Examined	Number Taking Latin	% of Total
1955	6,098	4,091	67
1965	11,651	6,537	56
1969	16,986	7,461	44
1979	35,510	1,769	5
1989	58,435	609	1

Similarly, in so far as it is possible to establish patterns over time, considerably more males than females continue to take physics and chemistry in the Leaving Certificate, with this gender gap being more pronounced in vocational, community and comprehensive schools, suggesting perhaps that social class, school location and traditions have a significant shaping influence on life chances in terms of subject choice and access to particular careers. Likewise, access to practical subjects – engineering, construction studies – are much more likely to be provided in vocational, community and comprehensive schools than traditional secondary schools. From a period when little or no provision was made for 'business' subjects, perhaps economics only, there has been a general proliferation of provision in this regard – accounting, business organization, economics, economic history – in all school types, indicative most likely of an entrepreneurial culture. Nevertheless, it is disappointing to note that the numbers of students who take art and music continue to be particularly low, despite 'STEAM' rhetoric and its hailed significance in more recent years as part of economic recovery, the promotion of creativity and imagination. More contentious still, in a policy context of 'inclusion', is provision for learners with additional or particular learning needs and the extent to which such educational responsibilities are distributed proportionately across the spectrum of school provision. Significant in this regard has been the provision of the Leaving Certificate Vocational Programme (LCVP) and the Leaving Certificate Applied (LCA) programme, which represent attempts to cater for a more diverse student population.[1] However, provision of these programmes has been extremely uneven, and allegedly avoided in many schools for fear of 'stigma', rather akin to earning a reputation for making

---

1   The Department of Education and Skills website provides the following brief descriptions of both programmes: 'The Leaving Certificate Vocational Programme (LCVP) is similar to the traditional Leaving Certificate Programme, with a concentration on technical subjects and some additional modules which have a vocational focus', while 'The Leaving Certificate Applied (LCA) Programme is a self-contained two-year course, intended to meet the needs of those students who are not adequately catered for by other Leaving Certificate programmes. It is a person-centred course involving a cross-curricular approach rather than a subject based structure' (<https://www.education.ie/en/The-Education-System/Post-Primary/>).

positive provision for special-needs learners, thus perceived as inimical to the 'image' and 'branding' of the school in a more competitive environment, while the legislation on Education for Persons with Special Educational Needs Act (EPSEN, 2004) Act sought to make provision for all students with learning needs.

The Celtic Tiger years, too, have made a distinct contribution to school curricula due to the presence of many immigrant children and native-born citizens whose cultural roots and language of the home are other than English and Irish. Consequently, it is interesting to note, beyond the more traditional German, French, Spanish and Italian provision in the Leaving Certificate, several additional languages are now included, as reflected in results for 2017: Arabic, Dutch, Portuguese, Russian, Czech, Polish, Latvian, Lithuanian, Hungarian, Romanian, Slovakian, Bulgarian and Croatian (*The Irish Times*, 16 August 2017). Such provision, despite its considerable expansion, may be open to the accusation of Eurocentrism and is likely to be challenged further in the near future to make provision for Mandarin – increasingly perceived as an economic necessity – or indeed the inclusion of more prominent West African languages.

Expansion of the system, the foregoing suggests, has not been immune to historical legacies, traditions and trajectories, and curricular provision in particular has the potential to reveal continuing inequalities of provision, but this is beyond the scope of the current chapter.

Legislative Reforms: Challenging Teacher Professionalism?

While the post-primary landscape has been transformed in a number of important respects, as indicated in general terms above, perhaps it is legislative reform that provides the most compelling requirements since compliance, rather than interpretation, is the consequence of legislative reform. As a prominent educator indicated to me some years ago, discussion and debate are over once legislation is passed; conformity or compliance become a requirement. Central in this regard is the Education Act (1998), since the system had been almost entirely devoid of legislation since the foundation of the national school system in 1831 (O'Donnovan, 2017). The Act indicates clearly that its intent is 'to make provision for the common good', itself a very contested concept, while it immediately indicates that such a commitment includes 'every person in the State' including those with 'a disability' or 'other special educational needs' (Ireland, 1998, p. 5). In one fell swoop, schools, boards of management, curriculum provision, education centres, parents, etc., were all brought into the same orbit. From a teacher perspective, school patrons are obliged to 'comply' under the Act, to make provision for 'the curriculum' and to permit and co-operate with regular 'inspection and evaluation by the Inspectorate', a practice largely absent from the post-primary sector at that time. While the legislation may be regarded as an important advance in modernizing the system, it is possible to suggest also that it represents a considerable centralization of powers in an otherwise very devolved system. Lest there be any doubt about the powers conferred on the Inspectorate under the legislation, the following, taken from the *Code of Practice for the Inspectorate* (Inspectorate, 2015), indicates clearly that:

> A person who obstructs or interferes with an Inspector in the course of exercising a power conferred on the Inspector ... commits an offence and is liable – (a) on summary conviction to a Class A fine, or (b) on conviction on indictment, to a fine not exceeding €100,000. (Section 13 (12a))

While such powers may be evoked only rarely, if at all, the very possibility contributes to a climate of conformity that runs counter to considerations of relative autonomy enjoyed by professionals and the discretionary judgement they require to live up to their professional responsibilities (Green, 2011; Sugrue and Solbrekke, 2011).

Following from the provisions of the Education Act (1998), the Teaching Council legislation (2001), drafted in 2001, had some of its provisions enacted in 2006, including the establishment of the council. Its purpose is 'to promote teaching as a profession' and, in the process of doing so, attend also to:

> ... The professional development of teachers; to maintain and improve the quality of teaching in the state; to provide for the establishment of standards, policies and procedures for the education and training of teachers and other matters relating to the teaching profession ... (Teaching Council Act, 2001, p. 5)

The council is a thirty-seven-member body, with a considerable majority of its membership from the teaching profession, primary and post-primary.[2] Teachers' initial reaction to the council's existence was rather negative since it became necessary to register with it, incurring an annual fee that was resented. This initial negativity has gradually yielded to a recognition of the necessity for registration to function in the system. The Disciplinary Committee of the council will investigate matters of professional conduct and as this work progresses it will be watched with interest by teachers and public alike. The combined 'force' of the Education Act (1988) and the Teaching Council Act (2001) has certainly, in the eyes of the profession, ratcheted up the 'accountability' agenda, while the decision in May 2006 by the then minister (Mary Hanafin) to publish School Inspection Reports on the DES website was interpreted by teachers as further evidence that 'professional autonomy' was being eroded – evidence of nascent neo-liberalism and its promotion by politicians and policymakers alike as part of New Public Management (NPM) (see Sugrue, 2015, pp. 25–42). The subsequent publication of Whole School Evaluation Reports (WSE) and more recently Management, Leadership and Learning (MLL) and subject inspection reports that may be on one or more subjects attest to the advancement of this accountability agenda (Sugrue, 2013a, 2013b) Having recently interviewed teachers immediately following a WSE in their school, I can certainly attest to the level of anxiety such encounters generate, major emotional labour, while similarly attesting to the sense of

---

2   The thirty-seven-member council consists of the following members: nine primary teachers, as well as two teachers nominated by their union (INTO), seven post-primary teachers, with an additional four being nominated by the post-primary unions (ASTI and TUI), four members from among initial teacher education providers, two nominees each from primary and post-primary managerial bodies, two nominees from the national parents' councils and five nominees of the ministers from trade unions and the private sector.

personal satisfaction and professional affirmation that accrue from receiving positive feedback. Nevertheless, the overriding emotion at the end of this heightened emotional state (a two- to three-week period) is one of exhaustion and relief. In this regard, it will be most interesting to document the impact on the teaching profession of the recent policy of School Self Evaluation (SSE); a policy that became mandatory in 2012 (Inspectorate 2012a, 2012b), introduced by the then minister, Ruairí Quinn, and revised more recently (Inspectorate, 2016a, 2016b).

There is considerable tension between the rhetoric of SSE and the external accountability exercised through the various external inspection mechanisms outlined above when the following is considered:

> School self-evaluation empowers a school community to identify and affirm good practice, and to identify and take action on areas that merit improvement. School self-evaluation is primarily about schools taking ownership of their own development and improvement. (Inspectorate, 2016a; 2016b, p. 6)

Apart from providing evidence of stealth reforms, beginning with 'pilot' or 'voluntary' interventions that over time become a requirement for all, evidence from elsewhere suggests that SSE was introduced in the UK context as a response by the profession to the impact of Ofsted (1992) (Office for Standards in Education), effectively a privatized inspection system. In publications such as *Schools Must Speak for Themselves* (MacBeath, 1999), as a counter to 'top-down' external evaluation, MacBeath (1999, p. 1) posited the following:

> There is an emerging consensus and body of wisdom about what a healthy system of school evaluation looks like. Its primary goal is to help schools to maintain and improve through critical self-reflection. It is concerned to equip teachers with the know-how to evaluate the quality of learning in their classrooms so that they do not have to rely on an external view, yet welcome such a perspective because it can enhance and strengthen good practice.

Finding an appropriate balance and trade-off between internal and external evaluation requires considerable trust between the parties involved, characterized by mutual regard, a sophisticated understanding of the nature of evidence, and, significantly, how such evidence should be interpreted in light of the particular circumstances of a school community. When

I engage in professional conversations with teachers from all sectors as an integral element of postgraduate programmes, they frequently draw attention to the asymmetry in terms of power relations between them as 'street level bureaucrats' (Lipsky, 1980) and the power positioning of the external evaluators, who can set aside the evidence provided by internal self-evaluation when it does not coincide with priorities determined at national level, even if the internal evidence supports particular priorities as determined by the school community. While it is important to recognize that a simple slide-rule approach to such tension is neither possible nor appropriate, since this approach would reduce complex professional decision-making characterized by professional judgement to a technical task, until such time as there is greater trust in the process *qua* process, teachers and principals are more likely to continue to regard the accountability demanded by WSE, MLL and subject inspections as issues to be endured rather than an opportunity to 'test' their professionalism and sense of professional responsibility. Such tensions are exacerbated by the seemingly endless demands for more change, allied to which is a constant demand for more policies and paperwork. This general drift, nay demand, for more paperwork, as evidence of 'being auditable', supports the view that 'the rise of auditing is as much about the cultural and economic authority granted to people who call themselves auditors as it is about what *exactly* these people do' (Power, 1999, p. xvii). This author observes further:

> The telling difference between an auditing and inspecting style of control concerns the substitution of internal for external agencies of inspection where the external inspector or auditor checks the system for self-inspection. (Power, 1999, p. 131)

However, with an increasing emphasis on paperwork as a 'measure' of stewardship in school communities, there is considerable risk that such exercises are reduced to ensuring 'the quality of your records, not the quality of your deeds' (Power, 1999, p. 131). Since human vulnerability, inherent to the process of personal and professional growth, is at the core of the teaching-learning process (Kelchtermans, 2011; Kelchtermans, Piot and Ballet, 2011), trust is essential in mitigating concerns about risk, while paradoxically the more trust in the educational process, the greater the risks it is possible to take in pursuit of enlightenment – for both students and teachers.

In summary, the dominant patterns evident fifty years after O'Malley's policy decision to introduce 'free' education to what was then referred to as the 'secondary' system include the almost total secularization of the system in terms of the absence, on a day-to-day basis, of religious personnel, the mainstreaming of 'other' schools (community and comprehensive), and particularly the vocational sector (ETB schools), significant increase in school size, considerable change in subject provision, but with evidence too of class divisions, while legislation has also contributed significantly to heightened tension between professional discretion, relative autonomy and external demands for accountability. This identification of patterns of change is not comprehensive. Rather, it focuses on the profession in general. A more comprehensive digest of various legislation, reports and demands on teachers is available in an 'Overview of the era, 1980–2016' in (see Coolahan, 2017, pp. 169–85). Collectively, these represent a considerable challenge to educational leaders both in and outside of schools and the forms they give to emergent professionalism that is fit for purpose within this changed and rapidly changing landscape. This is the focus of the chapter's final section.

Post-Austerity: *Cosán* to Emergent Professional Possibilities?

Elsewhere, I have addressed the impact of austerity on teacher salaries, morale and the necessity to engage in what I have termed 'transformative resistance' as a means of building professional commitment and a shared sense of professional responsibility in uncertain and challenging times (Sugrue, 2013a; Sugrue and Mertkan, 2016). While recognizing that curricular reform and the impact of austerity continue to be divisive, my focus here is on contemporary leadership and the possible pathways to creating professional futures that are fit for purpose, professionally responsible and yet remain open. No easy challenge.

The substantive issue is the 'formation' of student teachers, the ongoing formation of members of the profession, the formation of students and pupils in their care. While formation may be regarded as old fashioned, perhaps imbued with understandings of religious formation, thus less relevant in a secular age, the following argues the opposite – that there is a normative and moral dimension to professional formation:

> ... the term formation in professional education represents a process of change based on critical self-reflection and reflection around students' expectations and responsibilities. It describes the roles of teaching and experiences in helping students learn the knowledge, skilled know-how and professional responsibilities of their field, including the moral dimensions inherent to a profession and the societal responsibilities of professionals. (Sutphen and de Lange, 2014, pp. 411–12)

This approach to professional learning, growth and renewal frequently distinguishes between accountability and professional responsibility, whereby '"accountability" emphasises the duty to account for one's actions, and concerns what is rendered to another, while "responsibility" is a moral obligation assumed by oneself, or bestowed upon a person ...' (Englund and Solbrekke, 2011, p. 854). The distinctions these authors make between the language and logic of accountability and professional responsibility is helpful as a means of understanding the professional challenges faced by the teaching profession here in Ireland, with its own particular legacies and concerns (see Figure 10.3).

Professional Responsibility	Professional Accountability
based in professional mandate	defined by current governance
• situated judgement	• standardized by contract
• trust	• control
• moral rationale	• economic/legal rationale
• internal evaluation	• external auditing
• negotiated standards	• predetermined indicators
• implicit language	• transparent language
• framed by professions	• framed by political goals
• relative autonomy and personally inescapable	• compliance with employers'/ politicians' decisions
• proactive	• reactive

Figure 10.3: The types of logic and implications of professional responsibility and accountability. (Source: Englund and Solbrerkke, 2011, p. 855)

Needless to say, the policy context in which these different logics play out are shaped considerably by legacies, policies and the prevailing climate. Two policies are particularly pertinent in this regard: the Action Plan for Education 2016–19, published by the DES (2016), a centrally devised road-map for the system, and *Cosán Framework for Teachers' Learning* (Teaching Council, 2016). Arguably, these are the 'twin towers' or pillars between which the profession will build its capacity to lead and be professionally responsible in the immediate future. As key elements of both policy documents are discussed, the question of an activist profession will also be in focus – that is, the extent to which it is possible for the profession to be proactive, to enjoy relative autonomy and to build leadership capacity in a manner that is not merely being accountable, but life-affirming, enhancing, with an increased capacity for professional responsibility.

Both policy documents are, in different ways, symptomatic of the paperwork demanded by NPM: to be 'auditable' it is necessary to create a paper trail. This is not an argument against the necessity for planning, but rather draws attention to the reality that specificity and detail beyond a certain point become a prescription, a narrowing of possibilities, apart from the 'opportunity costs' entailed in the time, effort and energy that is currently being devoted to 'planning' and the production of paperwork. As the number of agencies proliferate in response to a more complex system, and the DES divests itself of responsibilities, which are given to agencies such as, for example, the State Examinations Commission (SEC), the National Council for Curriculum and Assessment (NCCA), the National Council for Special Education (NCSE), and, of course, the Professional Development Services for Teachers (PDST), all have an impact at the individual school and classroom level that may prove to be overwhelming for teachers and their coping capacity for both the demands for change and the pace at which they are expected to alter their pedagogical routines, while also transforming their professional dispositions.

The DES plan states its vision as follows: 'The central vision of our Statement of Strategy and Action Plan for Education is that the Irish Education and Training System should become the best in Europe over the next decade' (DES, 2016, p. 1). There is an inherent competitiveness in such aspirations, and while ambition is important from an individual and collective perspective, such rhetoric in the absence of adequate resource allocation is often perceived as rather hollow, doing little, as a consequence, for the morale of those whose responsibility it is to breathe life into such aspirations. There is recognition, however, that 'Ireland already has a top 5 position in Europe in several important spheres (for example, post-primary literacy, third level participation, take up of STEM at third level)', while 'there is significant ground to make up' in other areas. From a formation and professional responsibility perspective, there is recognition that 'success in education is built on the quality of leadership, the ingenuity in teaching', while such aspirations are inevitably tempered due to being 'constrained by the availability of financial resources' (p. 2). This ambition is translated into five 'high level' goals, and while all have implications for the teaching profession and its leadership, two are particularly pertinent: 'Improve the learning experience and the success of learners' and 'help those delivering education services to continuously improve' (p. 2). While the latter may be a laudable aspiration, there is a body of research which suggests that continuous improvement is a 'myth' (Bolton and Heap, 2002). Rather, as Hargreaves and Shirley (2012, p. 45) have convincingly demonstrated, sustainable educational transformation requires 'innovation and improvement combined'. In such circumstances, teachers become 'the designers of their own innovations' and in the process 'teachers also become its dynamos' (p. 200). They exhort teachers, not to 'be driven by data or anything else. Don't just deliver other people's ideas that have been invented somewhere else' (Hargreaves and Shirley, 2012, p. 200). This perspective is consistent with the language and logic of professional responsibility, to be proactive, to be an 'activist' (Sachs, 2004, 2016) professional. What these authors advocate is a considerable challenge to the teaching profession, particularly in an Irish context, where there has been a tendency to leave the 'leading' to others – principals, management, religious, policymakers, trade union activists or representatives. To all concerned, they insist that the challenges systems of schooling now face 'can only be undertaken together', but 'this does not absolve or exclude you from the individual responsibility that you have to exercise as well' (p. 201). How well positioned are post-primary teachers and the post-primary system to take up this considerable challenge? Is there too much emphasis on external prescription, data gathering and accountability, or will the Cosán framework outlined by the Teaching Council create sufficient space, time and opportunity to enable teachers and school communities to transform the sector?

While a *cosán*, as a metaphor, may be too narrow and meandering, as opposed to a highway, more conducive to collaborative endeavour, the framework does 'recognise teachers as autonomous and responsible learning professionals' (Teaching Council, 2016, p. 7), more consistent with a language and logic of professional responsibility. It also claims that the policy provides 'a flexible framework', something also to be welcomed, since there isn't just one 'path' to the future. As such, it envisages a broad canvas on which teacher learning will be enabled to flourish:

> Teachers' learning should be linked to teachers' needs, students' needs and school needs, and differentiated to suit the culture and context of teachers' work. The teaching profession is not a homogeneous group and the framework for teachers' learning takes account of 'teachers' individual career patterns, their priorities and their stage in life' as well as teachers' values, emotions, motivation and professional confidence. (Teaching Council, 2016, p. 7)

While this statement is relatively generous in identifying a professional learning agenda, there is an absence of attention to issues about the 'public good', and the kind of society we wish to create, issues that seek to connect teacher's values and dispositions to wider socio-cultural and economic issues. As educators, who take their normative remit seriously, and in a more secular and consumerist society, how are the values of respect, care, integrity and trust to be translated into the realities of everyday life in school? The framework is assertive in defence of teacher professionalism, teachers' autonomy, and discretionary judgement when it states:

> ... Cosán ... is a vision of teachers as professionals who are intrinsically motivated to take ownership of their professional development and steer the course of their own learning journeys. Cosán will respect the professionalism of teachers and allow them to exercise autonomy in identifying, and engaging in, the types of professional learning opportunities that benefit them and their students most. In turn, professional learning should further enhance teachers' professional autonomy. (p. 6)

While such assertions are open to the charge of being somewhat self-serving, more in tune with 'self' than 'others', they are nevertheless important for the morale of the profession: to assert a degree of professional autonomy and discretion, in the face of increasing external prescription. However, such words need to be accompanied by appropriate actions or the spaces and opportunities they aspire to create and appropriate will be closed down. The trust implicitly claimed in such assertions needs to be seen to be worthy, earned by adequate demonstration of commitment to and active concern for the other. It is necessary to recognize that contemporary 'performance cultures, premised on increased accountability and enacted through standards regimes' are more conducive to a 'conservative and risk-averse teaching profession, circumstances described as "compliant professionalism", devoid of the innovation deemed necessary above' (Sachs, 2016, p. 423).

As societies internationally become more polarized by extremes on the political spectrum, there are consequently repeated calls for more leadership. In the 'Rise of the Outsiders', Richards (2017, p. 118) argues that 'the ability to be a political teacher' is now 'an essential part of leadership'. In the Irish post-primary education sector, it is very definitely the responsibility of a lay leadership to take on the responsibility, and not merely the leadership, of school communities, but also to lead education debate, to inform public conversations on matters of educational import and to insist on the voices of the profession having their say. There are those who assert, not publicly, for the most part, that teacher unions have had too much influence on reform agendas, that they are a conserving, rather than a transformative, influence on the educational landscape, while others suggest that the onset of austerity has been used as a very blunt instrument to introduce unpopular reforms, particularly in the public sector. 'There is no other way' or 'there is no alternative' became something of a mantra, as a substitute for dialogue, deliberation and compromise, while simultaneously being exercised as a means of redressing power relations within the system. This is a legacy that prevails.

It is fashionable to extol the virtues of 'distributed leadership', even if substantial empirical warrants to support such policy espousal are less evident (Leithwood, Mascall and Strauss, 2009). Its espousal, too, ignores the issue of power relations and positional power within schools as

organizations and within systems (see Lumby, 2013). Nevertheless, understandings of professional responsibility insist that there is simultaneously
an individual responsibility, as well as a collective one, to uphold, promote
and renew the commitments that being professionally responsible entails.
Fifty years on from O'Malley's deviant decision, a core challenge, individual
and collective, is to be courageous in being an advocate for education, and
to have one's voice heard in classrooms and staffrooms, in the community
and the public sphere. Perhaps if Howard Gardner (1996, p. 11) were invited
to comment on O'Malley's deviant decision a half-century earlier, he may
well suggest that he was a '*visionary* leader', an individual who 'creates a
new story ... and achieves at least a measure of success in conveying this
story effectively to others'. For too long a culture of 'contrived silence', or
what Sachs has labelled 'compliant professionalism', has prevailed, whereby
'speaking up' and 'speaking out' has been left to others. In large measure,
this is an abdication of professional responsibility rather than its embrace,
a legacy that needs to be laid to rest.

Bibliography

Albertazzi, D., and McDonnell, D. (eds). (2008). *Twenty First Century Populism The
    Spectre of Western European Democracy* (London: Palgrave Macmillan).
Bolton, M., and Heap, J. (2002). 'The myth of continuous improvement', *Work Study*,
    51:6, pp. 309–13.
Coolahan, J. (2017). *Towards The Era of Lifelong Learning A History of Irish Education
    1800–2016* (Dublin: IPA).
Education (No. 2) Bill (1998).
Englund, T., and Solbrekke, T. D. (2011). 'Bringing Professional Responsibility Back
    In', *Studies in Higher Education*, 36:6, 847–61, DOI: doi.org/10.1080/030750
    79.2010.482205.
Fuller, L. (2004). *Irish Catholicism Since 1950: The Undoing of a Culture* (Dublin:
    Gill & Macmillan).
Green, J. (2011). *Education, Professionalism and the Quest for Accountability Hitting
    the Target but Missing the Point* (London and New York: Routledge).

Hallin, D. C. (1992). *The Uncensored War* (San Francisco: University of California Press).

Inspectorate (2012a). *School Self-Evaluation Guidelines for Post-Primary Schools Inspectorate Guidelines for Schools* <http://www.schoolself-evaluation.ie>.

Inspectorate (2012b). *School Self-Evaluation Guidelines for Primary Schools Inspectorate Guidelines for Schools* <http://www.schoolself-evaluation.ie>.

Inspectorate (2015). *Code of Practice for the Inspectorate* (Dublin: Department of Education and Skills).

Inspectorate (2016a). *SCHOOL SELF-EVALUATION GUIDELINES 2016–20 Post-Primary* (Dublin: Department of Education and Skills).

Inspectorate (2016b). *SCHOOL SELF-EVALUATION GUIDELINES 2016–20 Primary* (Dublin: Department of Education and Skills).

Jones, O. (2015). *The Establishment And how they get away with it* (St Ives: Penguin).

Kelchtermans, G. (2011). 'Professional Responsibility Persistent Commitment Perpetual Vulnerability', in C. Sugrue and T. Dyrdal Solbrekke (eds), *Professional Responsibility: New Horizons of Praxis* (pp. 113–26) (London and New York: Routledge).

Kelchtermans, G., Piot, L., and Ballet, K. (2011). 'The lucid loneliness of the gatekeeper: Exploring the emotional dimensions in principals' work lives', *Oxford Review of Education*, 37:1, pp. 93–108.

Leithwood, K., Mascall, B., and Strauss, T. (eds) (2009). *Distributed Leadership According to the Evidence* (London and New York: Routledge).

Lipsky, M. (1980). *Street-Level Bureaucracy Dilemmas of The Individual In Public Service* (New York: Russell Sage Foundation).

Lumby, J. (2013). 'Distributed leadership: The Uses annd Abuses of Power', *Educatinal Management Administration & Leadership*, 41:5, pp. 581–97.

Mac Laughlin, J. (1997). 'The New Vanishing Irish: Social Characteristics of "New Wave" Irish Emigration', in J. Mac Laughlin (ed.), *Location and Dislocation in Contemporary Irish Society Emigration and Irish Identities* (pp. 133–57) (Cork: Cork University Press).

MacBeath, J. (1999). *Schools Must Speak for Themselves:the Case of School Self-Evaluation* (London: Routledge).

McGarry, P. (2017). 'Church of Ireand attracts double the number training to be Catholic priests', *The Irish Times*, 26 September 2017.

Maher, E. (2017). 'Cultural legacy of Catholicism still very much alive,' *Irish Times*. 26/09/17.

Miller, K. A. (1988). *Exiles and Emigrants Ireland and the Irish Exodus to North America* (Oxford: Oxford University Press).

O'Connor, S. (1968). 'Post-Primary Education: Now and in the Future', *Studies*, LVII, pp. 415–43.

O'Connor, S. (1986). *A TROUBLED SKY: Reflections on the Irish Educational Scene 1957–68* (Dublin: Educational Research Centre, Drumcondra).

O'Donnovan, P. F. (2017). *Stanley's Letter: The National School System and Inspectors in Ireland 1831–1922* (Galway: Galway Education Centre).

Power, M. (1999). *The Audity Society Rituals of Verification* (Oxford: Oxford University Press).

Richards, S. (2017). 'The Rise of the Outsiders How Mainstream Politics Lost its Way' (Croydon: Atlantic Books).

Sachs, J. (2004). *The Activist Teaching Profession* (Buckingham and Philadelphia, PA: Open University Press).

Sachs, J. (2016). 'Teacher Professionalism: why are we still talking about it?' *Teachers and Teaching Theory and Practice*, 22:4), 413–25.

Schmidt, V. A. (2008). 'Discursive Institutionalism: The explanatory power of ideas and discourse', *The Annual Review of Political Science*, 11, pp. 303–26, DOI: 10.1146/annurev.polisci.11.060606.135342.

Sugrue, C. (2013a). 'Regimes of control and teacher educators' Janus face?', in L. Beckett (ed.), *Teacher Education through Active Engagement Raising the Professional Voice* (pp. 125–40) (London and New York: Routledge).

Sugrue, C. (2013b). 'Teachers' Lives and Work: Back to the Future?', in M. A. Flores, A. M. Carvalho, F. I. Ferreira and M. T. Vilaca (ed.), *Back to the Future: Legacies, Continuities and Changes in Educational Policy, Practice and Research* (pp. 39–56) (Rotterdam: Sense Publishers).

Sugrue, C. (2015). *Unmasking School Leadership: A longitudinal Life History of School Leaders* (Dordrecht: Springer).

Sugrue, C., and Mertkan, S. (2016). 'Professional responsibility, accountability and performativity among teachers: the leavening influence of CPD?' *Teachers and Teaching Theory and Practice*, 23:2, pp. 171–90, DOI: 10.1080/13540602.2016.1203771.

Sugrue, C., and Solbrekke, T. D. (eds) (2011). *Professional Responsibility: New Horizons of Praxis* (London and New York: Routledge).

Sutphen, M., and de Lange, T. (2014). 'What is Formation? A Conceptual Discussion', *Higher Education Research and Development*, 34:2, 411–19.

Teaching Council (2016). *Cosán Framework for Teachers' Learning* (Maynooth: Teaching Council).

Notes on Contributors

TOM BOLAND is an international education consultant and a partner in BH Associates. In August 2016, he stepped down from his role as Chief Executive of the Higher Education Authority, ending over two decades at the most senior levels in the Irish education system. The HEA leads the strategic development of the Irish higher education and research system. Prior to his role in the HEA, he served as Director of Strategic Policy and legal adviser in the Department of Education and Skills. He holds degrees in Civil Engineering (National University of Ireland, Galway) and Law (the Honourable Society of King's Inns) and was called to the Bar of Ireland in 1989.

JOHN COOLAHAN is Professor Emeritus of Education at Maynooth University. He qualified as a national teacher in St Patrick's College, Drumcondra, before obtaining a BA, HDE and MA from University College Dublin and an MEd and PhD from Trinity College Dublin. He was also awarded honorary doctorates by the NUI and Dublin City University. He taught at all levels of the Irish education system and has been heavily involved in major policy development initiatives sponsored by the Department of Education and Skills. He has also had extensive experience of educational policy internationally, particularly with the European Commission and the OECD.

MARGARET CREAN is Postdoctoral Research Fellow with the School of Education in University College Dublin (UCD). She holds undergraduate degrees in Science and Social Science from UCD, where she also completed a Master's and PhD in Equality Studies with the School of Social Justice. She has published book chapters and academic papers on a range of equality topics, including inequality in education, social class, gender and care.

BRIAN FLEMING spent twenty-five years of his teaching career as the principal of Collinstown Park Community College in Clondalkin. Following retirement, he completed a course of doctoral studies at the School of Education in UCD. His book, *Irish Education, 1922–2007: Cherishing All the Children?* (Mynchen's Field Press, 2016), is based on research carried out at that time. A subsequent publication, *Irish Education and Catholic Emancipation* (Peter Lang, 2017), traces the interaction between the campaigns for Irish education and Catholic emancipation in the early nineteenth century, outlining in detail the roles of Bishop James Doyle and Daniel O'Connell. Brian's first book was *The Vatican Pimpernel: The Wartime Activities of Monsignor Hugh O'Flaherty* (Collins Press, 2008 and Skyhorse Publishing, 2012). He is involved in a range of philanthropic activities. His current research interests are educational disadvantage and the history of Irish education generally.

JIM GLEESON is Professor of Identity and Curriculum in Catholic Education at Australian Catholic University, Brisbane. Once a post-primary teacher in Dublin and his native Tipperary, he spent much of his life as a teacher educator at Thomond College of Education (1981–91) and the University of Limerick (1991–2011). He was part of the External Evaluation Team for the first round of EU Transition from School to Adult and Working Life Projects (1979–82), leader of the SPIRAL 2 Transition Project at Shannon Curriculum Development Centre (1983–7), external evaluator of the European Studies (Ireland and Great Britain) Project (1988–91) and NCCA Education Officer for the Leaving Certificate Applied (1992–5). During his time at the University of Limerick, he served as head of the Education Department (1991–5) and course leader of the Master's in Educational Management (1993–2011) and as an Irish Universities Association (IUA) nominee on the Teaching Council (2005–12). His PhD is from the University of East Anglia and his main research interests include curriculum development and evaluation, education and curriculum policy, faith-based education and teacher education.

JUDITH HARFORD is Professor of Education, director of the Professional Master of Education (PME) and an elected member of the Academic

Council, University College Dublin. Her research interests are the history of women's education and education policy. She has served on several committees and working groups of the Irish state Department of Education and Skills and the Teaching Council of Ireland and has acted as an international advisor to the Social Sciences and Humanities Research Council of Canada, the Nordic Council of Ministers and the Estonian Research Council. She is a Fellow of both the Royal Historical Society (London) and the Massachusetts Historical Society (USA) and International Clinical Practice Fellow of the American Association of Teacher Educators. She is the Ireland Canada University Foundation Flaherty Visiting Professor (2017–18).

ÁINE HYLAND is Emeritus Professor of Education and former vice-president of University College Cork, Ireland. She has been active in education circles in Ireland and internationally for over fifty years. She started her career as a civil servant in the Department of Education in the 1960s, and was a secondary teacher in the 1970s. Since 1980, she has been involved in teacher education – in Carysfort College of Education, Blackrock, in the 1980s; University College Dublin from 1987 to 1993; and as Professor of Education in University College Cork from 1993 to 2006. She has been a member of various national education boards and committees and has published books and articles on the history of Irish education, educational policy, educational disadvantage and curriculum and assessment.

KATHLEEN LYNCH is the UCD Professor of Equality Studies, an Irish Research Council Advanced Research Scholar for 2014–17 and a member of the UCD School of Education. An academic and an activist, she is guided by the belief that the purpose of scholarship and research is not just to understand the world but to change it for the good of all humanity. She has published and campaigned widely on equality issues, both nationally and internationally. Her most recent co-authored books include *New Managerialism in Education: Commercialisation, Carelessness and Gender* (Palgrave Macmillan, 2015, 2nd edn) and *Affective Equality: Love, Care and Injustice* (Palgrave Macmillan, 2009). The latter has been published in Spanish (2014) and in Korean (2016).

D. G. MULCAHY is CSU Professor of Educational Leadership (Emeritus) at Central Connecticut State University and was formerly Professor of Education in University College, Cork. He is a past president of the Educational Studies Association of Ireland and of the New England Philosophy of Education Society. His books include *Curriculum and Policy in Irish Post-Primary Education* (Institute of Public Administration, 1981), *Knowledge, Gender, and Schooling* (Bergin and Garvey, 2002), *The Educated Person* (Roman and Littlefield, 2008), and *Pedagogy, Praxis, and Purpose in Education* (Routledge, 2015 and 2016) (co-authored with C. M. Mulcahy and D. E. Mulcahy). He has twice been awarded Fulbright Grants.

TOM O'DONOGHUE is Professor of Education in the Graduate School of Education, the University of Western Australia. He is also an elected fellow of both the Royal Historical Society and the Academy of the Social Sciences in Australia. He specializes in the history of education in the English-speaking world, with particular reference to the history of teachers and the process of education in faith-based schools. He is also concerned with examining the historical antecedents of various contemporary educational issues. His work is distinguished methodologically by the way in which it is informed by theoretical perspectives from the social sciences, especially those clustered under the label of 'interpretivist sociology'. He is a former president of the Australian and New Zealand History of Education Society and he has been Adjunct Professor in the Faculty of the Professions at the University of Adelaide and at Divine Word University in Papua New Guinea. He is currently Adjunct Professor at the Australian Catholic University. He has authored and edited over thirty academic books and 100 academic papers.

EMER SMYTH is Research Professor and head of the Social Research Division at the Economic and Social Research Institute (ESRI) and is Adjunct Professor of Sociology at Trinity College, Dublin. She has published extensively on her main research interests of education, school-to-work transitions, gender and comparative methodology. She has conducted a number of studies looking at young people's experiences of the schooling system and the factors shaping their post-school transitions. She is on the management team of the Growing Up in Ireland (GUI) study and has used GUI data to look at arts and cultural participation among children and young people, spatial variation in child outcomes and the transition into primary school. She has a strong interest in comparative research on education issues, and is currently involved in the education and stratification strand of the UK-based Applied Quantitative Methods Network, conducting comparative research on the influence of school curriculum on entry into higher education and employment.

CIARAN SUGRUE is Professor of Education at the School of Education, University College Dublin, where he is director of the postgraduate programme in educational leadership and chair of the school's research committee. He has served as teacher, school inspector, teacher educator and researcher in the Irish education system and also spent some years at the Faculty of Education, Cambridge University, UK. His research interests include teacher education reform in developed and developing country contexts, the continuing professional development of teachers and the teaching profession, school leadership and educational change, all with a policy focus. His most recent book (co-edited with Sefika Mertkan) is *Publishing and the Academic World: Passion, Purpose and Possible Futures* (Routledge, 2016).

Index

Figures and Tables are indicated by page numbers in italics, footnotes by the page number followed by 'n' and the note number.